Philosophical
Perspectives on
Developmental Psychology

Philosophical Perspectives on Developmental Psychology

Edited by

James Russell

Basil Blackwell

British Library Cataloguing in Publication Data

Philosophical perspectives on developmental
psychology.
1. Developmental psychology – Philosophy
I. Russell, James, *1948–*
128'.2   BF713
ISBN 0–631–14626–1

Library of Congress Cataloging in Publication Data

Philosophical perspectives on developmental psychology.
Includes index.
1. Psychology—Philosophy. 2. Intellect.
3. Cognition. I. Russell, James, 1948–   .
[DNLM: 1. Human Development. 2. Philosophy.
3. Psychology. BF 713 P568]
BF38.P445 1987 155'.01 87–825
ISBN 0–631–14626–1

Typeset in 10 on 11.5 pt Times
by Joshua Associates Ltd, Oxford.
Printed in Great Britain by
T. J. Press Ltd, Padstow

Contents

Contents

Preface

Given the nature – the disputed nature – of philosophy, it is possible to write and edit an almost infinite number of books using formulae of the following kind: 'Philosophy and X', 'The Philosophical Foundations of Y', 'Philosophical Perspectives on Z'. So why especially a book on philosophy and mental development?

The answer is quite simple. We cannot theorize about the process of mental development without doing philosophy and cannot tackle problems in epistemology and ontology without encountering developmental questions. In the first case a theory about how the mind develops will assume *some* philosophical position on the nature of mental entities and their relation to behaviour and to neural states. In the second, the enduring issues in epistemology boil down to questions about how the acquisition of knowledge is *possible*. And in doing ontology we face the problem of how mind can be said to emerge from matter – or at least we construct a framework within which it is not possible to describe mental development in this way.

In fact we do not even need to justify the interrelationship of the two disciplines in this abstract style: we can simply observe what developmental psychologists and philosophers actually do. To illustrate: in one memorable term of my undergraduate life I found myself (it being a matter of accident not design) having tutorials on Piaget during the same weeks as I was having tutorials on Kant, as well as tutorials on Vygotsky during the same weeks as tutorials as Wittgenstein. Well it seemed then, and it still seems now, that each member of these pairs had more in common with his partner than with many of his fellow 'philosophers' or fellow 'psychologists'. And so, for these reasons, a discipline that we might want to call something like 'genetic epistemology' can be said to exist. Genetic epistemology is rather a pompous term and it carries a heavily Piagetian flavour (in fact it was coined by James Mark Baldwin) but this should not make us reluctant to acknowledge its necessity.

But should we not admit that it is within the forum of 'cognitive science' (broadly, computational cognitive psychology) not genetic epistemology that the real cross-fertilization between the philosopher and psychologist is currently taking place? This is true, but it wrongly implies that there is a symmetrical conflict between genetic epistemology and cognitive science. There is no such conflict because, unlike cognitive science, genetic epistemology (excluding the specifically Piagetian use of the term) does not impose upon its practitioners any particular theory of the mind, any more than being a philosopher entails being a dualist or being a developmental psychologist entails being nativist. Consciously to regard oneself as a cognitive scientist, however, entails adherence to a very specific view of mental states (roughly, as functional states of an abstractly characterized mechanism) as well as adherence to a particular way of collecting data and interpreting them. So it involves no contradiction to describe somebody as doing genetic epistemology from the viewpoint of cognitive science.

It is not surprising, therefore, that many of the contributors to this volume have something to say about the bearing of the cognitive science metatheory upon issues in mental development. Now I am not trying to impose a consensus where one does not exist, but I think it is fair to say that many of them make the point that we cannot tell the full story of cognitive (let alone personal) development within the cognitive science framework. So the reader will find, in many of the chapters here, some good words being said (albeit qualified) on behalf of what cognitive scientists decry as 'folk-psychology'. Indeed in their overview chapter Feldman and Bruner bring this scepticism about cognitive science into very sharp focus, arguing for a principled agnosticism about the 'reality' of mental states, and suggesting that creative thought in science is stifled if we impose one ontology on its practitioners. As editor, I certainly agree with this position and hope that the reader will absorb from these chapters a liberal and pluralistic view of genetic epistemology – as an invitation to study the overlap between the philosophical and the psychological conceptions of development whilst remaining sceptical about any metatheory which tells you that *one* kind of process underlies it, be it equilibration, the elaboration of innate mental representations or whatever.

This volume would never have come into existence had I not been invited by the History and Philosophy Section of the British Psychological Society to convene a symposium at the society's annual conference in Swansea during the spring of 1984. My thanks to the section, and in particular to my colleague Sandy Lovie, for the invitation. At this symposium early drafts of the essays printed here by Adam Morton, Jim Hopkins, and by myself were presented. The discussant was Wolfe Mays, who also contributes a chapter. The commitment to the project shown by Philip Carpenter of Basil Blackwell also helped in getting the book under way.

My job as editor was more of a pleasure than a chore thanks to the enthusiasm of the contributors. In some cases this led them to boldly go into the cognitive–developmental literature where no philosophers had gone before! But I am particularly grateful to Carol Feldman and Jerry Bruner for taking on the considerable task of writing the overview chapter. In practice, this turned out to involve reading some pretty rough drafts as well as the finished products that you see here. Their overview chapter not only makes its own theoretical points but can be read as an introduction to some of the issues discussed in the book. A reader who is unfamiliar with the territory covered here may be advised to read the first half of the overview chapter before reading the chapters in sequence.

I would like to thank John Flavell, Harriet Haworth, Howard Robinson, Ray Tallis, Richard Latto, and especially Carl Johnson for reading and commenting on my own chapter. Finally, thanks to Anne Halliwell and Dorothy Foulds for coping with the typing and other secretarial chores with their usual, unfailing good humour.

J. R.
Liverpool

PART I

Issues in
Developmental Explanation

1

Describing the child's mind

Kathleen V. Wilkes

INTRODUCTION

The early months of a child's life are months of intensely rapid cognitive development. This is something which we, and developmental psychologists, need both to describe and to explain. But to what extent are the familiar everyday concepts, such as 'sees', 'believes', 'wants', 'thinks, 'fears', 'proves', 'guesses', 'realizes', 'infers' and their ilk appropriate, when we are talking about the prelinguistic infant?

It may seem that this is an unreal problem, and that common sense is all we need. For example, most would agree that there are terms and expressions that are clearly *in*appropriate: few would wish to describe a child of a few months' old as 'evaluating', 'forming an opinion', 'holding a prejudice'. Evidently, too, we will not ascribe to such a child any thought, emotion or belief that presupposes mastery of language – no creature without language can fear hell-fire or Friday the 13th. However, this surely does not suggest any major difficulty; admittedly there might be a few borderline cases, but by and large common sense, controlled by Lloyd Morgan's canon, will tell us what terms to use, and what terms not to use. *Prima facie*, terms like 'sees', 'fears', 'wants', 'believes' are clearly in order, whereas ascriptions like 'commits himself', 'preconceives', 'intolerant' clearly not.

Thus before attempting to solve the difficulty, let us first find out just what it is thought to be.

I

In most of what follows I shall talk primarily (although not solely) about the *beliefs* (or thoughts) of the prelinguistic child. This for two reasons: first, anyone who prefers can take my 'beliefs' as elliptical for 'beliefs, fears, guesses, wants, wishes ... etc.' Second, the ascription of practically any mental state or event presupposes some beliefs somewhere – the fear of a bull, or of a spider, presupposes the belief that something threatening is in the offing. Beliefs thus seem central to *almost* all psychological ascriptions. (They are not central to quite all; ascriptions of pain, for example, may *typically* presuppose that the person in pain has some relevant beliefs, but seem not invariably to do so.)

As the slogan has it, 'no entity without identity'. So let us consider the problem of identifying beliefs. Can the prelinguistic child have beliefs about *his mother*, when we are dubious about whether he has yet the idea that she is a spatially bounded persisting entity? Maybe the young child thinks of his mother as if she were discontinuous stuff like water: here's some mother, now no more mother, here's some more again. There is indeed some reason to think that an infant does go through such a stage; but if that were so, it would be odd to describe him as having beliefs *about that woman*. But then, the idea that she is a spatially bounded, persisting entity is, as expressed, a *highly* sophisticated thought, far more abstract and general than 'mother'; and the infant surely can be given mastery of the concept 'mother' *before* that of 'spatially bounded persisting entity'. Or consider the child who sees a cake and reaches out for it. We are tempted to say that he wants the cake. But does he have the concept 'cake'? Evidently he has no thoughts about the composition and origin of cakes; he may utterly fail to recognize, say, wedding cakes as cakes, or wrapped cakes as cakes; he may be unable to distinguish between biscuits and cakes ... the list continues. We do not know the extension of the ascribed concept 'cake' in the child's mind. Thus we cannot say what it is that the child thinks, or wants. But then, if we are unable to say what is the content of any belief he has when reaching for a cake, then we cannot say whether it is true or false; and once we lose *that* hook, we are at sea when discussing much more – we could not, for instance, say that he had made a rational inference from one belief to another, for rational inference is usually considered to be truth-preserving. More generally, the explanation of action adverts to beliefs and desires, and it explains by showing the action to be *rational*; and rationality is a matter of the content of the ascribed states.

Two diametrically opposed strategies for ascribing content both seem to fail. One allows that the content of a child's belief may be blurry – it hasn't quite got the concept 'cake', but it has something in the same *region*; and we can manage with blurry ascriptions at a pinch. We learn something when told that a tree is in the north-west part of a field, even though we get more information when informed that it is exactly 5 metres dead south from the left-hand gatepost. Consider the analogy of an exact circle (as an analogy for our adult concept 'cake'), with, overlapping it in part, an amorphous, shifting, amoeba-like shape (the child's concept). It is rough, but covers much of the same domain. However, the problem with this solution is that we need more; unless we can infer such things as 'he wants *the thing that his father gave him*', or 'he wants *something to eat*', or, alternatively, can deny that these are true, we have *arbitrarily* chosen just one of a number of logically incompatible content-ascriptions, each of which would explain the reaching behaviour with equal ease.

The other strategy, proposed by Armstrong (1973) for discovering the content of a dog's belief but one which we might attempt to use for our problem, is for 'generations of work by [animal] psychologists' so as to unearth 'the *exact* content' of the belief (p. 27; my italics). Thus we would try to pin some very precise content on to the child's thought: he wants something which is F_1, and F_2 or F_3, and F_4 or F_5 ... that is, he wants something *jammy or chocolatey* and *crumbly or soft* and *between 1 and 3 inches long* and *made of sponge or fruit* and *tasty* and so on. Evidently, this only makes matters far worse. If the child cannot securely be ascribed the concept 'cake', still less can he be ascribed concepts of length, of fruit, of crumbliness.

Nor is that the end of the difficulties. We have become increasingly familiar, primarily because of the work of Wittgenstein, with what is now generally termed 'the holism of the mental'. The phrase is loose, and loosely used; but for our purposes we can simply say that it draws our attention to the fact that mental ascriptions form a *web*, so that the ascription of one presupposes, or entails, or implies weakly or strongly, the ascribability of others. To illustrate: why doesn't a television camera really 'see'? Not because it is structurally too unlike the human eye – that could be rectified (indeed, the early pinhole cameras were of course designed on the basis of theories about how our optic system works). The reason, surely, is that camera 'seeing' has virtually no links to, hook-ups with, or implications for, other ascriptions. We can in a sense be said to 'record' much of what we see, and so does the camera; but then we sometimes eat, move, paint the seen objects; ignore them, throw them, describe them, circumnavigate them; talk to them, admire, fear or deplore them, bomb them. None of this can cameras do. Before we are going to get true artificial seeing – 'seeing' without a protective screen of scare-quotes – we will need a highly sophisticated robot that can be said to interact, physically and cognitively, in a fairly rich way with the objects its 'eye' scans. More generally, our notions of belief, thought, desire, hope, fear, expectation, and all other such terms, get their sense from their implicit surround. In other words, we are unable to ascribe content to any token belief state unless we can tacitly ascribe a fund of further related and backing beliefs, desires, attitudes, abilities, and so on and so forth.

Now this argument seems right; and it allows and explains the legitimacy of ascribing *seeing* to the prelinguistic child – the infant tracks seen objects with his eyes, reaches for them, tries to suck or chew them, drops them, picks them up. This is, early on, a sufficiently rich repertoire for un-problematic ascriptions of 'sees'. But *beliefs* about cakes, or about mother, wholly or seriously lack the backing cluster of ascriptions of further beliefs and desires; not only, then, are we unable to say what the content of such beliefs are – it seems even nonsensical to ascribe them at all.

Finally, Davidson (1975) in a well-known article argues that no creature lacking language could be said to have thoughts. He summarizes his argument thus:

> only a creature that can interpret speech can have the concept of a thought.
> Can a creature have a belief if it does not have the concept of belief? It seems to me it cannot, and for this reason. Someone cannot have a belief unless he understands the possibility of being mistaken, and this requires grasping the contrast between truth and error – true belief and false belief. But this contrast ... can emerge only in the context of interpretation, which alone forces us to the idea of an objective, public truth. (p. 22)

Believing that *p* probably cannot be distinguished from the belief that *p* is true (p. 23); infants cannot, however, be ascribed command of such fancy notions as truth, belief, mistake; hence they cannot be ascribed any beliefs at all.

II

Such a conclusion is, of course, disastrous. We are deprived of any way of describing the intricate and staggering cognitive development of the infant; behaviourism, and behaviourism of a fairly crude kind at that, is all we are left with either for infants or for non-human animals. It is also highly paradoxical, given that our conceptual apparatus (citing beliefs, desires, wants, fears, hopes, and so on) seems to work really very well most of the time. For example, there comes an interesting point in the child's development when he becomes aware that an object put (in his full view) underneath something – a piece of cloth, for instance – is still there even if invisible, and has not just vanished. We say, and it seems that we need to say, 'he now realizes that the object is out of sight beneath the cloth, whereas before he did not realize that'. This seems both informative and true. Analogously, suppose a dog chased a cat, which escaped up a tree and thence to another tree and to safety. If the dog persists in barking up the wrong (first) tree, then we say that it *thinks* the cat is still up that tree – and so, again, we need to say. Only in this way is the dog's behaviour explained.

Further, some of the arguments against ascribing beliefs to infants or non-human animals tend to prove far too much, which suggests that there is something deeply wrong with them somewhere. Consider the following: I have some, although not many, beliefs about sub-atomic particles. Physicists have more, and better-informed, beliefs. My beliefs about positrons stand to the physicists' somewhat as infants' beliefs about cakes stand to mine; if there are difficulties in specifying the content of the thoughts of infants or animals, there are, for precisely analogous reasons, problems in saying what it is that I believe about positrons.

More generally, *every* attempt to identify belief-content runs into familiar and fairly intractable dilemmas, all of which are familiar enough; so the slogan 'No entity without identity' may be too powerful. To show this, I shall just rehearse swiftly some of the principal knots in this area.

1 Should we construe beliefs *de re* or *de dicto*? Sometimes we need to choose one construal; sometimes, for slightly different purposes, we need the other; but they divide beliefs up in highly different ways. However, we do not have a tidy duplication of division; for even when beliefs are construed *de dicto*, if I believe the man in the brown hat is a spy, then I surely do also believe that Ortcutt is a spy – *if* I am well-aware at the time that the man in the brown hat is Ortcutt. Further, I may know that Ortcutt is the Mayor of Oxford, but that fact is not present in my mind now: can I be said to believe that the Mayor is a spy? I might say 'of course' when offered the proposition; but I might be astonished by the implication.

2 When is my belief the same as yours? For instance, when I believe that I am in Edinburgh and you believe that you are in Edinburgh, are those two tokens of the same belief-type? Or should we rather require you to believe that *K.V.W.* is in Edinburgh?

3 I think the stuff that I am drinking is H_2O. My *doppelgänger* on 'twin earth' planet Mirabile believes that the stuff she is drinking is H_2O. I am right, she is wrong (no substance on Mirabile has that chemical composition). Does my *doppelgänger* have the same belief as me? Mirabile is exactly like earth in all respects except that the stuff falling from the sky, lying around in lakes, glasses, bathtubs, used for washing and drinking, and falling regularly from cloudly skies, is not H_2O but XYZ (but is called 'water' and thought to be H_2O). My *doppelgänger* is exactly like me except that the watery part of her is XYZ not H_2O; otherwise her character, history, and (scanty) chemical knowledge is in all respects identical to mine. But of course they cannot be the same beliefs – not if one is true and the other false; or can they?

4 Indexicals. I believe that I am now in Oxford; I believe that K.V.W. is now in Oxford. Are these the same beliefs? Evidently I might forget my name, and so one of them seems more vulnerable to contingencies than the other. Compare: 'The meeting should be starting now' and 'The meeting

should be starting at 4.30 p.m.'. The truth conditions for these two can very readily vary.

5   *If* a true belief is a different belief from a false one (but is it?) then I can acquire and lose beliefs with no change in me, and without my knowledge. I now think that the leaning tower of Pisa leans. But the city council, let us suppose, had it secretly straightened last month, and the news has not yet got about (the tower is still shrouded in wrappings). So last month I acquired a new (false) belief. But did I?

6   Do you believe that cows do not eat concrete? I do. Since when? Well, roughly since the time that I could be said to believe that you cannot push medium-sized solid objects with string, that all female elephants are bigger than any male mouse, that daffodils are not drinkable, that most schoolchildren in Suffolk have eyebrows, that all Members of Parliament are mortal. These are banal, fatuous – but we can not ignore them completely. Assumptions, takings-for-granted, tacit presuppositions, trivial implications of other beliefs – any of these might occasionally come into question and need to be thought-out ('rethought'?). Moreover, they guide our actions and behaviour: when crossing a road we do not wonder whether the driver of an oncoming car is a homicidal maniac – we tacitly take it for granted that he is not, until forced to 'reconsider'. Do I 'have' the belief that *The Encyclopedic Dictionary of Psychology* does not contain the sonnets of Shakespeare? Or that it was not written by Homer? How are we to *specify* these tacit takings-for-granted – what is their content?

7   The preconscious. Suppose (an example that I have used before) you stumble at the top of a flight of steps. I say 'he thought' (or 'he must have thought') that there was another step. You say, dusting yourself down, 'I thought' (or 'I must have thought') 'that there was another step'. What are the truth conditions for such an ascription? What was running through your mind at the time, let us suppose, and thus making you more careless about stair-climbing than usual, were thoughts about booking a flight to Prague. None the less, we agree on the ascription as the correct way of explaining your stumble.

No doubt some of these knots can be disentangled; but even if so, few agree about the best ways of doing so. There are more than seven such knots, first because I have made no pretence at an exhaustive list, and second, because they can combine – for example, if we combine 1 and 7 above we start wondering whether to construe preconscious beliefs *de re* or *de dicto*. What they (cumulatively) show is that infants are not the only human organisms whose beliefs are difficult to specify. Worse than that, as already noted, what goes for beliefs goes for the rest of the so-called 'propositional attitudes', and indeed any intensionally characterized states.

Thus we should start from the beginning – *dismissing* the arguments of section I that impose unrealistically high conditions on content-identification, but searching for the conditions that *in fact* govern our ascriptions of intensional mental states.

III

We shall accept, then, the *brute* fact that parents, and developmental psychologists, have an unchallengeable right to exploit whatever terminology is necessary to describe and explain the behaviour and the development of the prelinguistic child. The answer to our problem now needs to be subdivided, one answer for the scientists and another for the parents; we shall consider the first in this section, and the second in section IV.

Developmental psychology is a science. Science is, as Quine insists, continous with common sense; but yet there are differences. These are differences of degree, because science is indeed 'continuous' with common sense; but differences of degree can be colossal. (In other words, to say debunkingly '*only* a difference of degree' needs justification. There is a difference of degree – only! – between the bumps in my lawn and the Himalayas.) The fact that the two are continuous allows for and indeed presupposes the further fact that somewhere in the middle of the continuum on which they lie there will be a broad band of statements which will not unambiguously be one rather than another (when does a hill become a mountain?) and therefore that there is no *sharp* non-arbitrary distinction. But this in no way casts doubt on the claim that there *are* significant and interesting differences between the two.

I have elsewhere (Wilkes, 1984) defended at length the claim that there are many significant and interesting differences between science and common sense, and shall not repeat my arguments here. Instead I shall concentrate on what this means for the terminology used by the scientist and the layman.

Science, in all domains, adopts terms from ordinary language – and then adapts them, trying to refine, define, and specify them; baking them in the theoretical kiln until they lose the vagueness, nuanced flexibility, and richness of connotation that they enjoy in everyday life – and which they need to enjoy for the multifarious purposes to which they are put. Pure science is concerned with only two aims: systematic description and explanation (where 'explanation' includes prediction). Our everyday conceptual apparatus sometimes describes and explains – although it rarely tries to give systematic or general accounts of anything – but equally it has to allow for joking, jeering, judging . . . and literally dozens of other activities. Thus flexibility, context-dependent nuance, overlapping shades of meaning, richness of connotation, and *lack* of sharp definition are needed by the layman; never believe any philosopher who suggests that the examination of ordinary language should start with a *definition* of terms! Science has to try to strip away this fluidity and fix terms precisely. For example, electrons 'spin'. But they do not go round and round, nor can one whip them. 'Information' is a perfectly good everyday term: mathematicians and computer scientists have given (and have needed to give) the term sharp definitions. So also with 'intelligent' – a term which every layman can use with ease, but which is in science the paradigm of a term picked out by a complex operational definition. The general point is obvious, and the list could continue long.

(I am not of course saying that all scientific terms *are* defined, clear, unambiguous – only that making them so is *one* of the prerequisites for a mature and successful theory. This clarification is often a difficult and lengthy process – as Newton-Smith (1981) points out, the terms 'field' and 'space-time', originally used very broadly, allow for just those experiments that help to fix their range more precisely. In all areas of psychology, there is at present more vagueness than clarity, as most psychologists would be the first to admit; a good example is the term 'representation' – arguably one of the key notions in cognitive science today – which no two people use in quite the same sense.)

So science has to search for the best and most perspicuous set of (theoretical and observational) terms in which to couch its descriptions and explanations; these are not 'given'. What we require of a conceptual apparatus adequate for developmental psychology is, I think, twofold. First, that it prove adequate to describe, predict and explain the fundamental, general and common factors that we hope to identify in cognitive growth. In Van Fraassen's (1980) terms, the theory must aim at 'empirical adequacy'. This is a bootstrapping operation, of course; both the terms appropriate for the *explananda*, and those for the *explanantia*, have to be sought together. Observation, insight and experiment give us pointers to what are, or might be, the critical and common factors during mental growth; the explanations we postulate serve to clarify, subdivide, specify more clearly what is being explained, and separate what is genuinely fundamental from what is 'noise'. Explanations – underlying regularities and general laws – inevitably focus the nature of the *explanandum* more determinately (another obvious point).

The second demand concerns the relation of child psychology to the neurosciences. The infant's mind develops at a staggering rate; one day (even if in the far future) we shall come to understand how it does so by virtue of what we know about the changes, connections, growth, biochemistry, and so on of the brain. Again there will be bootstrapping. The 'Channel Tunnel' model of the relation of psychology to neuroscience is wildly misleading – we do not have the psychologists, at the 'macro level', the 'top-downers', digging from one end, searching for postulated functions to explain psychological capacity; and the neurophysiologists, the 'micro level', the 'bottom-uppers' starting from individual nerve-cells and digging towards a grasp of cell *groups*, neural *networks*, and progressively larger cerebral structures. Of course there are, and should be, those working solely 'at the top'; and similary there are and should be those whose life work is in studying single-cell recordings; but there is a mass of work done at one of the numerous 'middle-sized' levels – studying the frontal lobes, or the comparator function, or the hippocampus, or cognitive maps. What one calls such work is wholly insignificant; 'neuro-psychology' will do. From conjectures about the brain one is stimulated to conjecture about 'cognitive' function; from observations about the development of transitive reasoning may come hints as to the structure and organization of the underlying cerebral systems. It is even misleading to talk of a 'co-evolution' of the two theories, since it is misleading to talk of 'two theories'; that suggests the Channel Tunnel again. There is a continuous search at many different levels (and we do not yet know what these 'levels' are going to be – they have to be discovered and described) which will advance *together*.

I hope that this too is an uncontentious and obvious point. (I find myself continually amazed, though, that is so often necessary to argue for it.) It does not even make a very strong claim about *the* mind–body relation; it would be compatible with many forms of dualism, so long as they allow for some forms of causal interaction between the mental and the physical. When we put it together with the first demand, though, we can see that the nature of the conceptual apparatus will be *constrained* by what we know or believe about the brain. In other words, the first demand alone is compatible with a denial of realism; it insists only that the developmental psychologists' theory must aim at 'empirical adequacy' – the phrase that Van Fraassen, who is avowedly an anti-realist, uses to characterize the ambition of scientific theories. But the second demand introduces the requirement of realism. Postulated psychological functions must not merely be competent to account for cognitive development; they must be functions which are really there – which the brain can and does perform. For we are all, I assume, realistic about the processes and structures with which neuroscience deals.

Thus the second demand on any adequate conceptual framework for developmental psychology deepens the impact of the first. The terminology that proves adequate to explain and describe the child's cognitive growth will have to be terminology that is infused by, or dependent on, or tractable to, or interlocking with, or helpful for, work in neuropsychology and neurophysiology. To illustrate by an extreme example: any theory that postulated, say, a telepathic power of the mind would be *falsified* if it could be shown that no cerebral system could possibly achieve such a thing.

Now the main question can receive its first answer. When we are thinking of the science of developmental psychology, then yes, we will need conceptual revision to describe the child's mind. But the answer is now (relatively) boring, in the sense that advances in all sciences require continual conceptual revision – whether of mass, of matter, of space; or of learning, memory, belief, emotion, or whatever. An implication that is possibly unwelcome, however, is the following: *no* armchair pontificating about what our ordinary language entails, suggests, presupposes, or implies is going to hold much interest. We cannot now predict what terms will be found useful and fruitful, nor how they will differ from the terms of everyday parlance from which they have been adapted. (They will probably prove to be very different indeed, very substantially adapted, simply because of the 'second demand' above, a demand which – it will shortly be argued – has no echo for everyday psychological terms.) No philosophy, except the philosophy of science, is relevant; and the least obstructive role that can be played by that branch of philosophy is to remind scientists continually that the mere fact that terms may have been *adopted* from everyday parlance may have no bearing whatsoever on the extent to which they have been *adapted*, and that what goes for ordinary language terms like 'belief' may not hold for those terms if, and when, they are used by the psychologist. (Curiously, scientists need reminding of this as often as do philosophers.)

IV

The original question subdivided, depending on whether we were considering the needs of psychologists or of parents: of science, or of common sense. Let us turn, then, to the difficulties that beset the non-scientist when he tries to describe what his child in the cot is doing. He is not, *qua* layman, concerned with building any general or systematic theory; unlike science (which seeks the common, the general, the fundamental) the descriptions and explanations of common sense aim to cope with the specific and particular: *this* child in just *this* playpen, after just *these* recent events involving *those* people, *that* smile or gesture, *this* achievement.

The non-scientist too needs something that is 'empirically adequate'. That is, he must have a way of talking about his infant that allows him to expect and predict certain things, a way of talking which makes sense of what he sees in his child. So some analogue of the 'first demand' discussed in the preceding section holds here as well.

What conspicuously does not hold is any analogue of the second demand. Parents in ancient Greece wanting to talk of their childrens' achievements needed an adequate mode of description just as much as parents do today; and many in ancient Greece would have believed, with

Aristotle, that the brain was an organ for cooling the blood. They were no worse off than we for that reason, though; or only marginally and insignificantly worse off. Virtually all of our incredibly rich, complex, intricate, and flexible psychological vocabulary stands in complete independence from any physiological facts; indeed, we can read and enjoy fiction that has rabbits, Pinocchios, ice-maidens, or robots as intelligent agents.

If the second demand does not hold, then we lose *that* argument for construing our common-sense psychology realistically. And now my claim is this: were we to take an instrumentalist construal of *much* (not all) of our everyday ascriptions of intentional states, then the other half of the original problem (the 'problem-for-parents') would dissolve; we have not solved it, but on the other hand we no longer have it. We can leave the thorny problems of propositional-attitude identification to those who like that sort of inquiry. The 'instrumentalist construal' I have in mind is the following: we need not require that expressions such as 'thinks that p', 'believes that q' (and so on) really refer to any state or process in the head; we need not require that statements involving such locutions are true or false 'by correspondence to the facts'.

Evidently, arguments need to be provided for such a (qualified) instrumentalism. I have tried to supply them elsewhere (Wilkes, in press) and will summarize them below. Since, however, the claim is one which many resist strongly, this summary may be considered inadequate; but I have no space for more.

1 I start with a concession. Not all of our everyday ascriptions are appropriate for a non-realist construal. Common-sense psychology cannot be said to constitute a 'theory' in the same sense that science has 'theories'; not being a 'theory', it would not be surprising if there were bits of it that needed to be considered realistically, and bits that do not. I am perfectly realistic about the existence of headaches, the capacity to see and hear, or thoughts and memories that 'run through the head', for example. Evidently, too, since science and common sense have a substantial overlap, in our everyday language we will often find ourselves talking about the same things that scientists talk about (gold, water, heat; emotion, fear, aggression); and whenever we do that, our terms will naturally refer – although perhaps more vaguely – to the same real things or capacities. It is rather the specific thoughts and beliefs (and so on) that we postulate or assume in order to explain someone's behaviour, for which instrumentalism is often more plausible than realism.

2 But just as there are statements in common-sense psychological talk that anyone would agree to be literally, realistically true, so there are many idioms and assertions that nobody would wish to so construe. For example, when we say that something 'weighs on', or is 'at the back of'

one's mind. Similarly, there are terms which most people would think did not genuinely refer to a 'mental state or event'; probably few today believe that 'there is such a thing as' the will, or willpower, although in the nineteenth century it was more common to be realistic about a *faculty* of willing. It is a trivial fact that not all noun terms refer (consider 'sake'), which does not stop them being useful. But if we admit that there is this host of useful but not literally true idioms in common parlance, and of useful but not literally referring noun terms, we have already stepped out in the direction I am recommending.

3   The arguments rehearsed above (section I) that illustrate the various and manifold problems in *identifying* beliefs can all of course be exploited to suggest the desirability of not *entifying* them. I shall say no more about this, although they add up to a compelling case.

4   Consider the beliefs that many might want to call 'preconscious', such as the example given above: 'I thought there was another step'. Do we really want to say, *and above all what would it mean to say*, that there 'really is' such a thought in my head? This question – what it would mean to assert this – is one for which I cannot imagine an answer. But the problem is worse than the example suggests; because what goes for such beliefs, thoughts (etc.) goes for virtually all others. Only thoughts or memories that 'run through the head' (perhaps in words), and which thus have a clear *temporal* 'fix', seem to escape the difficulty. In the physical world we can refer to spatio-temporally bounded objects and processes, so their ontological status is clear; we know what we are doing and saying. With ascriptions of beliefs we have nothing analogous. *If* our common sense ascriptions were tied to what is believed about cerebral processes (as I argued above the terms of scientific psychology are; *vide* the 'second demand') then we can make sense of thoughts and beliefs 'really being' in the head, because cerebral states and processes are suitably and spatio-temporally there; but they obviously and manifestly are not so tied. The second demand has no analogy in common sense. Of course information, of some sort, is *somehow* stored in the head, and so are mechanisms, of some sort, for using and exploiting, altering and adding to it; and about these (unknown) information-bits and information-processors I want to be perfectly realistic: science one day will have to identify and explain them. It does not follow, though, that science must or could find and explain my belief that MPs are mortal; indeed, it is difficult to understand what this could mean.

5   Common-sense explanation is an essentially context-dependent matter. There is a real sense in which scientific explanation is too, of course; but there the experimental contexts are 'fixed' in the sense that they are described precisely and are usually or at least typically repeatable, and thus the explanations are also, in another sense, context *transcendent*.

Moreover, science seeks to explain what is general, common, systematic, and so the *explananda* are context *independent* – the same in Wigan or Warsaw – to a very large extent. Now, the role of explanation is to remove puzzlement; and, in an everyday context, which may be richly specific, unique, well-nigh unrepeatable, what puzzles an inquirer will be in large part a function of *him* – of his background knowledge and ignorance (which may be highly idiosyncratic, tacit or implicit) of accidental details of this very situation and this particular baby. Thus an adequate explanation will depend not only on what may, or may not, be literally true of the infant whose behaviour is being explained, but must depend also on what holds of this very inquirer in the highly specific context of *this* explanatory enterprise. We need an account which the inquirer can use to make sense of what he has seen, in the light of what else he thinks or supposes. Put another way, all explanation is relational – explaining something *to* somebody; but in science the recipients of the explanation can be assumed to share the background against which explanations work, whereas they cannot in everyday explanation. The goodness of common sense explanations is therefore very largely a function of facts about *the audience*.

6   Not all explanation is causal explanation. We do indeed hold that actions are caused; we do indeed cite beliefs and desires in the explanation of action; but we need not conflate these two truths and suppose that beliefs and desires explain actions *because* they are causes of them. If beliefs and desires explain by making the behaviour fit a pattern that an inquirer finds intelligible, the argument that we must be realistic about propositional attitudes because they cause behaviour no longer has any bite.

7   Too loose a characterization of the instrumentalism I defend is that (i) the terms it construes instrumentalistically do not really refer, and (ii) that statements involving them are neither true or false. As thus loosely described, this may seem to suggest a *prima facie* objection to the argument; we do, after all, call many ordinary language explanations true or false. Points (5) and (6) above suggest that common-sense judgements use coherence when it comes to evidence; but one can surely run a coherence theory of *evidence* with a correspondence theory of *truth*, so our everyday judgements may yet be true (or false). Is not this a strong objection? No. Instrumentalism denies truth *by correspondence*, and is perfectly compatible with a looser (everyday!) notion of truth that allows correspondence, coherence, redundancy – and probably much else besides – to legitimize judgements of truth or falsity. Perhaps it is true that correspondence theories are the best *theories* of truth around; but it has yet to be shown (and how could it be?) that everyday English speakers use 'true' this way exclusively. The intricate and complex jelly of our everyday linguistic practices rarely fit well into the wire grid of systematic theories.

Suppose that the case for a qualified instrumentalism holds water (and I repeat that each of points 1–7 above should have had fuller defence). Then the parents no longer have any problem which common sense cannot handle. It matters not at all that we have no way of discovering *the* content of thoughts we ascribe to the infant. Whatever works – subject to the reasonable constraints of Lloyd Morgan's canon – will be acceptable. The common-sensical view illustrated in the introductory paragraph – claiming that there was no real problem here – thus emerges as half true. The layman can exploit the generous and tolerant richness of the language to describe the child's mind. That language, precisely because of its overlapping shades of meaning, nuance, and connotation, can be deployed in context to say specifically and exactly what we mean. No conceptual revision is needed here at all.

REFERENCES

Armstrong, D. M. 1973: *Belief, Truth and Knowledge.* Cambridge: Cambridge University Press.

Davidson, D. 1975: Thought and talk. In S. Guttenplan (ed.) *Mind and Language.* Oxford: Clarendon Press.

Newton-Smith, W. H. 1981: *The Rationality of Science.* London: Routledge and Kegan Paul.

Van Fraassen, B. 1980: *The Scientific Image.* Cambridge: Cambridge University Press.

Wilkes, K. V. 1984: Pragmatics in science and theory in common sense. *Inquiry,* 27, 339–61.

in press: Nemo psychologus nisi physiologus. *Inquiry.*

2

On the very idea of acquiring a concept

Andrew Woodfield

THE IDEA OF A CONCEPT

It may not be a miracle, but it is a marvel, how children attain concepts. Not all concepts are innate, so how are the non-innate concepts acquired? From experience. But the child has to organize and encode those experiences. Simply having the raw ingredients in front of you does not bake the cake.

Concept-possession is more than the ability to sort instances into one group and non-instances into another. The sorting has to be made according to the right criteria, and has to be represented at a properly conceptual level. There are pairs of concepts which, while they denote the same class of objects, classify the objects by distinct criteria. The concepts HUMAN BEING and FEATHERLESS BIPED are such a pair. A general concept has an intension as well as an extension; to master a given concept, the subject has to master the right intension. Also the representation must be of a kind that can figure in intellectual operations. The concept HUMAN, for instance, is not the same as the sensory capacity to discriminate human-ness. Certain biting insects have that.

Nor is it true, contrary to what some empiricist philosophers say, that 'a concept is a recognitional capacity' (Price, 1953, p. 355). The connection between acquiring the concept of a K and coming to recognize Ks is a very important factor in the ontogenesis of concepts for some observable kinds of K, but is quite unimportant in the case of concepts for theoretical kinds. Perceptual recognition is not identical with concept-exercising, because concepts are the ingredients of thoughts, judgements, beliefs, and other mental states that figure in processes of reasoning. In ordinary discourse, a sentence 'like Fido sees x as a bone' does not entail 'Fido has the concept BONE'. We, the speakers, show by our words that *we* have the concept BONE, but what we attribute to Fido is a representation of what a standard bone *looks like*, viewed from a variety of canine perspectives.

18 *Issues in Developmental Explanation*

Developmental psychologists, when asked how cognitive capacities develop, commonly distinguish two sorts of answer. One enterprise is to discover, by observation and experiment, what children of different ages can do. By generalizing across children in the same age-group, and then comparing different age-groups, they derive standard competence vectors charting the progress of an average child. The second enterprise is to pin down the mechanisms which account for the observed changes. In psychology, 'mechanisms' can mean a multitude of different things; practically any hypothesis will count as a hypothesis about a mechanism provided that it identifies a causal factor underlying the ordered changes, whether it be a rule, a procedure, or a functional structure.[1]

When the question at issue is how *concepts* develop, there is a further problem. A quick survey of the literature will reveal that different theorists mean different things by 'concept'. In the annals of twentieth-century psychology, there lies a vast corpus of material on concept-formation, classified under 'learning theory', and drawing upon the classical associationist tradition. The British empiricists had a seductive set of doctrines about how 'ideas' orginate, combine, and interact. Simple ideas, the building-blocks, were said to be faint copies of sense-impressions of simple qualities. This led empiricist psychologists to regard concepts as perceptual memory-traces, and to focus upon discrimination-learning.

On the neighbouring shelves we find 'cognitive development'. A great deal of the material here is written by, or inspired by, Jean Piaget. Piaget's approach, while informed by many sources, (biology, *Gestalt* psychology, Kant . . .), is ultimately rooted in a Thomistic conception of the soul. The young child is an active, abstracting intelligence, who interprets the world as it appears to him even before he is able to think symbolically. Reality throws up problems, the child strives to solve them in ways that are rational by his own lights, using his half-formed cognitive apparatus. As one might expect, given that Aquinas is one of the grandfathers of cognitive science, the same conception of mind is prevalent in artificial intelligence. Maybe the grandchildren should get together more – as Boden (1978) advocates.

Neither learning theory nor Piagetian theory has yet produced a satisfactory account of concept-formation. One wonders whether the problem has been properly formulated. Perhaps it is insoluble. The term 'concept' is a semi-technical term of folk psychology, and folk psychology, wedded to intentional idioms, may turn out to be an unsuitable framework for the scientific study of development. Paul Churchland (1981, pp. 75–6) likens the theory of 'beliefs' and 'concepts' to discredited, superseded theories, for example alchemy. Folk psychology, he says, is stagnant; it does not fit in with the rest of science. Folk psychology models inner states on sentences; but the inner states of a preverbal child are not sentence-like (Paul Churchland, 1979, pp. 127–37). Stephen Stich (1982, 1983) is another philosopher who argues that beliefs will not prove useful in cognitive science. They are individuated by their intentional contents, but content is not an objective property. Concepts are individuated by their contents, so Stich's attack is aimed at them too (as will be spelt out more fully below).

It is an open question whether content-based developmental psychology will gradually give way to a content-free, computational approach. At the present state of play, I think we ought to try and give concepts a good run for their money. This means making a serious effort to solve the problems that will now be stated.

THE PROBLEM OF THE LITTLE SCIENTIST

According to Saint Augustine, when children first learn a language, they learn to translate public utterances into private sentences that they already understand. The internal sentences belong to a system of cognitive representation – a language of thought – which must have as much semantic power as any public medium that the child learns. Wittgenstein (1953, section 32 and sequel) thought this view simply shifted the problem of understanding one step back. Jerry Fodor (1975, pp.55–64), on the other hand, argues that the Augustinian view, counter-intuitive though it may seem, must be correct. There is no serious alternative. The child masters a language by testing hypotheses about what the words might mean. Such hypotheses must be mentally represented; so the system in which they are framed must be rich enough to represent the meanings of public words.

This chapter is not primarily about language acquisition. Our problems arise at the very earliest stage of concept-formation, prior to the time when the child starts to talk. However, the 'little scientist' view can be applied to infants. If concept-formation, even at the earliest stage, is a process of learning that certain hypotheses are true, the infant needs to possess the concept being learned on a given occasion in order to frame the correct hypothesis. The argument is set out in careful form by Fodor (1981, pp. 266–9); it will be briefly summarized.[2]

Foder reserves the term 'concept-learning' to describe what goes on in experiments like the following. The subject S undergoes a series of learning-trials in which he is shown, say, pictures of triangles, squares, circles, and oblongs of various colours and sizes. Each trial presents him with four pictures, one of each shape; colours and sizes vary randomly. S is encouraged to select one. The experimenter has decided to reward S's responses to one of the shapes, say square, and to penalize responses to the other three. S has succeeded on the task when he responds consistently to just the stimuli that produce reinforcement. If S cottons on, the only explanation for his success is that he has tried out some hypotheses. *S* starts by *wondering* which class of stimulus he is supposed to select. Wrong hypotheses get discarded when they lead to penalties; eventually one hypothesis is hit upon which leads to consistent reward, and *S* regards it as confirmed. To hit on the correct solution, *S* had to frame the hypothesis that *squares* are the stimuli that he is supposed to be respond-ing to; he must mentally represent squareness to do this, hence he must possess the concept SQUARE.

This 'concept-learning' paradigm cannot explain how *S* acquired the concept SQUARE, for it presupposes that SQUARE is already *in situ*. According to Fodor, there is no theory of how a concept like SQUARE could get into *S*'s mind as a result of experience. Concepts like this, which are not synthesized by combining pre-existing simpler concepts, must, there-fore, be innate.

The conclusion seems incredible; surely there is something wrong with the argument. Are all its premises true? Is it really true that there exists no account of concept-acquisition that is not concept *learning*? If there really is none, then surely, as Patricia Churchland (1978) notes, someone had better hurry up and construct one, for such extreme innatism is contrary to common sense. One premise certainly looks very suspicious: the idea that concept-formation always involves framing and testing conceptualized hypotheses. It makes the infant too intellectually grown-up. We could try rejecting this premise. But we would need a radical alternative to replace it. It would be mere 'handwaving' to say that *S* 'does something *like* framing hypotheses and testing them, but ... he does not literally do so because, of course, he does not yet have a language in which to frame such items' (Patricia Churchland, 1980, p. 161).

THE PROBLEM OF NETWORK-DEPENDENCE

Concepts are not isolated from one another. They come in families, or clusters. There are two schools of thought about the structure of con-ceptual systems, and both imply that such systems are holistic.

Concepts, like general words, often have the job of dividing up a taxonomic domain, a spectrum, a dimension, or a hierarchy. Each concept does part of the dividing work and relies on others to do the rest. Concepts occupying the same taxonomic level tend to be mutually exclusive. When there is a hierarchy, a concept at a given level implies concepts at higher positions on its own branch, and is implied by concepts below it. Each concept implies the negations of concepts on other branches of the tree at or below its own level. Every language contains words for species and genera, determinates and determinables, and this fact surely mirrors a general truth about how the human mind classifies objects (see Keil, 1979; Macnamara, 1982).

Logical relations between concepts regulate their use in reasoning. For example, if S judges that x is a cat, S ought to be prepared to accept that x is a mammal, that x is an animal, that x is not a dog, and so on. The same logical relations, when viewed from a different angle, could be regarded as *constitutive* of the concepts in question. Thus, for a concept to count as CAT, it must occupy a position in a network where it implies higher-level concepts like ANIMAL and excludes same-level concepts such as DOG. This means that S must actually possess some concepts occupying the same level and higher levels.

Each concept has links to others which fix its proper role in inferences. Having a charactistic inferential role is part of having an intension; the inferential role of a concept is its totality of ways of interacting with other concepts, as includer or excluder, includee and excludee, and so on. In traditional semantics, the intension of a general word was held also to include everything in the word's definition. Thus, if 'cat' were defined as 'small furry mammal with whiskers and tail, which purrs', then all the properties mentioned would belong in this intension, as well as the genus (mammal). The same idea, when transposed from words to concepts, yields what may be called the 'Kantian' view: the concept for K is *constitutively linked* to every concept which stands for a nominally essential (that is, defining) characteristic of K.[3]

Natural kind terms, however, are hard to define in words. It was never clear which characteristics of any given natural kind were nominally essential. The intuitive idea is that a characteristic C is nominally essential to a kind K if and only if it is true that a person who did not know that all Ks have C would not really understand what it was to be a K. In the case of kinship terms, which are easier to define, the Kantian view becomes somewhat clearer. For example, the concept FATHER is constitutively linked to the concepts MALE and PARENT certainly, and possibly to ADULT. It is also contitutively linked, in virtue of its inferential role, to MOTHER, FEMALE, and perhaps CHILD.

Because it draws a rigid distinction between essential and non-essential characteristics, the Kantian view has the corollory that not all the links enjoyed by a given concept are constitutive links. Suppose that S knows that all cats have lungs. S's CAT concept 'stands in connection' with his concept LUNG. But if 'has lungs' is not part of the definition of 'cat', S could have acquired CAT without connecting it with LUNG, indeed S could possess CAT without possessing LUNG. The absence of that particular link would not affect the identify or integrity of S's concept CAT.

Quine (1953), in his well-known argument against the analytic–synthetic distinction, cast doubt upon the traditional doctrine of definition. The second school of thought about conceptual structures, which may be called the 'Quinean' view,[4] correspondingly rejects that rigid distinction between constitutive and non-constitutive links. Instead, the identity of a concept is loosely tied down by a multifarious array of links which extend to concepts for other kinds of thing and concepts for characteristics, both defining and non-defining. Some links will be more important than others. If an important link to the concept of K is broken, there may be a question as to whether the severance results in a concept that is no longer the old concept of K. Such questions sometimes have no right answer; if an answer has to be decided upon, certain global properties of the whole system – such as coherence, economy, and simplicity – will have to be taken into consideration. No single link is absolutely essential, nor is there a definite, minimum number that must remain intact: concept-survival is a matter of degree. The tendency of the Quinean view is to heighten the holism. Any link is potentially relevant to the identity of the linked concepts; moreover, every concept could be linked to all of the others, if we take account of indirect, mediated links, Quine (1960, p. 13), plays down what he calls 'excessive holism' by noting that 'some middle-sized scrap of theory usually will embody all the connections that are likely to affect our adjudication of a given sentence'.[5]

A parallel qualification, espoused by the Quinean view of concepts, is that S's network has an inner organization of smaller networks such that links *within* a sub-network have higher weight than links that *cross* from one sub-network to another. Hence CAT will probably not have much to do with CATHODE RAY, for instance. Some such view, incorporating a graduated holism, is currently the orthodoxy in Anglo-American philosophy.

In both the old view and the new, concepts come in bundles by their very nature. This fact imposes a tough constraint upon any theory of concept-acquisition. Given the graduated holism, it makes no sense to suppose that there was ever a time when subject S possessed just *one* concept, and no sense to suppose that constitutively linked concepts were acquired *one by one*. Consider a baby who has no empirical concepts at all. Network-dependence means that the baby has to 'jump' into a network endowed with a certain size and logical structure, without going through any intermediate states in which the network was smaller. Whereas the baby's physical development is gradual, psychological development appears to involve a saltation. Yet it is difficult to see how a baby *could* go from having no concepts to suddenly having a lot. Is it sparked off by a special event, rather as a car windscreen, when hit by a stone, becomes opaque all over? Is 'catastrophe theory' relevant?

According to Wittgenstein (1969, section 141), 'When we first begin to *believe* anything, what we believe is not a single proposition, it is a whole system of propositions. (Light dawns gradually over the whole.).' The last sentence is a metaphor for which Wittgenstein offers no further elucidation, and which fares poorly under close scrutiny. However, it presents a challenge to us. It appears that the acquisition of a minimal system of concepts is *not* a gradual process in which parts of the system are acquired at different times, precisely *because* the system is holistic. Yet any observer of children will say that light does dawn gradually. How is this possible?

THE PROBLEM OF ASSIGNING CONTENTS TO JUVENILE CONCEPTS

Psychologists, and parents, want to know which concepts the child possesses at which age, how the set gets bigger over time, and what effects the new ones have upon the old ones. We normally specify concepts in terms of their contents, by a method that is irremediably approximate (see Woodfield, 1982). This may be good enough for the parents, but it is doubtful whether it is good enough for developmental psychologists.

Consider the case of 1-year old Susie, who is well-acquainted with Tibby the family cat. Susie has routines for handling Tibby; she picks him up, strokes him in a special way, listens out for his purr, gives him saucers of milk, and so on. Susie has met several other cats, whom she is disposed to treat to the same routines. One day, the neighbours introduce her to their pet rabbit; Susie reacts to it pretty much as she reacts to Tibby and the other cats. Her parents exclaim, 'Susie thinks the rabbit is a cat!'. In ascribing this false belief, they intend to claim that Susie exercised the concept CAT.

Difficulties begin with doubts about whether the parents are justified, by scientific standards, in making this claim. Susie's behaviour suggests that she has classified the rabbit in the same category as the cats. No doubt she can see that the rabbit does not look exactly like the cats, but no two cats look exactly alike, and for all Susie knows, some cats might have big, floppy ears. Would it not be plausible to say that Susie has a half-formed concept whose extension includes some cats plus a rabbit? If so, it is not the concept CAT. English does not have a special word to name the mixed class, but we could invent one, 'catrabbit', whose extension exactly matches Susie's hypothesized concept. Then the parents could say 'Susie thinks the rabbit is a catrabbit', and their thought would be true. Why do the parents not consider this possibility?

It could be that they prefer to use 'cat' because they think that the concept in question will mature into a concept which Susie will herself express, later on, by means of the word 'cat'. They may think it is destined to turn into the concept CAT. Aristotle was happy to classify growing things into the kinds to which they will belong later; he says, for example, that a rose-bud has the form of a rose *potentially*. Such prolepsis is a familiar taxonomic device in embryology (cf. 'limb-bud', 'presumptive neural plate'). Yet it would be risky to place much weight on what the parents say in this case, for their expectations about how the concept will develop may be wrong.

The total behavioural evidence actually available always underdetermines the choice between various hypotheses about Susie's conceptualization. Furthermore, this underdetermination never goes away. Suppose that Susie, after learning that the rabbit is very different from Tibby and the other cats, comes to classify it as a member of a different kind. To chart her progress, we need to specify her two later concepts. The difficulty about specifying her original concept carries over to the later stage, for there is no guarantee that the two separate concepts correspond exactly to CAT and RABBIT. When presented with new animals, a Pekinese dog, for instance, she might overextend one or other of the two concepts in order to cover the dog.

A further difficulty arises. It is tempting to say that her later concept (CAT, we shall suppose) is a refinement of the original (which we shall suppose was CATRABBIT). Perhaps the cues she first used were quite good ones for picking out cats, and she sticks to those but supplements them with additional criteria that rule out floppy-eared rabbits. We are tempted to say that one and the same mental representation exists before and after, but that it has narrowed its scope. In folk psychology, however, a concept is type-individuated by its content. Because CATRABBIT and CAT have different extensions, they have different contents, and must be counted as numerically distinct. They could be regarded as ancestor and descendant, perhaps, but they are certainly not the same concept, nor phases of the same concept. This fact undermines any attempt to treat concepts as individuals that modify their contents as they grow. The notion of a developing individual is that of a temporally persisting substance which undergoes property-alterations. 'This arm has grown', for instance, implies that the arm referred to, now a certain size, is the very same arm that was, at an earlier time, smaller. Similarly, 'This concept has become more sophisticated than it used to be' implies that the concept referred to is the very same one that used to be less sophisticated.

The difficulties do not end here. Stich (1983, p. 79), building upon certain insights of Quine (1960, especially p. 219), and of Davidson (1974), has offered an analysis of what goes on when a person ascribes content to a subject's beliefs. The analysis is complex; there is no space here to go into all the details. The basic idea, however, is: 'In saying what someone else belives, we describe his belief by relating it to one we ourselves might have.' The relation in question is a complex *similarity* which admits of degrees along several dimensions. For an ascription of the form '*S* believes that *P*' to be deemed true, there must be a doxastic similarity between the ascriber and *S* that is *sufficient* in the light of the context and the purpose of the utterance. Since beliefs are network dependent, *S* cannot truly be said to have the belief which the speaker ascribes on his own understanding of '*P*' unless *S* and the speaker share a large number of background beliefs and concepts. In other words, the two have to be 'ideologically similar'. They must also be 'functionally similar' in the sense that their inferential mechanisms must operate in similar ways. The more dissimilarity there is, the more difficult it becomes for the ascriber to convey S's state of mind. Accuracy decreases, in cases where the subject has very few of the same concepts as the speaker, to the point where content cannot sensibly be ascribed to S at all. This critical point is approached, or passed, when we try to capture the beliefs of people very alien in life-style to ourselves, or the beliefs of animals (Stich, 1983, chap. 5, sections 4 and 5). The intuition is simple: if *you* conceive the world in a totally different way from *me*, I cannot say (or conceive) how you conceive it.

At the beginning of *The Child's Conception of the World*, Piaget (1929) asks, 'Does the child, in fact, believe, as we do, in a real world and does he distinguish the belief from the various fictions of play and of imagination? ... What conceptions of the world does the child naturally form at the different stages of its development?' If Stich is right in his analysis, no scientific answers to these questions are possible. There is no saying, in English, French, or any other adult language, what the child conceives the world *as*.

Of course, a sentence like 'Susie believes that this porcelain receptacle contains H_2O' can be deemed true if it is *construed loosely*. A speaker may use a term in a 'that' clause to pick out an object without claiming that Susie thinks of the object under the mode of presentation that is suggested by that term. Predicates in 'that' clauses can function transparently also; speakers do not always aim to capture the way in which S conceptualizes properties and categories. Armstrong (1973, chap. 3) exploits this in his account of animal beliefs. We can, he says, ascribe beliefs to dogs, though our attributions have to be construed transparently, 'because we do not know the exact content of their beliefs'. Very often, the focus of our attention is the state of affairs believed in, rather than the subject's representation of it. Unfortunately, this truth offers little comfort to psychologists who do aim to specify the child's mode of presentation. For a person who is interested in Susie's mind, the sentence cited above is useless on the loose construal, and simply false on a strictly psychological construal.

Content-ascription, then, poses a threefold problem. Identifying a juvenile concept by this method is unsuitable for psychological purposes because: the extention of a concept is impossible to determine by behavioural tests; the concept cannot change its content over time without becoming a different concept; and the intension of a child's concept cannot be expressed in indirect speech unless the speaker shares roughly the same conceptual framework as the child – but infants evidently do *not* think like adults. To cap the problem, there seems to be no other way to talk about a concept except by specifying its content; content seems to be its most essential feature. So much the worse for concepts, says Stich, and for any theory of concept-formation.

WHAT IS TO BE DONE?

Philosophical objections to a scientific enterprise can vary greatly in weight and status. Sometimes they strike the scientists as 'merely verbal'. Such objections can be dealt with at the stroke of a pen, by altering a phrase without altering the theory, or by coining a metaphor. Alternatively, an objection may be felt to be valid, but nit-picking. It is to be defused, neutralized, put in perspective. Then again, an *a priori* objection can sometimes be so damaging as to call for a complete revamping of the theory.

Several of the present difficulties could be circumvented by the introduction of new, perspicuous terminology. Concepts cannot, by definition, change their contents. Fine. Let developmentalists drop the term 'concept' and replace it by a term that is free from this restriction. Concede that we cannot specify S's subjective contents until the time when S is conceptually similar to ourselves. Concede that concepts are intrinsically network dependent. Put the two concessions together and accept that it is wrong to describe any of the child's representations as 'concepts' until they form an inferentially integrated network like our own. Still, the child could possess representations that are not yet concepts (because they fail this condition), but which are, so to speak, destined to attain that status later. Let us call these precursors 'protoconcepts'. Protoconcepts start off not having that high degree of holistic intentionality which is essential to concepts. We can express hypotheses about their identity-conditions and persistence-conditions without getting tangled in knots. By a verbal reform, the problems of holism, and ideological and functional similarity, are sidestepped, at least for a while.

With respect to the 'little scientist' problem, Fodor's challenge should be met by looking for alternatives to the 'concept-learning' paradigm. S must acquire certain representations very early in life, before the time when he can represent hypotheses. The sort of representations wanted are *recognition-schemas*. The notion of 'schemata' dates back to Kant (1787). Many cognitive and developmental psychologists have seen the usefulness of some such notion.[6]

The principal desideratum is that the process of forming a schema should *not* be a matter of testing hypotheses couched in the same representational medium as the schema. On the notion that I favour, schemas are formed by a process of adaptation to the objective groupings that are found in S's environment. That such groupings exist at the 'basic' level of categorizataion has been established by Rosch et al. (1976). Schemas are not products of hypothesis testing at all. It would be an intellectualist fallacy so to describe a process of environmentally steered *growth*. In cases where the structure of the brain is permanently and irreversibly altered by environmental influences, 'epigenesis' seems the appropriate term to use, in psychology as in embryology (see Bower, 1979, especially chaps 2 and 3).

To be logically adequate, a theory of schemas must not only define them, it must explain how it is possible for them to be epigenetic products yet representational at the same time. To be empirically adequate, the theory should describe how schemas do actually get formed in the human infant's mind/brain (and in the brains of other animal species perhaps). This is the first step in a multi-step project.

The next step is to devise a theory of protoconcept formation. It would have to say precisely what protoconcepts are, say which aspects of them are innate (if any), and what sort of system they belong to. Then, it would, in my view, show how certain protoconcepts get anchored to schemas, and acquire there by a kind of natural reference. to the category to which their schema is sensitive.

A further step will be an account of the various ways in which proto-concepts turn into concepts. Concepts are like members of a highly integrated society governed by social rules. An individual protoconcept develops, under favourable circumstances, into a concept, rather as a human neonate develops into a socialized person. Each protoconcept is launched into the system having a natural semantic value mediated by its schema. It has minimal intension at first; it builds up an inferential role gradually, by incorporating a dossier of accumulated information.

How? I wish I could offer a properly worked-out theory. Alas, my theory is still in foetal form, unready to see the light. The prospects for achieving an abstract formulation that solves the three problems are, I believe, good. Nevertheless, the construction of a precise *empirical* theory of concept-formation calls for a joint effort on the part of philosophers, artificial intelligence workers, and psychologists.[7]

NOTES

1   This twofold division is an over-simplification on my part. At each stage of development there is a structure or process which underlies the competence, and which generates the performance characteristics of that stage. There could be a series of hypotheses about *different* functional mechanisms that are in control at different stages. At a level below this, there might be another mechanism or process which causes the functional mechanisms to change. In cognitive development, there is no limit to the complexity and number

    of the things to be explained; my modification, therefore, is over-simplified too.

2 Fodor's essay is required reading for anyone interested in the philosophical background to theories of concept-acquisition. It is full of surprises; the debate between empiricists and rationalists is shown in a new light.

3 'Kantian' because of this celebrated dictum: 'Either the predicate B belongs to the subject A, as something which is (covertly) contained in this concept A; or B lies outside the concept A, although it does indeed stand in connection with it. In the one case I entitle the judgement analytic, in the other synthetic' Kant (1787, Introduction IV, p. 48).

4 I do not say that Quine himself would subscribe to this view. In fact, he is altogether sceptical of 'ideas' and 'concepts'. See, for example, Quine (1974, section 9).

5 This remark has been taken out of context; it is about confirmation rather than meaning. But there is a close connection between these. It should also be registered, in connection with Quine's real views, that sentences vary in the degree to which they rely, for their continued acceptance, upon support from the sentential network. Some are closer to the 'periphery' than others, that is, are more closely tied to perceptual evidence (see Quine, 1960, p. 13). However, no sentence is immune to intra-network pressures. Hence Fodor's (1983, p. 107) choice of the word 'Quinenian' to name a holistic aspect of belief-fixation, the aspect whereby 'the degree of confirmation assigned to any given hypothesis is sensitive to properties of the entire belief system'.

6 Piaget (see Flavell, 1963, pp. 52–8, for a summary of Piaget's views), Bartlett (1932, pp. 199–214), Kagan (1970, 1971), and Neisser (1976, chap. 4) have all zeroed in on the idea of a primitive, pre-conceptual type of representation, though their conceptions are all slightly different. Harris (1983) goes into some of the differences between Piaget and Kagan. Rumelhart (1980) uses the term 'schema', though schemata in his sense are quite complex, frame-like representations. They are more like the things we have called 'protoconcepts', or like *combinations* of protoconcepts and schemas (see Woodfield, forthcoming).

7 I should add that in the past decade a great deal of interesting research has been carried out by cognitive psychologists on conceptual categorization, though not from a specifically developmental point of view. Important discoveries have been made about prototypes, family resemblance, and graded structure. Unfortunately there is not enough space to comment on this work here. For useful reviews, see Smith and Medin (1981), Mervis and Rosch (1981), and Medin and Smith (1984). These findings must clearly be integrated with any developmental theory of the future.

REFERENCES

Armstrong, D. M. 1973: *Belief, Truth and Knowledge*. Cambridge: Cambridge University Press.
Bartlett, F. C. 1932: *Remembering*. Cambridge: Cambridge University Press.

Boden, M. 1978: Artificial intelligence and Piagetian theory. *Synthèse*, 38, 389–414.

Bower, T. G. R. 1979: *Human Development*. San Francisco: W. H. Freeman.

Churchland, P. M. 1979: *Scientific Realism and the Plasticity of Mind*. Cambridge: Cambridge University Press.

  1981: Eliminative materialism and propositional attitudes. *Journal of Philosophy*, 78, 67–90.

Churchland, Patricia S. 1978: Fodor on language learning. *Synthèse*, 38, 149–59.

  1980: Language, thought, and information processing. *Nous*, 14, 147–69.

Davidson, D. 1974: On the very idea of a conceptual scheme. *Proceedings and Addresses of the American Philosophical Association*, 47. Reprinted in *Inquiries into Truth and Interpretation*. Oxford: Clarendon Press, 1984.

Flavell, J. H. 1963: *The Developmental Psychology of Jean Piaget*. New York: Van Nostrand Reinhold.

Fodor, J. A. 1975: *The Language of Thought*. Brighton, Sussex: Harvester Press.

  1981: The present status of the innateness controversy. In *Representations*. Brighton, Sussex: Harvester Press, chap. 10.

  1983: *The Modularity of Mind*. Cambridge, Mass.: MIT Press.

Harris, P. L. 1983: Infant cognition. In Paul H. Mussen (ed.), *Handbook of Child Psychology* 4th edn, vol. II (edited by M. M. Haith and J. J. Campos). New York: Wiley.

Kagan, J. 1970: The determinants of attention in the infant. *American Scientist*, 58, 298–305.

  1971: *Change and Continuity in Infancy*. New York: Wiley.

Kant, I. 1787: *Critique of Pure Reason*, trans. Norman Kemp-Smith (1929 edn). London: MacMillan.

Keil, F. C. 1979: *Semantic and Conceptual Development: An Ontological Perspective*. Cambridge, Mass.: Harvard University Press.

Macnamara, J. 1982: *Names for Things: A Study of Human Learning*. Cambridge, Mass.: MIT Press.

Medin, D. L. and Smith, B. B. 1984: Concepts and concept formation. *Annual Review of Psychology*, 35, 113–38.

Mervis, C. B. and Rosch, B. 1981: Categorization of natural objects. *Annual Review of Psychology*, 32, 89–115.

Neisser, U. 1976: *Cognition and Reality*. San Francisco: W. H. Freeman.

Piaget, J. 1929: *The Child's Conception of the World*. London: Kegan Paul, Trench, Trubner.

Price, H. H. 1953: *Thinking and Experience*. London: Routledge and Kegan Paul.

Quine, W. V. 1953: Two dogmas of empiricism. In *From a Logical Point of View*. Cambridge, Mass.: Harvard University Press.

  1960: *Word and Object*. Cambridge, Mass.: MIT Press.

  1974: *The Roots of Reference*. La Salle, Ill.: Open Court.

Rosch, E., Mervis, C. B. Gray, W., Johnson, D. and Boyes-Braem, P. 1976: Basic objects in natural categories. *Cognitive Psychology*, 8, 382–439.

Rumelhart, D. E. 1979: Schemata: the building blocks of cognition. In R. J. Spiro, B. Bruce and W. F. Brewer (eds), *Theoretical Issues in Reading Comprehension*. Hillsdale, NJ: Lawrence Erlbaum.

Smith, E. E. and Medin, D. L. 1981: *Categories and Concepts*. Cambridge, Mass.: Harvard University Press.

Stich, S. P. 1982: On the ascription of content. In A. Woodfield (ed.), *Thought and Object: Essays on Intentionality*. Oxford: Clarendon Press.

1983: *From Folk Psychology to Cognitive Science*. Cambridge, Mass.: MIT Press.

Wittgenstein, L. 1953: *Philosophical Investigations*, trans. G. Anscombe. Oxford: Basil Blackwell.

1969: *On Certainty*, ed. G. E. M. Anscombe and G. H. Von Wright. Oxford: Basil Blackwell.

Woodfield, A. 1982: On specifying the contents of thoughts. In A. Woodfield (ed.), *Thought and Object: Essays on Intentionality*. Oxford: Clarendon Press.

forthcoming: Schemas and protoconcepts: a 'dual-representation, dual-process' model of concept-formation. Unpublished manuscript.

3

The development of 'introspection'

William Lyons

INTRODUCTION

In philosophy, and in psychology since behaviourism, there have rarely been extended studies of introspection and it is no longer a topic treated in psychology textbooks. If the word 'introspection' appears in the index of a textbook, the reference will be to introductory pages where introspectionism is executed in summary fashion and buried outside the graveyard. Certainly there have been general theories in philosophy about the relation between mind and body where the proponents have felt the need to explain or explain away the 'difficult case' of introspection in terms of the new theory. There have been theories about the nature and scope of psychological methodology where the exponents have explored the efficacy of the new methodology in explaining the nature of introspection. On the other hand, introspection has rarely been approached as a topic worthy of investigation in its own right. Further, it can safely be said that in both psychology and the brain sciences theorizing about the nature of introspection is at a rudimentary stage in comparison with, say, theorizing about the nature of perception or memory.

However, introspection continues to intrude. While introspection itself is not a central topic in philosophy or psychology, it seems impossible to escape giving some attention to it. Often the hope is that a quick by-the-way explanation, or better still an 'explaining away', will be enough, so that one can get on to important matters. Unfortunately even to attempt a by-the-way account of introspection forces one's hand in a way that few other theoretical enterprises do, for to attempt such an account is to reveal a great deal about one's view of mind.

In one particular area of psychology, developmental psychology, it could be argued that the concept of introspection intrudes more noticeably than in any other, yet paradoxically receives less critical treatment than in any other. For while in developmental psychology, the concept of metacognition has been given considerable employment in recent years, most often it is not clear at all what is being discussed under the label 'metacognition'. Sometimes it is defined very widely as 'the monitoring and regulation of information-processing- strategies' (Lawson, 1980, p. 145) where it is not at all clear that the 'monitoring' referred to is in any sense at all a second-level conscious monitoring process in relation to first-level mental processes or events. At other times it seems to be used, more or less synonomously with the traditional concept of introspection, as a second-level 'reflective awareness' in relation to first-level mental processes as they are occurring (Pratt and Grieve, 1984, pp. 141–3). Sometimes (as in Flavell, 1981, pp. 37ff.) there is a distinction made between 'metacognitive experiences', the concept of which seems to amount to the traditional concept of introspection, and 'metacognitive knowledge', the concept of which covers any knowledge at all (however gained) of our own or others' cognitive processes. Discussion of the latter concept of metacognition would presumably include mention of the former, so that the relation of 'metacognitive knowledge' to 'metacognitive experience' is the relation of whole to part (or of genus to one of its species) rather than, as initially one might have expected, a division (or dichotomy) delineating two exclusive types or categories of metacognition. However, in subsequent discussion, Flavell's concept of 'metacognitive knowledge' sometimes seems to have been interpreted as excluding 'metacognitive experiences' (Butterworth, 1982, p. 4), while at other times it is taken to include it (Robinson, 1983, pp. 107–8).

Often it is simply not clear at all what is being discussed when the term 'metacognition' is used. Definitions such as 'self-knowledge about cognitive states and processes' and 'metacognitive awareness' (Borkowski and Kurtz, 1984, pp. 193, 197) and 'all those capacities which entail reflection upon one's own mental powers' and 'an increasing sensitivity to one's own mental state' (Harris, 1983, pp. 261, 278) are not very revealing. Sometimes the account – 'predicting . . . checking . . . monitoring one's ongoing [overt problem-solving] activity' (Brown and DeLoache, 1983, p. 282) – seems to bear little or no relation to what most others mean by it, as it seems to bear little or no relation to monitoring inner cognitive processes. On the other hand, when metacognition is glossed as 'introspective knowledge' (Harris, 1983, p. 273), it seems as if what is meant by 'metacognition' is still more or less what was meant by the term 'introspection' from the seventeenth century to the middle of the twentieth century.

Faced with this conceptual morass, the term 'metacognition' will be left aside altogether and the much narrower, relatively clear, classical term 'introspection' used instead. There is no denying that this term also meant different things at different times, but the history of this concept in mainstream theoretical psychology and philosophy wil be briefly and critically documented, before the important question of what in fact might be going on when someone claims to be introspecting, and the implications of this for accounts of the development of introspection (and so at least some of the accounts of the development of metacognition) is discussed.

So this account of the nature and development of introspection begins paradoxically with a brief sketch of the development of *theorizing* about the concept and nature of introspection. Another reason for doing so is to maintain that, despite arresting changes of costume, the unequivocal accounts of introspection in mainstream philosophy and psychology that are still 'hanging about' in the last quarter of the twentieth century are little changed from the accounts available in the time of Augustine. For one way or another it is still believed or assumed that we have a second-level (or second-order) sense, or mechanism, or facility for gaining immediate direct information about our first-level perceptual and cognitive–appetitive–affective life. And it is still believed that this sense, or mechanism, or facility operates by an internal process of perceiving, or monitoring, or registering, or retrieving data from these first-level mental or brain events. This core model which underlies the local variations is, I believe, fundamentally mistaken.

THE DEVELOPMENT OF THEORIZING ABOUT THE NATURE OF INTROSPECTION

While it is arguable that the ancient Greeks had no conception of introspection,[1] there is no doubt that the concept was firmly in place in the fourth century AD[2] and that the basic picture was that we have direct, immediate, reportable access to, and so knowledge of, our own mental operations gained especially by a second-level process of inspecting those operations. From Augustine to the demise of introspectionism in psychology at the beginning of the twentieth century, the general picture was that there was a first-order stream of consciousness which either forced itself on our attention from time to time like a sort of mental fluorescence that one could not help but notice (self-consciousness), or could be actively focused on by a separate second-order act of attention as if one had focused a mental torch beam (introspection) on to the stream.[3] There were grave theoretical and practical difficulties with the attempt to make introspection thus understood the basic method of a scientific psychology. These difficulties exposed the weaknesses in this account of introspection. If one took the model or account seriously, then it would seem that the very act of introspecting would upset its own target (the stream of mental conscious processes), for the attention previously engaged in these first-level mental processes would be drawn off by the second-level act or introspection. With ingenuity, John Stuart Mill (1882,

p. 64) and, following his lead, William James (1950, vol. 1, p. 189) reinterpreted introspection as retrospection (or the introspection of merely remembered conscious events), for, by means of this theoretical adjustment, the theoretically awkward split in attention was avoided. The target stream of consciousness was now rendered down into a static flowchart stored in memory, and only the process of introspection itself remained conscious. But this tinkering with the classical model of introspection created as many problems as it solved. It made introspection subject to the frailties of memory and seemed to spoil the whole purpose of introspection by emasculating its target, that is by taking the stream out of the stream of consciousness.[4]

Historically however, besides the baroque nature of introspective experiments themselves (see Boring, 1953) and the elaborate if not bizarre rules governing them (see English, 1921), it was the unreliability if not uselessness of the data of introspection (see Boring, 1946, 1953; Humphrey, 1951, chap. 4) which led to the successful takeover bid by the behaviourists. By and large the behaviourists would have liked to have put introspection to one side for good and to have ignored, if not forgotten about it, for ever. But either as a result of the backlash from the outraged introspectionists or because of a belief that behaviourism, in order to be comprehensive and consistent, had to have some account of what was going on when people claimed to be introspecting, the behaviourists grudgingly gave their own accounts of this phenomenon.

J. B. Watson, after initially suggesting that all we should say is that introspection can play no part in a scientific psychology (Watson, 1913, p. 158) came to adopt the view that consciousness and introspection were a complete myth (Watson, 1920, p. 94).[5] Later behaviourists were not convinced by this blunt response and, while admittedly given to explaining away many cases of alleged introspection as just the misdescription of the observation and analysis of ordinary overt behaviour, they gradually adumbrated what came to be the classical behaviourist account of introspection proper. This classical behaviourist account described introspection as a person's recording and reporting of his or her own inner or covert cognitive activities which were in turn to be explained as being inner truncated forms of ordinary outer linguistic or cognate behaviour (see, for example, Jones, 1915; Lashley, 1923; Tolman, 1922). Thus, thinking to oneself was explained often as stopped-short speech, or 'speech' which did not evolve beyond the inner abortive activation of the mechanisms of speech. This, in turn, might amount to nothing more than movements in the larynx or in the muscles of the tongue. Introspection was the internal registering of, and reporting upon, these movements. How this registering or recording was achieved was never made quite clear, though Skinner (1965, chap. 17) suggested at one stage that it was achieved in terms of proprioceptive feeling, that is, the feelings involved in being aware of the position of one's body and the tension and the movements in one's own muscles and limbs.

Unfortunately science proved to be no friend of behaviourism in this matter, for the experimental results that are available point to the fact that such paradigm introspectible events as talking to oneself, or reading to oneself, or composing a tune in one's head, are not always accompanied by movements or even significant electrical activity in the mechanisms and muscles of speech (Woodworth and Schlosberg, 1955, chap. 26). Besides, even if better results had been obtained, it seems unlikely that proprioceptive stimulation would be sufficiently fine-grained to distinguish, say, a thought about Tottenham Hotspur from a thought abut Harry Hotspur, and there would remain to be explained the enigma of how we report in the language of thought, belief, desire, hope, and intention what must (on this view) reach our recording apparatus in the 'language' of feeling.[6]

At any rate, behaviourism's failure to solve what Skinner has called 'the problem of privacy'[7] (the problem of explaining the nature of inner private thought and how we come to know about it) was one of the factors which led to the rise of current centralist (that is, brain centred) psychologies and philosophies. In recent years in psychology, centre stage (at least in theoretical matters) has been hogged by latter-day cognitivist psychologies (that is, computational cum artificial intelligence accounts of what goes on *between* environmental input and non-reflex behavioural output in the human organism). In philosophy, centre stage has been occupied, until recently, by eliminative and reductive materialism (that is, by the complete theoretical elimination of the mental in all its forms or merely the reduction of the reference of mental terms to reference to certain sorts of brain states and processes). Now, in both philosophy and psychology, functional materialism (the interpretation of the mental in terms of the abstract, functional, or 'program' properties of the brain) seems to be emerging as the dominant theoretical position.

On the whole the modern philosophical (and psychological) reductive and eliminative materialists[8] presumed that there would be no difficulty in delivering an account of introspection in terms of brain states and processes and then excused themselves from producing any such account. A notable exception was David Armstrong (1968, chap. 6, sections 10, 11, and chap. 15) who suggested that introspecting was the literal scanning of one set of brain states or processes by another though the scanning was reported in the language of beliefs, desires, intentions, and the like rather than in neurophysiological terms. If this account turns out to be correct, Armstrong points out, introspective knowledge is in principle neither indubitable nor privileged. The introspector's claims can be checked and, if necessary, overruled by the neuroscientist of the future.

Unfortunately this account turned out to be incompatible with certain facts. In the first place it would seem to be the case that, if this account were correct, then introspective data (like the data from radar scanners) should be (though still neither indubitable nor privileged) remarkably reliable and more or less foolproof, and not, as the early history of psychology displays only too well, remarkably unreliable. Secondly, if introspective data were data about the brain's states and processes, obtained in a more or less foolproof mechanistic manner, then such data ought to be remarkably useful as a source of knowledge about the mind cum brain. But the more we learn about the brain, the less it seems that there is any correlation of an informative kind between the output of our introspective reports – in terms of beliefs, intentions, desires, and so on – and the cognitive operations of the brain as revealed by neuroscience. Indeed the suggestion that our introspective data should be construed as information resulting from a literal scanning of discrete localized states or processes seems radically mistaken. In whatever manner it is that the brain 'believes' (if to talk in that way makes any sense at all), it seems more likely to turn out to be the activation of an 'electro-chemical system' or 'systems' than a process or event occurring in a particular discrete area of the brain (see Luria, 1973, p. 29; Pribram, 1982, p. 281). The same thought – that I should go home now – may activate parts of the brain on Monday which are quite different from those which are activated on Tuesday though, introspectively speaking, the thought is the same. So the upshot is that there is little or no basis in fact for any account of introspection as a literal reporting, no matter in how roundabout a way, on discrete brain states or processes.

If these difficulties are not sufficient to sink this account of intro-spection, the final push to submersion point will result from some more basic theoretical reflections. For, if we allow the 'literal brain scanning' story, it seems to force upon us the invention of an additional intervening and dubious entity – a translation centre – whereby the neurophysio-logical data resulting from the brain scanning is translated into the language of beliefs, desires, intentions, and the like, by means of which we report the data from the brain scanning. In brief, one wonders how we could have evolved so as to receive pure empirical data about the brain but then proceed to cloak it in mentalist mysteries.[9]

At any rate it was these difficulties, particularly those of the former sort, which led to contemporary functionalist accounts of the mind.[10] To give a functionalist account of the mind is to give an account of the events in our 'mental world' purely in terms of the operations that we are presumed to perform inwardly between environmental input and behavioural output, when those operations are described purely functionally. To put this another way (in computer jargon) one could, so to speak, explain the mental in terms of the brain's 'machine table', that is, in terms of a table or matrix which would show the brain's outputs at the intersection of rows of current states (described purely in program or logical terms) and columns of inputs. The catchcry is that the functional or 'program' properties of a computer are in relation to its structure (say, electronic properties), as the mind of a human is to his or her body. Describing 'the mental' in this way would avoid having to say anything at all about the composition or nature of these inner processes or states. It would avoid the need to say whether these processes are just brain processes or whether they are something else. Or would it?

The worry is that a functionalist account of introspection – that is, an account of introspection in terms of some computer-like data-retrieving routine or other similar series of operations (such as in Dennett, 1969, Part 2, chaps 5 and 6; and especially Dennett, 1979; Ericsson and Simon, 1980; Thomas, 1978, Part 1, section 5) – might accord well with what we know of the relevant human perceptual input and behavioural output, but give a completely distorted picture of what is really going on when humans claim to be introspecting. This generates a dilemma for functionalism. If functionalist accounts of mental processes (such as introspection) are just 'free floating' inventions of a plausible operational cum computational story of what might be happening between perceptual input and behavioural output, then they must accept the resulting status of being just that, pure inventions. Alternatively, if functionalists seek to turn these invented accounts into true descriptions of what human brains do, by enlisting the help of neurophysiologists, they run the risk of their accounts failing to be substantiated in just the way that the brain scanner accounts failed. Put even more bluntly, it is not clear what information (if any) about the real nature of introspection, we are being given in these functionalist accounts; and it is not surprising that the extant versions look surprisingly like reiterations of orthodox, but discredited, accounts in cognitive cum computational dress. For example, for introspection as 'inspecting or scanning or recording and then reporting' there is substituted 'data retrieval and then publication' (see Dennett, 1979b). The basic story – that in introspection we have direct, immediate, and reportable knowledge of inner states and processes – remains intact.

Indeed the basic story has remained intact throughout the twentieth century. When they were allowing that there was something internal going on when we claim to be introspecting, the behaviourists substituted the recording of internal truncated movements in the speech-producing muscles for the introspectionist's inspection of our conscious cognitive processes. In turn the eliminative cum reductive materialists substituted literal scanning of the brain. Then the functional physicalists substituted the immediate computer-like retrieval and publication of data about first-level cognitive cum computational processes. No one, not even for a moment, appears to have doubted that humans possessed some sort of second-level monitoring facility called 'introspection'. The differences of opinion were merely about whether its object (or target) was the brain, or the mind, or internal muscular movements, or computational data; and about whether the monitor itself was an inner sense, or inner scanner, or inner computer-like retriever-of-data.

TOWARDS A NEW ACCOUNT OF INTROSPECTION

In the first instance, I want to proceed on the basis of the available ground-level data – admittedly very thin on the ground – about introspection. I want to start from the ground up and, in so far as this is possible, to ignore the mind–body problem and questions of methodology in psychology. I shall attempt to build up a theory or model of the nature and functioning of what we normally label 'introspection' by paying as much attention to data about introspection from normal and abnormal psychology, anthropology, and the brain sciences as to the discussions of philosophers and those engaged in artificial intelligence. The solution I seek to the problem about what we are really doing when we claim to be introspecting will be at the psychological level (at the level of talk about perception, beliefs, memory, imagination) not at the neurophysiological level. Even if I were capable of seeking a solution at the latter level – which I am not – it seems to me far too early to look for one and that, anyway, as we shall see, it may be the wrong place to look for one.

A phenomenological point

If to introspect were in any literal sense to employ an inner sense,[11] then it would have its own phenomenology.[12] Just as tasting is different from touching, and this difference provides us with different sets of unique predicates, so we should expect that if to introspect were to employ an inner sense then introspecting would involve a *sui generis* experience with its own phenomenal qualities and would generate its own unique set of predicates when we came to describe these qualities in words. But when we come to describe our alleged introspectings, we do so in terms of *what* we introspect not in terms of *what it is like* to introspect. Any experiential qualities in introspecting seem to be borrowed from the content of introspection. Any experiential qualities in introspecting a patch of blue seem to be borrowed from the first-level experience which is perceiving the patch of blue.

Even when we introspect with our eyes closed the result still seems, phenomenologically speaking, to be much the same. We 'see' introspectively our childhood nursery or 'hear' grandmother's voice again. When we introspect our thoughts, it is in terms of a language and words. In so far as they are words, they are words seen or heard, not words introspected. Later, when the positive side of this account of what it is we are really doing when we claim to be introspecting is given, it will be argued that 'introspecting' is intimately tied, and in unrecognized ways, to perception.

So phenomenologically it seems impossible to detect our introspections; and if *we* cannot do so who could? At this point it is salutary to remind ourselves that, while the failure to discover something is not a demonstration of its non-existence, no observer of the brain has ever found, and few nowadays would want to suggest, that there is any special organ of introspection or even any special 'introspection centre' in the brain.

A hint from developmental psychology

There is not a great abundance of work in developmental psychology about how and when children develop any conception of their having an ability to introspect. On the other hand, what research there is available is very suggestive not merely of what introspection is not but of what it might be.

Nor merely is it arguable that children are not born with anything which could be construed as a specific physiological basis for any special faculty, or sense for internal scanning or monitoring or inspecting, children take a long time to develop any conception at all of introspection. This is in sharp contrast to their swift development of their conception of the ordinary outer senses and their function.

There seems to be a reasonable measure of agreement among developmental psychologists that a child acquires the ability, and some recognition of the ability, to do what goes under the label 'introspect' – which is generally construed in this context as the 'awareness and verbalization of one's own thought processes' (Ginsburg and Opper, 1979, p. 175) – somewhere around the age of 8 years.[13] Moreover some at least seem to conclude from this sort of enquiry that 'such work does illustrate the fact that we are not born with some sort of inward eye that informs us about our own mental processes. We learn about these gradually just as we gradually attain a better knowledge of the behaviour of things outside us' (Lunzer, 1979, p. 12). That is, there is the explicit claim that research in this area should incline us to the view that the learning that does take place in regard to introspection is not in terms of fully developing and maturing a physiological mechanism by means of which we are enabled to look inwardly at mental events or gain access to brain processes. The maturation that occurs is in terms of the child learning to use already existing abilities in more sophisticated ways. The child learns to analyse its own overt actions and to ' "reconstruct" them on the plane of thought'

(Ginsburg and Opper, 1979, pp. 176–7) or, as I would put it, on the plane of perceptual memory and imagination, and in 'folk psychological' terms.

The age of 'introspection' should not be construed like the age of puberty, and the appearance of 'introspection' like the appearance of facial hair and deep voice in the male adolescent. The ability to do whatever it is we do when we claim to introspect develops in a child in much the same way as does the ability to see and make jokes. The ability to 'introspect' is connected with the gradual growth of understanding and is enhanced no doubt by the putting of that understanding to work verbally, though it is undesirable to equate the beginning of the alleged ability to introspect with the beginnings of the ability to talk *about* what one 'introspects', one gets the impression that this conflation does occur at times in the literature of developmental psychology (Ginsburg and Opper, 1979, pp. 176–7).

A warning note from anthropology

There is some reason to think that as regards 'introspection' we not merely find what we expect to find, but that we claim the very ability to introspect occurrent mental or brain events because it is embedded in our culture that we have the ability to do this. And as has already been remarked the word 'our' should be emphasized here. While it is arguable that the ancient Greeks of fourth and fifth century BC Athens did not make such a claim, it seems clear enough that more or less since the time of Augustine, western culture has enshrined the belief that we are able to introspect more or less in the way described by the traditional core model; that is, that we are able to look in on, monitor, or gain access to mental or brain events and then publish the resulting information. However, there is no such tradition in some other cultures. While it is notoriously difficult for a European to translate and fully comprehend terms in languages which are not based on any of the languages or proto-languages of Europe, and while it is acknowledged to be a very slippery inference from what are terms in a language to what are the conceptions in the thinking of those that use the language, and from what is conceived in thought to what exists, what is clear is that some cultures have no words that readily translate into our word 'introspection' nor employ descriptions that could be taken to refer to or circumscribe in any way what we traditionally understand by the process labelled 'introspection'.

The Balinese, for example, or at least those of them untouched by western culture, seem to have no terminology for a private self with an inner private mental life, and so no terminology for introspecting the events of that inner life. In Bali 'it is *dramatis personae*, not actors, that endure; indeed, it is *dramatis personae*, not actors, that in the proper sense really exist' (Geertz, 1976), though it is possible that this should be interpreted as, not that the Balinese do not introspect but that they try to suppress that side of life in favour of an ideal, stylized life where a person lives out a role assigned by birth and circumstances, and which can only be sustained when the sort of individuality that is nourished by introversion is deliberately squashed. But even so, what was long ago a deliberate act, once it is anchored to what has become a basic attitude in the culture as a whole and become a fixed disposition over many centuries, can become such that the agent could not do otherwise. The Balinese may well be blind to any inner self. There are also grounds for thinking that, if they have any conception of introspection at all, the Maori and the Ifaluk of the Pacific regions have at most a very wizened one in comparison with the western notion (Lutz, 1982; Smith, 1981). In regard to the Maori, Johansen writes:

> Psychology did not interest the Maori very much. The main classification is made according to kind and degree of bodily perceptions, through which things are united which to us are quite different, and the word which covers our word 'mind' best, viz. *ngakau*, is just expressing a whole ['a total picture of man in a situation'] which is not analysed. ... Conflicts in the mind, un-conscious motives, or the like are never mentioned. (1954, p. 249)

What is certain is that Nicholas Humphrey's claim that, 'there is, so far as I know, no language in the world which does not have what is deemed to be an appropriate vocabulary for talking about the objects of reflexive consciousness, and there are no people in the world who do not quickly learn to make free use of this vocabulary' (1983, p. 8), is unsupported by what we do know of some non-European cultures. This assertion will probably not lead to many doubts if we note that Humphrey believes that 'the gist' of 'a remarkable convergence in the accounts which people of all races and all cultures give of what reflexive consciousness reveals to them' is that 'in association with my body there exists a spirit, conscious of its own existence and its continuity in time. This is the spirit (mind, soul . . .) which I call "I".' (1983, p. 9).

Even if a majority of people in our culture claimed to have a very strong conviction that they had an ability to introspect in an immediate and non-inferential way occurrent mental or brain events, it may only be the case that – and this is a truism – people in western culture have accepted uncritically their culture's belief that every adult human normally has the ability to introspect according to the traditional proto-model of intro-spection. However, it may be that any poll of the whole population, or of a judiciously selected sample of it, would not reveal a wholesale commit-ment to a belief in introspection as described traditionally. Partly, perhaps, because most people would not even know what was meant by the word 'introspection' in the pollster's question. Generally speaking 'introspec-tion' is a term reserved for the debates and theories of philosophers and psychologists. As Ryle put it,

'Introspection' is a term of art and one for which little use is found in the self-description of untheoretical people. More use is found for the adjective 'introspective', which is ordinarily used in an innocuous sense to signify that someone pays more heed than usual to theoretical and practical problems about his own character, abilities, deficiencies and oddities; there is often the extra suggestion that the person is abnormally anxious about these matters. (1949, chap. VI, p. 163)

Of course, as Ryle pointed out, it does not follow from the fact that ordinary people do not employ the term 'introspection' that they have no alternative 'ordinary expressions' nor any conception of something which corresponds to the references of this term in technical discourse nor any belief in its reality. But equally it does not follow that they do hold anything approaching the traditional doctrine as found in philosophy and psychology, for even if ordinary people speak about inner mental events, and direct knowledge of occurrent ones, it is most likely that they have no clear picture at all of what such knowledge consists of nor of how it has been gained. The existence of the term 'introspection' in the academic reaches of our culture, in other words, does not guarantee very much at all.

It is also worth reminding ourselves that psychologists and philosophers only came to have a reasonably precise and formal *account* of what exactly is going on when we claim to be introspecting when it became important to do so. That is, when it became important, particularly to psychologists, to explain and defend the claim that introspection was the unique method whereby investigators seeking facts about our mental life could gain direct access to mental entities and events. Up to the time of Brantano and Wundt, or thereabouts, there only existed a rather amorphous concept of self-reflection. It was when psychology became separate from philosophy and, aspiring to align itself rapidly alongside the traditional natural sciences, set up laboratories and started discussing experimental methods, that the details of introspection as we now talk about it came into being.

Some unsettling suggestions from experimental psychology

Though contemporary psychologists, philosophers, brain scientists, and those working in artificial intelligence all refer to the 'data of introspection' from time to time, there is a growing body of work in psychology which should be unsettling to anyone who still maintains a belief that 'introspection' is some kind of direct private access to occurrent mental or brain states or events which in turn bestows special status if not unique reliability upon 'introspective evidence'.

There is, for example, plenty of evidence to show that we report on incoming sensory information and, via 'introspection', its use in ensuing deliberations and decisions with unfounded certainty in the reliability of that sort of immediate reporting. Because our ability to attend to what is pouring into our sensory receivers is severely limited, we can only concentrate on very little of it. Often we fail, or are simply unable in principle, to concentrate on the salient fetures, the features which turn out to be the ones that influence our subsequent beliefs and behaviour. For example, the following sort of experiment has been performed many times and with many variations (Lackner and Garrett, 1972). An ambiguous sentence, such as 'The bank was destroyed' is fed through an earphone at a reasonably loud level into one ear. Another sentence which makes clear which sense of the word 'bank' is being referred to, say a sentence like 'Because the river was in spate', is fed through an earphone into the other ear at a level of five or ten decibels less. Because of the limitations of attention, one can only attend to the louder, more insistent sentence, 'The bank was destroyed', that is, attend in the sense of being able subsequently to repeat the sentence. The other sentence, the disambiguating sentence, is unattended in this sense. The subject in the experiment cannot say what is coming in through the so-called unattending ear; the subject cannot even be sure in what language the information was couched or whether it was information. Yet, when asked for the meaning of a sentence like 'The bank was destroyed', subjects invariably interpret it in terms of the information coming though the unattending ear.

The general point, of course, is that this experiment is merely a precise illustration of what happens all the time. We can readily report on what took up our attention when it was on the way in to our head, but not on the wealth of unattended information, though this latter may have formed the basis for the cognitive states and acts which governed subsequent action. What was attended to may have been only the most insistent as regards attention, not the most important in causal terms. A more homely example would be someone's apparently giving an account of why he or she did something, say giving an account of his alleged deliberations which led to the choice of this toothpaste rather than that one. What made him and most of those asked choose this toothpaste rather than those other ones on the market researcher's tray might have been because this was was placed on the right. Because English speakers read from left to right and so tend to scan from left to right, whatever is on the far right is that which is seen last and so has a preeminent status in regard to choice. Yet he tells the market researcher that he chose it because its taste had something special to it which the others did not (Laird, 1932; Nisbett and Wilson, 1977).

It might turn out that we are remarkably unrealiable whenever we give 'introspective reports' – no matter how immediate and 'on the spot' – on deliberations which precede choice or action. We come up with the choice or engage in the behaviour, and we produce a convincing account or rationale for why we did so, but the superimposed conviction that we have privileged access to the cognitive and appetitive moves which produces the choice or behaviour seems to lack evidence, for the regularities of choice and behaviour seem better explained in other ways.

The same may very often be the case with accounts of how we came to remember something. Very often we can remember but are at a loss to say why. The sorting, sifting, or shuffling which preceded the recollection seems to be hidden from us. 'If a person is asked, "What is your mother's maiden name?", the answer appears swiftly in consciousness. Then, if a person is asked "How did you come up with that?" he [or she] is usually reduced to the inarticulate answer, "I don't know, it just came to me" ' (Nisbett and Wilson, 1977, p. 232). He or she cannot say whether he referred to a stored file of family names which included an entry for his mother's maiden name, or replayed in memory an occasion when he saw his mother's maiden name written on her old school Latin text, or whether he asked himself what was the name of his maternal grandfather. Though if asked how he did recall his mother's maiden name, he might well reply in terms of one of these manœuvres. Indeed some philosophers and psychologists have been so impressed by what we do not know about our cognitive and appetitive processes that they have adopted the startling dictum, 'No activity of mind is ever conscious.'[14]

When we claim to introspect the deliberations that precede our choices and actions, and in general make claims to be privy to our own cognitive and appetitive processes, what we seem to be doing is more like adopting a likely rationale for *a* person exercising a choice in such a situation or deciding to act in such circumstances rather than engaging in any process of observation of internal cognitive and appetitive events or retrieval of information. It is more like producing a machine simulation of some cognitive process of Smith's without knowing, or being *able* to know, whether it resembles in any way what Smith in fact did in cognitive–appetitive terms.

In experimental psychology there is also evidence that when subjects are asked to give an account of the considerations which they tossed about in their mind and which influenced them to take the course of action they in fact took, and when the requests are made 'within seconds of their occurrence', they not only give an account which can be shown to be at variance with what in fact must have been the cognitive–appetitive processes behind their behaviour but they also give a remarkably stereotyped account (Nisbett and Wilson, 1977, pp. 248ff; Latané and Darley, 1970). For example, it can be shown that the likelihood of a person going to the aid of another person in distress varies more or less inversely according to the number of other people there are about and in a position to see anything the 'rescuer' might do. Yet when such persons are asked for an account of what went on in their minds before their action or inaction, they make no mention of the influence of bystanders. The account they give is in terms of the plight of the victim and their own power (or supposed lack of it) to lend aid and comfort, and is in terms of what we would all like to think would be our cognitive (appetitive) processes on such occasions, namely processes which make sympathy and altruistic action the prime considerations. The true account of our cognitive processes would probably be in terms of items from the following list; shyness, hesitancy, worry about what others would think, hopes that someone else would make the first move, wonderings if others would see through any attempt to pretend that one did not see or hear the victim, or that one had a broken arm, and so on. All in all it is hard to resist the conclusion that frequently we delude ourselves when we purport to give introspective reports on the cognitive processes that precede choice and action, and that what we are doing very often is much more like making reference to a stereotype or conventional model of someone's cognitive processes in such situations.

It is also hard to resist seeing the whole unhappy history of introspectionism in psychology as pointing towards this conclusion as well. Introspection fashioned its own disrepute not only by so multiplying the conditions under which 'introspective experiments' could be considered valid and by making them so intricate that the whole routine became bizarre, but also because even trained 'introspectors' from the same culture could not agree on any results from these 'introspective experiments'. What agreement there was seemed to go along with previous theoretical agreement or allegiance to some school of introspectionist psychology. Wundtians agree amongst themselves, so did the followers of Ach and Bühler, and so did the disciples of Titchener. But there was little or no agreement on particular issues that could be sustained across all schools (Hebb, 1969).

None of the points that have been made in this section are 'knockdown' arguments in regard to what has been called the orthodox core account of introspection that has lasted right up to the present time. Rather they were brought forward as considerations, based none the less on a variety of facts, which may make us conscious of the fragility of our conviction that we have immediate introspective access to the contents and workings of our own mind or brain. It is doubtful whether there are ever QEDs or anything of that sort in philosophy of mind or theoretical psychology. What is more likely to happen is a gradual shift in our theoretical picture or model, but even this can have profound and far reaching effects.

In these considerations, it has been alleged, there are hints that introspection when explained as any form of monitoring or inspecting or scanning or immediate retrieval of data in respect of cognitive–appetitive processes is a myth of our culture, an invention of our 'folk psychology'.

The alleged introspection of perception is another sort of myth, by and large a concoction derived from 'sense data' theories of psychologists and, especially, philosophers, though this will barely be referred to again.

THE REPLAY THEORY OF 'INTROSPECTION'

An outline of the theory

An epigraph for this section could well be the following passage from Wittgenstein's *Philosophical Investigations*:

> It makes sense to ask: 'Do I really love her, or am I only pretending to myself?' and the process of introspection is the calling up of memories; of imagined possible situations, and of the feelings one would have if ... (1958, section 587)

Though I would not want to be so rash as to say how Wittgenstein himself would have interpreted this passage, one interpretation illustrates what I want to say about introspection; namely that, when we 'introspect' in order to discover things about our cognitive, appetitive, and affective lives, we engage in a process of perceptual 'replay'. We 'replay' or re-create – at least 'with edited highlights' or 'in dramatized form' – what we think we said, or would have liked to have said, or did or felt. For example, if we 'introspect' in order to discover whether we love someone, we 'replay' how we looked or reacted, and what we said or did (or how we thought we looked or reacted, and what we believed we said or did, or might have, or were going to, or had it in mind to) when he or she, the beloved, was present, or the topic of conversation, or when the beloved was noticeably absent. For 'introspection' is not a special and privileged executive monitoring process over and above the more plebeian processes of perception, memory, and imagination: it is those processes put to a certain use.

It has already been mentioned how in certain circumstances we may be led into thinking that we are introspecting when we are simply perceiving. For when we are looking at a red tomato or a yellow daffodil, and if we are influenced by certain philosophical theories of sense data, we may report our perceptions in terms of seeing round red patches and bell-shaped yellow presentations.

Leaving this sort of case aside,[16] the central contention here is that 'introspection' is our employment of perceptual memory and imagination to 'make suggestions' (to ourselves) about our motives, thoughts, hopes, and desires, and so on, by finding out about our motives, thoughts, hopes, and desires as revealed in speech, gesture, expression, and behaviour, for these latter are all that we have conscious access to. From our point of view, what we can experience and directly know about and so use to build up our picture of 'mind' (including *our* 'mind') is the world-as-perceived and the world-as-processed by the perception-based processes of memory, imagination (and the cognate processes of dreaming, day-dreaming, and hallucination), the rest lies hidden in the brain.

To put it starkly, it is suggested that 'to introspect' our cognitive and appetitive and affective processes is

1   to employ perceptual memory and imagination,
2   so as to produce substitutes for our ignorance of our brain's (or 'mind's') cognitive, appetitive, and affective life,
3   These substitutes take the form of edited, or interpreted, or imaginatively reconstructed, 'replays' of experienced or perceived, overt public intelligent performances,
4   especially overt intelligent performances employing language (or codes or calculi), or significant gesture, or expression.
5   In particular the 'replay' will be in terms of our own or others' recalled or imagined talk, or written performances, or communicative expressions.
6   These utterances, written texts, and expressions, in turn, are formed and understood inevitably against the background of a shared, stereotyped, orthodox, culture-based, amateur, 'folk psychological' account of human 'mental life'.
7   Thus any creativity or novelty in our 'introspective' performances is only so within and against that shared 'folk psychological' background.

The intimate relation between introspection and perceptual processes

What is being suggested is that, if we were to make a survey of human perceptual and cognitive processes, we should consider the first level to be perceptual, that is all the various avenues for gaining perceptual information and, when they occur, perceptual experiences. We should not forget that a lot of perceptual data never reach the level of attention, and so never become experiences, maybe even the majority of them never do. Then, more or less at the same level, there are the processes parasitic on perception, namely perceptual memory and imagination, which are experiential in character.

But arguably as least as important from the point of view of the life of the human organism are what in 'folk psychology' are called deliberating, desiring, choosing, planning, intending, loving, and so on. However, the detailed processes underlying such 'folk psychological' talk (or for that matter our more sophisticated functional or 'information processing' talk of the same) lie permanently hidden from our experience, and take place unmolested in the labyrinth of the brain. Unless we are enlightened by the brain sciences, these processes remain a mystery to us.

The suggestion then is that perception is the first and most important level in the account of 'introspection'. For part of that level the processes are symbiotic with perception, namely perceptual memory and imagination, which involve editing, interpreting, elaborating, filtering, constructing, reconstructing, concocting, and then storing 'artefacts' made out of perceptual material. 'Introspection', thus conceived, is to be found here. For leaving aside the alleged cases of introspecting our perceptions or sensations, 'introspection' is to be explained in terms of operations by perceptual memory and imagination when their operations are at the level of conscious attention. To 'introspect' our higher or mental processes is to model – by means of perceptual memory and imagination or, in general, perceptual 'replay' in edited and interpreted and elaborated form – the hidden cognitive life of our brain in terms of our non-hidden, overt intelligent acts. To 'introspect' is to use the first level in its experiential mode to model the second level which never reaches experience.

The traditional story about introspection that has lasted through the ages is dual-levelled in that it posits a special act of inner perception (or scanning or retrieval) in regard to a first level of inner processes in the brain, or mind, or consciousness. This new model is dual in a very different way. It describes the perceptual level (albeit as perceptual memory and imagination) as the model-maker in respect of the hidden second level. The second level does not monitor in any way the first level, for it has no access to it; instead, in its acknowledged ignorance, it substitutes a working model or dynamic picture for what it cannot know first hand. We might think that we are catching ourselves monitoring or inspecting or scanning our acts of thinking, or hoping, or deciding, or loving, or needing when in fact all that we are doing is replaying internally to ourselves or imaginatively constructing for ourselves a model version made out of overt behaviour, gesture, and expression, which we describe in our 'folk psychology' in terms of thinking, hoping, deciding, loving, and needing.

'Introspection' and 'folk psychology'

Many cases of 'introspection' will be relatively straightforward 'replays' of 'static' perceptions or of perceived performances, operations, or episodes. When we 'introspect' what we remember of our nursery, the 'replay' is likely to be simple and clear-cut. We simply 'replay' an edited or, if necessary, an elaborated version of what we believed we saw in our childhood in a particular room.

Even the 'introspection' of certain cognitive processes or episodes will be relatively straightforward. When we 'introspect' our doing of mental arithmetic, what we are doing is to 'replay' a tidied-up, reconstructed, or (more likely) creatively constructed, 'edited highlights' version of some of our (or other's) overt arithmetical performances in speech, in writing, on a blackboard, or printed in a book. It is a reconstruction of what we ourselves or someone else has done. Or it is an invention of what we believe, or surmise, we or someone else would do if asked, and so on.

But the matter is more complicated than this. Most often mental arithmetic itself *is* such a 'replay'. It itself is doing arithmetic in a quick, neat, and 'edited' way via perceptual memory and imagination. That is what the teacher was trying to teach us, to do the sums 'in our head' (in our imagination) using the methods he teaches us out loud or on the blackboard (that is with the help of perceptual memory). So 'introspecting' our doing of mental arithmetic will be, so to speak, a case of 'Play it again, Sam', or a 'replay' of a 'replay'.

On the other hand the 'introspection' of other cognitive processes will be far from straightforward. The 'introspectively discovered' versions of cognitive acts such as those of deliberating, finding out one's motive, producing an intention, coming to a decision, weighing up reasons, discovering needs, and so on, will very often be highly elaborated. Yet also highly stereotyped. 'Deliberation', 'motivation', 'intention', 'decision', 'reason', 'need', are 'folk psychological' terms (part of our folk theory of the mind). They are, thereby, far removed from being just labels for relatively simple perceivable scenarios, behavioural episodes or events, in the way that one's 'picture' of one's nursery or one's doing of mental arithmetic are. To impute a reason or intention to someone, is to interpret the perceivable according to a quite elaborate folk theory or 'folk psychology'. Intentions, decisions, plans, wants, and so on are at the highly interpreted and abstracted level of talk about behaviour, not at the simple level of description of perceived (or perceivable) episodes of behaviour. 'Folk psychology' is the web of concepts – such as belief, desire, intention, decision, plan, deliberation, and so on – by means of which we explain our own or other's behaviour. We 'picture' our behaviour in 'folk psychology' as 'targeted' by 'inner mental items' such as beliefs about our immediate environment, long-term or short-term goals, perhaps values, which in turn generate behaviour via the 'propulsions' of wants, desires, needs, or wishes. This is the merest outline. The scene is also peopled by reasons, proposals, presumptions, fears, doubts, guesses, forecasts, hopes, insights, inspirations, and the like.

So as soon as our 'introspecting', or anything else for that matter, involves this web of concepts, it is also inevitably involved in a certain stereotyped, culture-based outlook. Thus our 'introspection' of our motives, or desires, or deliberations, or plans, or decisions, or intentions, will be coloured by and adapted from our own particular culture's 'rough and ready' view of the mind and its operations. In that respect our 'introspections' will employ alleged 'processes' and reveal alleged 'processes' borrowed from this general 'folk psychological' viewpoint, and not differ very much from everyone else's 'introspections'; for everyone else will borrow in much the same way from much the same source, and with much the same expectations in regard to the 'data of introspection'. In a culture with a highly developed and centralized education system, common language, a readily accessible store of knowledge and speculation, and constant widespread social intercourse, this 'folk psychological' viewpoint will be continually buttressed by the fact that we learn much the same accounts, methods, procedures and explanations in regard to anything of a cognitive–appetitive–affective sort.

There is an important caveat to be tabled here. I am not suggesting that all our thoughts, desires, motives, deliberations, decisions, intentions, and so on, are stereotyped. Of course not, otherwise nothing novel would ever be produced. There could be no science nor poetry nor philosophy worth the having. What I am suggesting is that when we claim to introspect the steps, moves, processes, methods, and means, by which we produce the novel theory or poem or conclusion, by and large we give a stereotyped 'folk psychologial' account of how we produced the theory, poem or conclusion. How could it be otherwise, for we do not know how our brain did the job. We have merely learnt how to produce the 'folk psychological' account or some more rigorous, amended, academic version of it.

Even so, this is still not the whole story. For within the confines of our 'folk psychological' (or cognate account) of the workings of our mind, there is still room for novelty of explanation, model, theory, or thesis. Presumably that is what most 'insights' in philosophy of mind and psychology are. Yet in a real sense, even when a novel explanation or theory about the workings of mind is produced, it is only novel when seen against the background of the existing orthodox, stereotyped, culture-based, 'hand me down' account, whether couched in naïve or sophistic-ated terms. Further it is built on the existing orthodox model or models. It is novel against that background and in that connected-to-the-background sense. It is novel in so far as someone, conversant with the culture's view of the mental, has then gone on to produce an original account of some aspect of the mind within that broad cultural viewpoint.

'Introspective reports'

If it is agreed that we can report immediately – without intervening mind or brain apparatus – on our seeings and hearings and so on, then it would seem to follow that we can immediately report, again without intervening apparatus, on its 'blood relations': our perceptual recallings and imagin-ings. I am not for a moment wanting to deny that there might be a mystery about *how* we report on what is in front of our eyes or nose – I await the details from neurophysiology as eagerly as the next person – I am just saying that, however we do it, the achievement will be much the same in respect of our reporting on our perceptual recallings and imaginings. On the other hand, what I am wanting to deny is that in either case there is theoretical pressure or need to believe in that Loch Ness Monster of Philosophy of Mind, a faculty or facility or mechanism or device for introspecting.

Now this 'package deal' can be best illustrated by the central case of 'introspecting' what in our 'folk psychology' we call the cognitive acts of our mind, such as our deliberating, planning, reasoning, intending, deciding, inferring, composing, wishing, hoping, wanting, and so on. In so far as we 'introspect' these, then we have engaged in producing internally a 'folk psychological' model of these acts which is in the form of perceptual 'replays'. These 'replays', as we have seen, are highly elaborated or edited, faithfully recorded or wholly invented, versions of our public perceived versions of cognitive acts. What will have been perceived, and will be the perceptual basis for the modelling, will be spoken or written 'folk psychological' comment on matters mental or episodes of intelligent behaviour, gesture, or expression, or some complex amalgam of some or all of these. But, abstracting from the immense complexity of these individual pieces and how they come to play their part, the fact remains (at least according to my theory) that at the heart of this form of 'introspecting' is once again perceptual 'replay'. So reporting in the sense of giving a 'running commentary' on this 'replay' will be direct and immediate and, more importantly, without need for postulating introspective apparatus.

However this account has another level to it. When I 'introspect' my so-called cognitive episodes, say in order to find out whether I love someone, or what my motive was in telling such a lie, or whether I really believe in God, or why I feel that way about a woman, I may well engage in perceptual 'replay' of a quite elaborate kind. I may do this in order to form a 'picture' of my relationship with someone or my attitude to something. On the other hand I might *report*, to myself or someone else, in quite a summary way. I might say merely 'Yes, of course, I do love her' or 'Well, I suppose I must have been jealous'. Here I am making a final judgement via my 'introspective replays', not giving a blow-by-blow account of them.

In our 'introspective' reports of our cognitive life, we can be wrong in our recall of what we said and did, or mistaken in our fanciful constructions of what we would say or do in certain circumstances. Even if we do not go wrong at this level, we might err in our interpretations of our expressions, words and deeds in the light of the 'folk psychology' of our culture. Moreover, if our stereotyped orthodox 'folk psychological' account can be corrected in the light of a more rigorous psychologist's account, then any 'introspective' report based on the 'folk psychological' account is similarly open to correction. Hercule Poirot or the psychologist might notice more details, or have a better memory for the details, or have a better grasp of what is relevant and significant, or make no mistakes of inference or analysis, or do all of these things better than I.

Put simply, if, for various reasons, someone else's account of my cognitive activities is based on a better model than mine or on a better interpretation of the modelling – which is not merely conceivable in respect of all of us but highly likely if I am a child or just poor at such perceptual model building and interpreting – then he or she is in a position to correct my report of my cognitive activity.

Of course I retain a corner of incorrigibility. I can have privileged access to *my* version or *my* 'replay', however mistaken, of what I believe are the significant episodes which reveal my motivation, or belief, or hopes, or what have you. Also I have privileged access to *my* judgement (what I make of those 'replayed' episodes) and could refrain from publishing it. But this sort of privilege is very thin indeed in this context and does not bring with it any real epistemological privilege. One is not in a better position to give a correct 'folk psychological' account of one's own cognitive states. All that one knows better than others is what one's stored and perhaps flawed account is.

It might be argued that I have overplayed the extent of the corrigibility of our 'introspective' reports on our cognitive–appetitive life. For after all, it might be objected, I am in my own company more than others are in my company, and so I cannot help but notice more of my own doings and sayings including the crucial significant episodes upon which a correct 'folk psychological' or cognate account of my cognitive life must be built. But this is balanced, unfortunately, by the fact that I can all too easily still miss things that others see. First of all, in the literal sense. They can see my expressions and gestures, which I usually cannot notice. Then, in a non-literal sense, they will often 'see' more than I do. In regard to what both of us see, they might 'read the signs better'. Quite likely, also, I will be biased in favour of myself when I come to interpret the public episodes in my life; they are much less likely to be.

Few, I imagine, will be convinced by my scepticism in respect of all the versions of the orthodox account of introspection, for a belief in introspection is so basic to our culture. Moreover, introspection seems so fundamental both to our knowledge of and to our concept of our self – for introspection is held to give us direct knowledge of the self at work, especially in its higher, truly human, cognitive, appetitive, and affective functions, and part of the concept of a human ego is that it is self-inspecting. So the belief in introspection will not easily be given up. Indeed it is quite frightening to think that others might know more about our self and our mind than we ourselves do. To admit that they do might seem to some to be a way of assassinating the self.

However, as I will endeavour to make clear at least in a very brief way, the picture is not as gloomy as it seems. 'Introspection', as I have explained it, has an important, probably crucial part to play in our lives.

THE POINT OF INTROSPECTION

Particular attention should be drawn to introspection's part (that is, introspection as understood here) in helping us predict the behaviour of others, so as to come to understand them and in that sense at least make them less alien. For, and this follows from the suggestion that our models of cognitive activity are culture based and biased, it is notorious that we can fail to understand 'the mind' of people from another culture. We have not observed them, or observed them often enough or perceptively, and so have not formed a model (or at least an adequate model) of their mind. A good illustration of this occurs in the experiences of those who were the prisoners of war of the Japanese. The following extract is from the second of two BBC radio programmes about what it was like to be a prisoner of war in the Far East, and is based on the remembered experiences of those who were such prisoners.

> Such a background [of Japanese militarism and resentment of colonial empires] on its own is quite enough to account for a large part of Japanese behaviour, but in the actual day-to-day encounter of captor and prisoner there were other elements still. Perhaps these were best summed up by a survivor of the infamous Burma–Siam Railway, who remarked to me: 'We simply couldn't understand the reasoning processes behind the things they did. We never could and never did; there was just something completely different, they were totally unpredictable, in our view'. (Wade, 1983, p. 8)

What is more, there was little possibility of quickly building up models of the Japanese way of thought (or cognitive life). For a start there was the language barrier. Few of the Japanese soldiers spoke any English and few of the Allied prisoners spoke any Japanese, and there were usually no interpreters on hand. Those that were, were 'interpreters' in name only. In addition, as the cliché has it, the Japanese seemed inscrutable in a literal sense. One could not read their faces. Gesture and facial expression – though generally speaking they have their effect more or less unnoticed by us – are almost as powerful a medium as language for expressing someone's beliefs, thoughts, desires, and values. When we frown, or laugh, or smile, or show sorrow or disgust, or perplexity or anger, we do so at something or other, and in doing so very often reveal our outlook or standpoint. But if someone cannot 'read' another's face or gestures – another race's face and gestures – a huge gulf in comprehension develops between the two. The 'unread' face appears expressionless, inscrutable, impassive, cold, and unheeding. Or when it suddenly, and unaccountably, erupts into a recognizable laugh or display of anger, the result is both frightening and baffling.

> They [Japanese faces] seemed expressionless . . . you couldn't make out how the owners were reacting or what they might do next. It may well be, of course, that the guards experienced the same problem with the prisoners: some had never seen a European in the flesh before they found themselves in charge of large numbers of them. The result was, in one opinion, that each side was always making the most terrible mistakes in interpreting the other and this provoked the most profound insecurity in the Japanese, who were in any case inclined to be jumpy and hysterical. They also constantly suspected they were being laughed at – as indeed they occasionally were: there is something deeply comic in the sight of such very small soldiers dwarfed by their own rifles and fixed bayonets. In fact, it is likely that neither side had much idea of what made the other side laugh, while what the Europeans observed was often anything but reassuring: a Japanese factory girl, for instance, lost one foot in a machine and her workmates giggled. All these circumstances paved the way to violence. (Wade, 1983, p. 9)

So far I have concentrated on what might be called the social purpose of what I understand by 'introspection', whereby, by a process of forming a general model of that sort of person's mind from observation of that sort of person's behaviour, speech, and gesture, one person gains insight into the mind of another; that is, an insight into his or her character, views, values, needs, and behaviour. But part of the purpose of 'introspection' is connected with the formation of what in psychology is often called our own 'self-concept'. Just as we have a model of our body such that, if a foot is amputated, we have to learn by degrees not to locate our present pain in the non-existent foot, so we concoct a model of our own mind and character, which in turn is related to the way we think and behave, what we believe and care about, or in general what we are like. Again it is only by degrees that we come to form such a model, and only by degrees that we can adjust it to new information. We can learn, say, that we hold views we did not believe (or could not even imagine) that we held. To our horror, we can realize that we are racist, or sexist, or selfish, or mean, or patronizing, or neglectful. Often this realization creeps over us gradually, but it can dawn on us suddenly and traumatically. In neither case is such knowledge gained by instant access to some inner self giving private performances for our own benefit, rather the process is of garnering information from available hints and clues, and then putting it together – perhaps imperceptibly, perhaps suddenly and dramatically. Certainly the gathering and garnering will quite likely involve replaying incidents or imagined incidents in perceptual memory or imagination, and in that sense involve 'introspection', but there is no internal peering at some internal inhabitant suddenly caught in the spotlight and recognizable as 'The Self'. The concept of one's own mind, or character, or person is the result of making something reasonably continuous and coherent in the biographical sense, and something reasonably consistent and integral in the logico-psychological sense, out of the *mélange* of our knowledge of our own everyday acts, reactions, and our knowledge of others' actions and reactions to ourselves.

The 'introspective' processes of perceptual memory and imagination help to produce a self-concept in an evaluative sense as well. We not merely need to build up an *holistic* concept of ourself – a descriptively coherent and consistent concept of ourself – but we also need to build up a *healthy* self-concept which in turn implies a certain modicum of self-esteem or self-respect. While a healthy self-concept does not necessarily imply blindness to one's faults or shortcomings, but may result from one having come to terms with them, nevertheless, the process of 'coming to terms', at least for some people, may involve an underestimation of one's faults in relation to those of others, or even a disinclination to think in terms of faults much at all.[17] An idealized view of the self may be necessary for the psychological health of some people; in some cases, in regard to the self, ignorance may be more likely to lead to bliss.

So while we do not need to revert to some Cartesian introspectionist model of the mind, as ordinary persons we may need *some* macro model of the cognitive, appetitive, and affective activities of the brain. Certainly we could make very little of direct access to our own raw brain and its neuronal activities, for its vastness and complexity would overwhelm us. The brain works much better without interference from us. The brain is a way-station, a switching post that receives, sifts, stores, and sends off electrochemical signals, and all its energy is aimed at producing appropriate output (behaviour) now or later. For us to know directly and immediately about the workings of our brain is about as useful as it is for a clock to have direct and immediate information about its own mainspring. If we had immediate access to and knowledge of the brain, we would be gaining knowledge about neuronal firings and the state of the neurone-protecting glial cells, and the intricacies of cerebral processes and states in general, but would learn nothing about our mental life.

But we may not be able to do without some sort of macro and admittedly inexact model or series of models of what the brain achieves cognitively speaking. Presumably, forming such a model is the role of much of our 'folk psychology'. If we had no account at all, we could not even talk of ourselves or others in respect of our cognitive activities and achievements. We could not, for example, mention or make use of the cognitive antecedents of action which, in turn, means that we could not operate with concepts of deliberating, deciding, choosing, evaluating, believing, hoping, wishing, wanting, desiring, planning, forecasting, predicting, intending, and so on and on. Probably we would be reduced permanently to very crude behaviourist explanations wherein one could make no mention of anything but present behaviour and probabilities of future behaviour computed by reference to correlations observed in respect of past behaviour, for this is what happened when psychology gave up, at about the same time, introspectionist, associationist, and faculty explanations and was unwilling to put anything of a centralist nature in their place. As we have seen, behaviourist theories and explanations, by and large, have given way to centralist (that is, brain-centred or mind-centred or cognition-emphasized) theories and explanations in both philosophy and psychology, precisely because we seem to have a need to make mention of something other than behaviour and its stimulus conditions in the environment. We need to mention something cognitive between environmental input and behavioural output, if we are to produce adequate accounts of human psychology.

Macro modelling for use in ordinary social intercourse is just modelling in terms of concepts such as deliberating, deciding, wanting, and so on. On the other hand psychology, at least in the future, may need to work with a macro model (or models) couched in more technical and more sophisticated terms which psychologists themselves will have to generate. The former ordinary person's macro model may be data for the psychologist's model, and in turn the psychologist's model may influence the ordinary person's model and perhaps, in the distant future, may even come to replace it in whole or in part. The gap between ordinary amateur 'folk' psychologizing and proven psychological explanations may be reduced to a crack.

'INTROSPECTION' AND MENTAL DEVELOPMENT

This essay has been highly critical of behaviourism and its struggles with introspection but as regards 'introspection' it could also be argued that the behaviourists were closer to the truth than their rivals. For behaviourism held that 'introspection' was somehow derived from the analysis of perceived behaviour. However I am not backsliding into a behaviourist position. The differences between my account of 'introspection' and a behaviourist account may become clearer through a discussion of a suggestive passage in Ryle's *The Concept of Mind*. Ryle wrote that

> The combination of the two assumptions that theorising is the primary activity of minds and that theorising is intrinsically a private, silent and internal operation remains one of the main supports of the dogma of the ghost in the machine. People tend to identify their minds with the 'place' where they

conduct their secret thoughts. They even come to suggest that there is a special mystery about how we publish our thoughts instead of realising that we employ a special artifice to keep them to ourselves. (1949, chap. 2, p. 27)

When this passage is shorn of any behaviourist nuances of thinking being just internalized, stopped-short speech, I think that it points us in the right direction. For as we saw earlier (pp. 39–40), it is true that children slowly form a concept of the mind and the mental. But this is true not because they have laboriously to learn the 'trick' of reducing speech to inner stopped-short 'speech' (as the behaviourists would have it) and then learn to monitor it and other forms of internalized behaviour, but because they learn quite late the ability to analyse their behaviour and that of others in the light of 'folk psychology'. They have to learn the 'trick', so to speak, of seeing the cognitive in what they do and say and how they react, and in what others do and say and how they react, and understanding it to the extent of being able to build a series of 'folk psychological' models or accounts of how they come to do and say such things. It is arguable that it is just because young children do not have a large experience – or if very young, no experience at all – of behavioural and linguistic performances on which to draw for the production of the 'replays', and because they also lack the ability to 'filter' out the important features in the required way as they have yet to learn the 'folk psychology' of their culture, that they engage in little or no 'introspection'.

Part of the 'trick' or 'artifice' which the child learns is, certainly, close to what Ryle and some of the behaviourists would want to say. Often the child, and the adult for that matter, will commit to memory and be able to replay on demand an account of a series of moves or techniques by which he or she was taught and has learnt to do some task, for this account would constitute a model or constructed version of the cognitive strategy embedded in the task. Putting it in memory is internalizing it, and remembering or recalling it without telling anyone is keeping it private. Thus, for example, if a child is asked to give an 'introspective' account of how he did subtraction in respect of some simple arithmetical problem, quite likely he will reply in terms of just such a replay. He will reply in terms of the moves he learnt recently on his mother's lap, or on the blackboard, or in his own school textbook. He will have stored in memory, on high quality, non-decomposing 'film', a 'picture' of himself doing subtraction sums.

If the problem is to take 642 from 1397, we either do it on paper or do it in our head by 'picturing' ourselves doing it. If the latter we might 'see' ourselves writing down 1397, then placing 642 underneath it with the 6 under the 3, the 4 under the 9, and the 2 under the 7, then we might 'see' ourselves substract in single vertical columns beginning from the right, and so on. What is not stored are 'pictures' of mothers' laps, blackboards, ruled exercise books, and ballpoint pens. What is stored is an abstraction from the myriad perceptual data we processed when learning subtraction. Also what is internalized is not a covert, reduced, and unemitted form of our doing subtraction sums in old school exercise books or of someone else doing it for us on a blackboard, nor is it some more mysterious 'as if' or anticipation of the doing of subtraction sums. What I do when I 'introspect' my subtracting one number from another is quite simple and unremarkable. I produce in the edited, 'rounded off', internalized 'replay' of visual memory and imagination a partly correctly recalled and, most probably, a partly imaginatively constructed version or model of my or someone's doing a relevant subtraction sum.

We must not fall into the trap of thinking that when 'introspection' is in the form of a perceptual 'replay' in memory or 'dramatisation' in imagination or most likely both, it must always be in 'pictorial' form, that is, always in terms of *visual* perception. The term 'perception' in this context is meant to cover all the forms of perception including kinaesthetic sensations. So I am not committed to the view that our internalized model of the performances of mental arithmetic or, in general, thinking to oneself, must be in the form of a 'pictorial' replay. One of our perceptions – arguably the most important in this context because most intimately connected with speech – is hearing. We can hear ourselves or others do mental arithmetic out loud, or ourselves reading from a text out loud. So another form of modelling in terms of edited, tidied-up, perceptual replay of overt cognitive performances will be in terms of the heard and spoken word. Our model of our thinking to ourselves might well be in the form of a replay of our own heard words once spoken but now imaginatively reconstructed. Our speech is internalized, not in literal movements of the mechanisms of speech as some behaviourists would have it, but in an edited version of the memory of the heard speech or in an imaginatively constructed and recalled version of heard speech. For example, since I learnt my arithmetical tables in English by bellowing them out loud in unison with the rest of the school class and in time with the primary teacher's first thumping the desk, it is quite likely that, if I am asked to multiply 11 by 12, then I will 'hear myself' say 'Eleven twelves are 132' or, more likely, I might have to start a bit farther back at, say, 'Seven twelves . . .' and so approach 'Eleven twelves . . .' smoothly and at speed.

Some research by developmental psychologists in America (Johnson, 1982, pp. 468ff) suggested that children from at least one area of America – when they had developed what could be called a clear concept of mind – initially associated the mind in particular with the sensory by-products, dreaming, and imagination, and only secondarily with thinking, deciding, making plans, and solving problems. Even so, thinking and cognate activities were often associated with inner speech or inner voices. Feelings were sometimes also associated with the mind. In general it seemed that the mind 'appeared' as a source of 'inward fantasy' in contrast to the brain's role of control centre for bodily movement and personal action.[18] It was only much later that the concept of mind came to be associated with the concept of the self, and this development seemed to coincide roughly with the development of the quite sophisticated ability to form an abstract concept or model of the mind with a clear set of faculties and activities or, in general, mental events. Along with this more abstract model came the employment of it in talk about others as well as oneself.[19]

In short, the underlying moves in the development are that children abstract the concept of mind from concepts of the elusive, immaterial, or at least ethereal aspects of dreaming, imagination, and internally heard speech. This in turn becomes solidified into a concept of *a* mind which is the source of these activities, and finally this is used to communicate with others about our inner cognitive life and to come to an understanding of the inner cognitive life of others. Perhaps this latter stage should be put in reverse, that we generate an abstract sophisticated concept of mind under pressure of the need to develop an explanation of our actions and the actions of others that includes reference to internal cognitive activities. I suspect that parents in particular may contribute to this pressure when they ask such questions as 'Why did you do that?' and are not satisfied until they get answers that refer to acceptable, or at least understandable, 'folk psychological' beliefs, evaluations, and wants. The child defends his action of climbing up on to the shelf in terms of 'I was hoping to find Teddy' and 'I thought that this was where Daddy hid the biscuits' or merely 'I wanted to see what was up there'. Then the child learns to ask such questions as 'Why did you smack me?' and to receive explanations in terms of her parents' beliefs, values, demands, or wishes. A child also constructs a cognitive life for her cat, doll, and the menacing dog next.

Mental development, including the development of 'introspection' – it is suggested – involves developing sufficient maturity to understand and take part in our 'folk psychology'. Consequently it will go hand in hand with the development of whatever is necessary to grasp the quite sophisticated concepts of belief, evaluation, want, decision, plan, forecast, deliberation, reason, and all the other artifacts of 'folk psychology'. It will also go along with the development of the sophisticated ability to concoct explanations of behaviour in terms of these artifacts, and of the ability to make models of our and others' 'minds'. Many of these, as I have endeavoured to explain in some detail as regards the case of 'introspection', will involve also a maturity and sophistication in the employment of perceptual memory and imagination.

1 There is a section in Aristotle (1941 edn, book 3, chap. 4, see especially pp. 429b–30a) where it might be suggested that he is saying we can reflect on our own mental states; but a good discussion of this whole question can be found in Wilkes (1978, chap. 7).

2 For example, Augustine (1955 edn, book 10, section 7, p. 80) remarks, 'What then can be the purpose of the injunction, Know Thyself? I suppose it is that the mind should reflect upon itself.' (See also p. 85.)

3 The most famous version of this distinction is probably that of Brentano (1973 edn, book 1, section 1, p. 3) where he distinguishes 'inner perception' (Wahrnehmung) from 'inner observation' (Beobachtung).

4 For a fuller account of my view of the theoretical difficulties associated with the introspectionist view of introspection, see Lyons (1983, pp. 327–30; 1986, chap. 1).

5 G. H. Mead (1934, pp. 2–3) suggested that Watson's attitude to consciousness and introspection 'was that of the Queen in *Alice in Wonderland* – "Off with their heads!" – there are no such things.'

6 For a fuller account of this critique, see Lyons (1983, pp. 330–5; 1985a; 1986, chap. 2).

7 See Lyons (1984) which includes a reply from Skinner.

8 An example of an early fairly explicit eliminative materialist position in psychology is Boring (1946), though there are elements in his work which seem closer to contemporary functionalism (p. 192).

9 For a fuller critique of reductive (and eliminative) materialism and introspection, see Lyons (1983, pp. 335–41; 1986, Part II, chap. 3).

10 The classical sources for functionalist accounts of the mind are Putnam (1975) and Deutsch (1962). The notion of a 'machine table' is most clearly explained in Putnam's paper 'Minds and machines' (1961; in Putnam, 1975). On this matter see also Hodges (1983, chap. 2, pp. 96ff).

11 Churchland and Churchland (1981, pp. 128ff), Churchland (1984, p. 74), and Quinton (1977, section 13), all seem at least to toy with the idea that introspection does really involve some sort of inner sense, though I take it that Quinton eventually discards it.

12 I suspect that this point is very much 'a philosopher's approach'. I take this point from McGinn (1982, pp. 50–1), though Wittgenstein (1958, Part 2, p. 231) made a similar point in regard to remembering.

13 See, for example Broughton (1976), Ginsburg and Opper (1979, pp. 175–7), Lefebvre-Pinard (1983), Lunzer (1979).

14 Karl Lashley (1958) coined the dictum and it has been echoed by Dennett (1979a, p. 165; 1979b), Hebb (1980, p. 20), Mandler (1975, p. 43), Miller (1962, p. 56), and Neisser (1967, p. 301).

15 Hebb (1969) made this point and it is also to be found long before (for example, in Dodge, 1912, p. 223).

16 I think that it has received adequate treatment in Austin (1962), Ayer (1956, chap. 3), Hirst (1967), and Ryle (1949, chap. 7).

17 Cf. La Rochefoucauld: 'We lack the courage to say, as a general statement, that

we have no bad qualities and our enemies no good ones: yet on specific occasions we almost believe as much', 'We try to glory in those failings which we are unwilling to correct' (1665, maxims 397 and 442).
18 See also Wellman (1985, pp. 172ff).
19 On this last point, the reader might consult Baron-Cohen et al. (1985).

REFERENCES

Aristotle 1941 edn: *De Anima* (c. 330 BC), in *The Basic Works of Aristotle*, ed. R. McKeon. New York: Random House.
Armstrong, D. 1968: *A Materialist Theory of Mind*. London: Routledge and Kegan Paul.
Augustine 1955: *De Trinitate* (399/419), in *The Library of Christian Classics*, vol. 8, *Augustine: Later Works*, trans. and ed. J. Burnaby. London: SCM Press.
Austin, J. L. 1962: *Sense and Sensibilia*. Oxford: Clarendon Press.
Ayer, A. J. 1956: *The Problem of Knowledge*. Harmondsworth: Pelican Books.
Baron-Cohen, S, Leslie, A. M. and Frith, U. 1985: Does the autistic child have a 'theory of mind'? *Cognition*, 21, 37–46.
Boring, E. G. 1946: Mind and mechanism. *American Journal of Psychology*, 59, 34–48.
— 1953: A history of introspection. *Psychological Bulletin*, 50, 169–89.
Borkowski, J. G. and Kurtz, B. E. 1984: Metacognition and special children. In B. Gholson and T. L. Rosenthal (eds), *Applications of Cognitive-Developmental Theory*. Academic Press, New York.
Brentano, F. 1973: *Psychology from an Empirical Standpoint* (1874) International Library of Philosophy and Scientific Method, ed. P. Kraus and J. McAlister, trans. Rancurella, Terrell and McAlister. London: Routledge and Kegan Paul.
Broughton, J. 1978: Development of concepts of self, mind, reality, and knowledge. In *Social Cognition* no. 1, ed. W. Damon. New York: Jossey-Bass.
Brown, A. L. and DeLoache, J. S. 1983: Metacognitive skills. In M. Donaldson, R. Grieve and C. Pratt (eds), *Early Childhood Development and Education*. Oxford: Basil Blackwell.
Butterworth, G. 1982: A brief account of the conflict between the individual and the social in models of cognitive growth. In G. Butterworth and P. Light (eds), *Social Cognition: Studies of the development of Understanding*. Brighton, Sussex: Harvester Press.
Churchland, Paul 1984: *Matter and Consciousness*. Cambridge, Mass.: MIT Press.
Churchland, Paul and Churchland, Patricia 1981: Functionalism, qualia and intentionality. *Philosophical Topics*, 12, 98–112.
Dennett, D. 1969: *Content and Consciousness*. London: Routledge and Kegan Paul.
— 1979a: Towards a cognitive theory of consciousness. In *Brainstorms: Philosophical Essays on Mind and Psychology*. Brighton, Sussex: Harvester Press.
— 1979b: On the absence of phenomenology. In D. F. Gustafson and B. L. Tapscott (eds), *Being, Mind and Method*. Berlin: Reidel.

Deutsch, J. A. 1962: *The Structural Basis of Behaviour*. Cambridge: Cambridge University Press.

Dodge, R. P. 1912: The theory of limitations of introspection. *American Journal of Psychology*, 23, 214–35.

English, H. B. 1921: In aid of introspection. *American Journal of Psychology*, 32, 404–14.

Ericsson, K. A. and Simon, H. A. 1980: Verbal reports as data. *Psychological Review*, 87, 215–51.

Flavell, J. H. 1981: Cognitive monitoring. In W. P. Dickson (ed.), *Children's Oral Communication Skills*. New York: Academic Press.

Geertz, C. 1976: From the native's point of view: on the nature of anthropological understanding. In K. H. Basso and H. A. Selby (eds), *Meaning in Anthropology*. Alburquerque: University of New Mexico Press.

Ginsburg, H. and Opper, S. 1979: *Piaget's Theory of Intellectual Development*. Englewood Cliffs, NJ: Prentice-Hall.

Harris, P. L. 1983: The child as psychologist. In M. Donaldson, R. Grieve and C. Pratt (eds), *Early Childhood Development and Education*. Oxford: Basil Blackwell.

Hebb, D. O. 1969: The mind's eye. *Psychology Today*, 2, 42–61.

1980: *Essay on Mind*. Hillsdale, NJ: Lawrence Erlbaum.

Hirst, R. J. 1967: Sensa. In P. Edwards (ed.), *Encyclopedia of Philosophy*, vol. 7. New York: Collier Macmillan, The Free Press.

Hodges, A. 1983: *Alan Turing: The Enigma*. London: Burnett Books.

Humphrey, G. 1951: *Thinking: An Introduction to its Experimental Psychology*. London: Methuen and John Wiley.

Humphrey, N. 1983: *Consciousness Regained: Chapters in the Development of Mind*. Oxford: Oxford University Press.

James, W. 1950: *The Principles of Psychology* (first published 1890), 2 vols. New York: Dover.

Johansen, J. P. 1954: *The Maori and his Religion in its Non-Ritualistic Aspects*. Copenhagen: I Kommission Hos Ejnar Munksgaard.

Johnson, C. N. 1982: Acquisition of mental verbs and the concept of mind. In *Langauge Development* vol. 1, *Syntax and Semantics*, ed. S. Kuczaj. Hillsdale, NJ: Lawrence Erlbaum.

Jones, A. H. 1915: The method of psychology. *Journal of Philosophy, Psychology and Scientific Method*, 12, 102–24.

Lackner, J. R. and Garrett, M. F. 1972: Resolving ambiguity: effects of biasing context in the unattended ear. *Cognition*, 1, 359–72.

Laird, D. A. 1932: How the consumer estimates quality by subconscious sensory impressions: with special reference to the role of smell. *Journal of Applied Psychology*, 16, 93–102.

La Rochefoucauld, F. duc de 1665: *The Maxims of the Duc de la Rochefoucauld*, trans. C. Fitzgibbon (1974). London: Millington.

Lashley, K. 1923: The behaviouristic interpretation of consciousness, Parts 1 and 2, *Psychological Review*, 30, 446–64.

1958: Cerebral organization and behaviour. In *Proceedings of the Association for Research in Nervous and Mental Diseases*, vol. 36, *The Brain and Human Behaviour*. New York: International Universities Press.

Latané B. and Darley, J. M. 1970: *The Unresponsive Bystander: Why Doesn't He Help?* New York: Appleton-Century-Crofts.

Lawson, M. J. 1980: Metamemory: making decisions about strategies. In J. R. Kirby and John B. Biggs (eds), *Cognition, Development and Instruction*. New York: Academic Press.

Lefebvre-Pinard, M. 1983: Understanding and auto-control of cognitive functions: implications for the relationship between cognition and behaviour. *International Journal of Behavioral Development*, 6, 42–53.

Lunzer, E. A. 1979: The development of consciousness. In G. Underwood and R. Stevens (eds), *Aspects of Consciousness*, vol. 1. New York: Academic Press.

Luria, A. R. 1973: *The Working Brain: An Introduction to Neuropsychology*. Harmondsworth, Middx.: Penguin.

Lutz, C. 1982: Ethnopsychology compared to what? Explaining behaviour and consciousness among the Ifaluk. In preparation.

Lyons, W. 1983: The transformation of introspection. *British Journal of Social Psychology*, 22, 327–42.

 1984: Behaviourism and 'the problem of privacy' (a commentary). *Behavioural and Brain Sciences*, 7, 251–2.

 1985a: The Behaviourists' struggle with introspection. *International Philosophical Quarterly*, 25, 46–59.

 1985b: Dennett, Functionalism, and introspection. *Canadian Journal of Philosophy*, Monograph Collection in Philosophical Psychology, no. 11, 121–34.

 1986: *The Disappearance of Introspection*. Cambridge, Mass.: MIT Press.

McGinn, C. 1982: *The Character of Mind*. Oxford: Oxford University Press.

Mandler, G. 1975: *Mind and Emotion*. New York: John Wiley.

Mead, G. H. 1934: *Mind, Self and Society: From the Standpoint of a Social Behaviourist*, ed. C. W. Morris. Chicago, Ill.: University of Chicago Press.

Mill. J. S. 1882: *Auguste Comte and Positivism*, 3rd edn, vol. 1. Trübner.

Miller, G. A. 1962: *Psychology: The Science of Mental Life*. New York: Harper and Row.

Neisser, U. 1967: *Cognitive Psychology*. Englewood Cliffs, NJ: Prentice-Hall.

Nisbett, R. E. and Wilson, T. de C. 1977: Telling more than we can know: Verbal reports on mental processes. *Psychological Review*, 84, 231–59.

Pratt, C. and Grieve, R. 1984: Metalinguistic awareness and cognitive development. In W. E. Tunmer, C. Pratt and M. L. Herriman (eds), *Metalinguistic Awareness in Children: Theory, Research, and Implications*. Berlin: Springer.

Pribram, K. 1982: Localization and distribution of function in the brain. In J. Orbach (ed.), *Neuropsychology After Lashley: Fifty Years since the Publication of 'Brain Mechanisms and Intelligence'*. Hillsdale, NJ: Lawrence Erlbaum.

Putnam, H. 1975: *Mind, Language and Reality, Philosophical Papers*, vol. 2. Cambridge: Cambridge University Press.

Quinton, A. 1971: In defence of introspection. *Philosphic Exchange*, 2, 43–59.

Robinson, E. J. 1983: Metacognitive Development. In S. Meadows (ed.), *Developing Thinking: Approaches to Children's Cognitive Development*. London: Methuen.

Ryle, G. 1949: *The Concept of Mind*. London: Hutchinson.

Skinner, B. F. 1965: *Science and Human Behaviour* (first published 1953). New York: Collier Macmillan–The Free Press.

Smith, J. 1981: Self and experience in Maori culture. In P. Heelas and A. Lock (eds), *Indigenous Psychologies: The Anthropology of the Self*. New York: Academic Press.

Thomas, S. K. 1978: *The Formal Mechanics of Mind*. Brighton, Sussex: Harvester Press.

Tolman, E. C. 1922: A new formula for Behaviourism. *Psychological Review*, 29, 44–53.

Wade, D. 1983: The ultimate offence: to be taken prisoner of war. *The Listener*, 109, no. 2796, 21–4.

Watson, J. B. 1913: Psychology as the Behaviourist views it. *Psychological Review*, 20, 158–77.

   1920: Is thinking merely the action of language mechanisms? *British Journal of Psychology*, 11, 87–104.

Wellman, H. M. 1985: The child's theory of mind: the development of conceptions of cognition. In S. R. Yussen (ed.), *The Growth of Reflection in Children*. New York: Academic Press.

Wilkes, K. V. 1978: *Physicalism*. London: Routledge and Kegan Paul.

Wittgenstein, L. 1958: *Philosphical Investigations*. Oxford: Basil Blackwell.

Woodworth, R. S. and Schlosberg, H. 1955: *Experimental Psychology*, 3rd edn. London: Methuen.

PART II

The Development of Perception

4

The explanatory depth of propositional attitudes: perceptual development as a test case

Adam Morton

As children develop their capacities as agents, slowly acquiring the skills that mark the socialized adult, they also develop their suitability as objects of psychological ascription. That is, they develop in such a way that the complex network of mental words that we use in ordinary life – what recent philosophers have called common-sense or folk or vernacular psychology – can profitably be applied to them. As adults we describe and explain one another in terms of desires, beliefs, emotions, memories and a host of other such concepts, using subtle principles associated with them which are very hard to make explicit.[1] It is hard to know quite how well this works: one needs to ask 'How accurately do we predict each other's actions?', which is a difficult empirical question, and also 'How accurately do these terms capture our real states of mind?', which is in part a difficult conceptual question.

These are questions about the status of the concepts of common-sense psychology. And one can ask similar questions about the concepts found in psychological theories. How well do they describe and predict behaviour? What mental or physical or behavioural realities can we take them as referring to? Questions of the first sort are at the heart of what psychologists say when comparing rival theories. Questions of the second sort are more to the taste of philosophers. Recent work in the philosophy of mind has tended to buy safety for the postulations of scientific psychology at the expense of those of common sense. The line is, very crudely: psychology (some psychology, anyway) is on the right track, and describes an intelligible domain of real facts, and in seeing why this is so we are forced to admit that common-sense ideas about mind have only a social function, that they give us nice useful labels for ourselves without describing the real causes of our actions. That is especially true of the work of Paul Churchland and Stephen Stich, who will be my main targets here. (It is also true of Patricia Churchland and J. A. Fodor, whom I will not discuss.) But other writers too have emphasized the great difference between the two kinds of postulation, and the difficulty of relating them. K. V. Wilkes has called this 'the mind–mind problem'. Before going on to describe the work by Churchland and Stich and my worries about it, I should explain why it is natural that these issues are discussed in a volume on mental development.

Vernacular psychological ideas, the everyday understanding of mind, applies best to normal people in a normal physical and social context, when they are not undergoing any deep changes. It can provide satisfactory, if sometimes rather shallow, explanations of why people quarrel and make up, how people go about solving complex (but not simple) problems, why people adopt various sensible means to their explicit ends, and so on. But it does not throw much light on either the abnormal or the particular. By 'abnormal' is meant not just the pathological but also whatever is not part of a steady routine: originality and development, behaviour under unfamiliar conditions, disruptions of the social context. And by 'particular' is meant the ways in which people do the component acts which common sense takes for granted: raise teacups to their lips, see the bullseye on the dartboard and so on (see Wilkes, 1978, chap. 3).

It is hoped that these remarks seem obvious vague and harmless. Recent psychologically minded philosophers have tried to develop them, though, in a way that makes them very much less anodyne. In particular, when Churchland and Stich are arguing that there is little hope for much continuity between vernacular psychology and *real*, scientific, psychology they both make central use of the claim that our ordinary psychological concepts of belief, desire, emotion, and the like cannot be used to throw much light on the ways in which the human organism develops in its first years of life.

There is a natural objection to this. We certainly do use the vocabulary of belief and desire, hedged around with some warnings and restrictions, when describing very young children. And we use much of the vocabulary of perception and emotion with practically no restriction at all; we speak of what an infant sees and hears and recognizes, and we speak of rages and depressions and excitement. (The vocabulary is restricted, but we use the restricted vocabulary unrestrictedly.) Moreover we can make perfectly respectable explanations of infant behaviour in these terms: 'she is screaming because she is afraid of the man with beard, who she does not recognize as her father'. Such explanations may be not deep, systematic, and context independent in all the ways that one would want a scientific explanation to be, but they are of a piece with the explanations we give of adult behaviour, for all their imperfections.

This objection does in the end tell against the position that this chapter attacks; but there is a definite way in which this objection misses part of the point of that position. For Stich and Churchland are arguing not that we cannot ascribe common-sense mental words to the very young (or the damaged, or those in crisis or transition) but that it is not in terms of these words, or generalizations expressed in terms of them, that we are likely to extend our understanding of what is going on with such people. Churchland's version of the claim focuses on the importance in the common-sense mental vocabulary of terms for propositional attitudes: words such as 'believes', 'wants', 'remembers', 'hopes'. The characteristic of such verbs is that they are completed not by noun clauses but by embedded sentences: Mary believes that *James is blocking her promotion*; Stephen fears that *the tax people have rumbled him*; no one wants *there to be a nuclear war* (that is, according to orthodox linguistic philosophy, 'No one wants that *there is a nuclear war*'). They seem to be at the core of the common-sense strategy for understanding thought and action. Churchland (1979) thinks that this is a bad strategy. He stresses the unlikeliness – he would say impossibility, I think – of getting an explanation in terms of assumptions about propositional thought ('sentential parameters', in his terminology) of how a child comes to be capable of propositional thought. He calls this the 'infralinguistic catastrophe'. In his words: 'sentential parameters cannot be among the primitive parameters comprehended by a truly adequate theory of rational intellectual development, and the relevance of sentential parameters must be superficial or at best derivative even in the case of fully mature language-using adults' (p. 128).

Stich's version focuses not on all propositional attitudes but on a few central ones, in particular that of belief. His arguments are meant to show that the differences in thought and behaviour between a child in an earlier stage of cognitive development and one at a later stage are unlikely to be expressible in terms of concepts like those of belief. To understand such things as mental development one will need, he thinks, some more theoretical and more specific concepts. And in particular, according to Stich, the feature of common sense that will have to be jettisoned is the description of psychological states in terms of symbols – either words or less obvious symbols – and their identification in terms of those symbols' reference or meaning.

Now put in this way Stich and Churchland's defence of the independence of psychology from common sense may seem not only plausible but perhaps even platitudinous. *Of course* psychology has to invent its own ideas, *of course* the whole point is to get a better grasp of what and how and why people act than one can get in vernacular terms. Who could doubt that? The only doubt might be about the extent to which the enterprise may succeed. (But that is another matter.) The further conclusions each of them draw from this position – variations on the theme that the common sense idea of mind is referentially vacuous, purely instrumental, and not such a good instrument at that, analogous to ancient talk of witches or spirits – may indeed seem more worth worrying about. But while doubting this one might also wonder at the effort taken over these apparently obvious premises.

They are not obvious. For the claim is not just that psychology *may* have to develop and in part break with the vernacular conception of mind, but that the signs are that it *will* have to. If this is right, then the moral many of us drew from the rise of cognitive psychology and cognitive science, that philosophical analysis could be part of a channel through which the common-sense concepts of our culture could be refined into a form in which they come to be of use in the scientific explanation of thought and motivation, is wrong. And, surely, it is not yet obvious that it is wrong.

The issue has been set up in this dialectical 'on the one hand, but on the other, but then again . . .' way, in order to bring out the subtlety of what is at issue. The question is one of the extrapolation from on the one hand the present situation of psychology – the theories presently being entertained, their degrees of success, the directions that look promising – and on the other hand philosphical accounts of the nature of the everyday conception of mind – about which there is considerable diversity of opinion – in order to make a projection about the future relations between the two.

My own view is that it is too early to come to a conclusion. It is not just that we have not enough to go on, either about patterns of success and failure in psychological theorizing or about the nature of vernacular psychology, to come to any definite conclusions, but also something rather more definite. We *do* know enough to begin to see what it is that needs to be settled, and we can see that the issues focus on psychological questions which are as yet unanswered. I will try to illustrate this, in the particular case of the 'infralinguistic catastrophe' with particular emphasis on perceptual development (see Kitcher, 1984, for a more general attack on these ideas).

INFANT PERCEPTION

There is not much explicit common-sense lore about perception. People see, hear, and smell things, and in so doing usually have sensations and acquire beliefs. That is just about all there is to it. There are of course subtle philosophical elaborations of these simple truths, and they have their purposes, but they do not uncover much more of a detailed implicit common-sense doctrine.[2] But perception is obviously an extraordinarily complex affair, and in the past century or so a lot of hard data and very well-confirmed generalizations have emerged. And so one would expect that the Stich–Churchland line, claiming the lack of continuity of common-sense and scientific psychological concepts, should be at its strongest here. Or to put it differently, every little dint that can be made in the position as applied to human perception should count for a lot.

The argument used here will be based on an account of human vision in artificial intelligence terms, that of David Marr (1982). It serves its purpose well because it is based on a lot of hard data, is intellectually rigorous, and is a very live contender among contemporary perceptual theories. The theory cannot be summarized here, but the essential features of it are that it describes first of all 'bottom-up' mechanisms, which take visual input and process them in such a way as to produce 'representations' which are of a more symbolical or cognitive character. The main accomplishment of the theory, besides its unified treatment of a number of perceptual phenomena, is that it shows one way in which very raw, stimulus-like, material can be processed into a product having the appearance of symbolic structure. The model of perception that emerges is of a fairly mechanical process proceeding from the 'bottom' – visual input – 'upwards' towards an articulation accessible to verbal reporting and encodable in long term memory. Now there obviously also are 'top-down' processes, which take as input items from memory and perhaps occurrent thoughts and use them to interpret perceptual input. But on Marr's account these are of secondary importance, at any rate in the 'early' stages of perception, those more directly connected to sensory input.

If this picture is right two probable consequences follow. First, there is almost certainly going to be a stage of processing below which top-down processes do not reach; the effect of thought and memory on perception will go down only so far. And the exact location of this stage will almost certainly vary from individual to individual. Second, in the development of the individual the location of this stage will change; in early childhood top-down processes will be less common and reach less far down, and they will become more influential with increasing age and sophistication.

It is this second consequence that concerns us here. It is a definite and fairly plausible proposition about cognitive development, for which there is not yet unambiguous independent evidence. Some of the work on the development of drawing skills in children seems to support it, in that it demonstrates that children less than 10 years old have little access to the richness of *immediate* visual data stored in short term memory, and must direct their drawings by their more *conceptualized* representations in long-term memory (see Phillips et al., 1985). Thus, in the absence of direct, top-down access to their visual representation the children will be forced to make use of their conceptual knowledge when drawing the object. The study of perspective systems used by young children supports a similar conclusion: the drawing conventions they adopt represent on paper not the visual appearance of the object, the patterns of occlusion and foreshortening, but the structure that the object is thought to have. A story told by Willats (1985) illlustrates the point:

A young girl was asked to draw a ball . . . [her drawing], in the form of a circle, hardly surprises us, and is just what an adult would have produced; so we naturally assume that the line in the child's drawing denotes the smooth edge or occluding contour of the ball. However, the child wanted to go on and draw the mould mark on the surface of the ball, produced by the meeting of the two halves of the mould when the ball was made. An adult would probably have produced a drawing [in which a shape representing the mark is within the circle]. However, the child first drew a line *outside* the first circle, saying as she did so 'I can't draw it here because it's not outside the ball'. She then drew a line *inside* the circle, saying 'I can't draw it here because it's not inside the ball'. Finally she drew a line on top of the first circle, saying 'And I can't draw it here because it won't show up. So I can't do it'. It is hard to resist the conclusion that for this child the shape enclosed by the circle stood for the whole volume of the ball, while the circle itself stood for the surface of the ball, dividing the inside of the ball from the space outside. If this is correct, then it makes perfect good sense to draw the mould line where it belongs, on the line representing the surface of the ball – except that a line drawn there 'won't show up'. (p. 90)

The child in this story is not trying to draw the visual appearance of the ball in front of her. What she is doing is instead to draw a ball, with pictorial symbols representing the facts about the ball as she knows and sees them to be. Visual information for use in drawing is only accessible to her at the very 'top' of the visual system, in the form of knowledge about the structure of the ball. In a few years' time she will be able to make use of information at much lower levels of processing, allowing her to represent occlusions and other features of visual appearance.

More direct experimental evidence for the main proposition ('bottom-up dominates over top-down more in children than adults') may emerge from work now being done by Norman Freeman and his colleagues at Bristol.

AGAINST CHURCHLAND

We are now in a position to present two kinds of doubts about Church-land's position, a fairly straightforward one and a more speculative one. The straightforward line of doubt is that it clearly *is* possible to formulate laws of psychological development in propositional terms. The laws may not be obviously true – only time can tell – but they are clearly respectable and intelligible. The basis of one such set of laws is the movement, mentioned above as a pretty safe conjecture, of the point of contact between bottom-up and top-down processes in visual perception. The crucial point is that in small children this point will be further up. As a result, the influence of verbal stimuli on some intermediate stages of visual processing will not be found in young children. For example, if you show children a photograph such as the well-known 'dalmatian on a dappled background' photograph reproduced on p. 101 of Marr (1982), then, if the presentation is short, you cannot expect a line to be seen along the ridge of the dog's back. But if you say 'See the dog?' while presenting the photo, then you can expect more older children than younger children to make out the line. In an experimentalists' dream world there would be a confirmation for a specific generalization of the form: there is an age A and a time t such that a presentation of t seconds will cause this line to be perceived by more than 50 per cent of children above age A and less than 50 per cent of children below A. In the real world problems about attention, comprehension, and the interaction of experimenter and subject make things less tidy, but, still, there is a law of development here which can be roughly stated and which could approach precision as more other relevant phenomena are understood. That is – *if* Marr's theory and the conjecture about the movement of the point of contact between bottom-up and top-down processes are correct – the output of a particular channel of visual processing should be proposition P (there is a line from $p1$ to $p2$ of visual space) under these conditions for subjects of greater age than A and proposition Q (there is no such line) for subjects of age less than A. This would be a law of psychological development, marking a stage along the route to full cognitive capacity, whose formulation is essentially propositional. And it is clear that the more basic laws from which this one results are of the same sort.

Examples such as this make it pretty likely – just about certain, in fact – that there are developmental laws which are best expressed in terms of propositional attitudes, and in fact that some of these laws concern the development of the child towards capacity for adult propositional thought. There is a way, though, in which this is consistent with some of what Churchland wants to claim. For it could be that although there are such laws, paying attention to them will give only rather superficial understanding of psychological development. The really deep general underlying laws – assuming that there are such and that human beings are capable of formulating them – may take quite different forms. Now this topic is inevitably extremely speculative, and no conclusion at this stage can be worth much compared to what we will eventually learn just by going out and seeing what laws we manage to find. But there are reasons for thinking that some pretty basic psychological laws may be expressed in propositional attitude terms. This is the second and more speculative worry about Churchland.

The idea to be attacked is that the more we learn about mind and brain the less useful we find it to describe their functioning in terms of attitudes to propositions. (And thus, assuming this to be the central strategy of common sense, the more we distance ourselves from it.) Moreover, this is undermined by Marr's description of how something like propositionality arises out of a natural and neurologically plausible information-processing model.

Marr is pretty explicit that his visual processes yield results that can profitably be taken to be symbolical. He is less explicit about what it is about them that is responsible for this. But it is fairly clear in outline what is going on. Symbols emerge from the processing of non-symbolical input because of the simultaneous operation of simplification and modularity. To take each in turn. Simplification: perceptual input is 'filtered', put through channels which eliminate a lot of detail and emphasize some special aspects. The natural example is that of the 'zero crossing' filters Marr is particularly fond of, which in effect highlights the points at which a change in intensity occurs. Modularity: such filters can be set up and tuned in many different ways; at each stage of processing the signal is run through a number of different channels, in parallel, which simplify and highlight in different respects. The result is a collection of 'features', of final products of series of different simplifications. This can be presented just as an unorganized collection, or with some final structuring imposed upon it.

These features can reasonably be considered as symbols for three reasons. First, they are typically causal effects of corresponding features of the environment, though not direct copies of them, and can function in the organization of action directed at those features of the environment. Second, they are on the way to being discrete elements of an all-or-nothing sort: the filtering that results in them reduces, and in the limit eliminates, intermediate results between the full presence and full absence of such a feature. Third, these processes extract them from the swirl of visual input, so that they can be – and require to be – embedded in some other organizing framework. In the case of visual processing this framework is typically three-dimensional perceptual space (not to be confused either with physical space or with the two two-dimensional retinal inputs). But visual features are also directly inserted into more linguistical syntaxes. (As when one glances around a roomful of people and knows that someone has smiled at one, but has no idea where in the room the smile came from.)

This provides material for some doubts about Churchland's claims. Most obviously, it allows us to see how the ascription of propositional attitudes to people might join naturally with a neurological account of their mental functioning. For example, the output of a certain level of visual processing might be *that* edges are located at places $p1$ and $p2$ in visual space, oriented in directions $d1$ and $d2$, respectively. *That* indicates a proposition: the output cannot be represented just as 'edge 1, edge 2, place $p1$, place $p2$, direction $d1$, direction $d2$', for it also gives specific relations between the edges the places and the directions. This propositionality is implicit in the second and third of the reasons for taking the results of visual processing to be symbolical which I gave, extracted from Marr, in the last paragraph.

I have given this simply as an argument against one of Churchland's conclusions, but it can also be seen as pointing out the implausibility of one of his premises. Folk psychology uses propositional attitudes, he seems to assume, as a result of an internalization of propositional speech. People speak in sentences and many of their mental states can be correlated with dispositions to produce particular sentences, as in the case of beliefs or desires, or can be seen as analogous to overt linguistic activities such as discussion, as in the case of thought and deliberation. One might then suppose, following Sellars, that there is an implicit strategy in common sense, embedded deep within our and other cultures, of describing people in terms of their relation to sentence-like objects – propositions. This would explain why the core of our mental vernacular consists of verbs expressing propositional attitudes. And if this were the strategy of common sense it would be clearly a quite superficial one: dispositions to produce tokens of spoken language will only go so far down into human thought and motivation, and the analogies between thought or deliberation and conversation are obviously pretty delicate. So one might well suspect, might indeed be fairly confident, that any significant advance over common sense would have to jettison propositional attitudes.

But we can now see the weak spot in this argument. It might be an intrinsic feature of some neurological processes that they result in propositional states; that is, states which are best described as having as content a number of symbols organized in some definite way. (Obviously more would have to be said than this to provide a real definition.) I would like, in fact, to go out on a limb and suggest that we might well look for such states whenever neural organization is modular, and this modularity can be given a functional significance. For then one will have to have something like communication, the handing over of information, from one module to another. And the three conditions for symbolism that have been extracted from Marr will be met.

1   Causal relations to features of the environment: the information thus transmitted will be related via the functional significance of the module to aspects either of the environment or of yet prior stages of processing.

2   Discreteness: the information will have to be specific, that is the variety of features in the input to the 'transmitting' module and in its internal workings will be reduced to those relevant to the operations of the 'receiving' one.

3   Embedding in a syntax: to the extent that the information has been 'filtered' to a more specific form, it will have been separated from its original context; disparate elements will need to have a common presentation imposed upon them.

If anything of this sort is correct, then in chancing upon propositional attitudes common sense hit upon something very basic about what it is to be human, indeed what it is to be a creature with a nervous system at all like ours. No wonder it has stuck with it so long.

The examples of developmental laws in visual processing which were used for the first, less speculative, doubts about Churchland, can also be used as the basis of an argument against Stich's rather more moderate claims. His conclusions are directed against the semantic aspect of propositional attitudes rather than the mere appeal to sentences or propositions. He accepts – indeed makes great use of – the fact that psychological theories will relate people to symbols – some of them the symbols of our spoken languages and some of them inventions of the theories themselves. But his view (and Fodor's) is that in sufficiently developed psychological theories only the syntactical properties of these symbols will be appealed to, and not their meanings or their relations to objects in the environment (see Stich, 1983).

Now there is quite a lot of force to Stich's arguments for these; he may be right. But I have reservations. I can put my reservations into the form of an argument. It is rather abstract, and I am not quite sure what to make of it, but it seems to me that there is something possibly quite important going on here.

Consider the psychology of a person who has developed in such a way that bottom-up and top-down perceptual processes interact at various stages of visual processing. It is assumed that this will happen as a response to the need to acquire various perceptual and mechanical skills, for example in learning to draw in a grown-up way, and not as a result of the inherent tendencies of the visual system. As a result the exact location and nature of the connections between the two will vary somewhat from individual to individual. Let us try to express this in computational terms. We have a program which begins with a cognitive input and at some stage incorporates the results of some bottom-up perceptual processing. So at a certain stage of computation the program will, say, have to look for edges with a certain orientation. This will be, in effect, what in some programming languages is represented by GOSUB command: the program will under certain conditions receive the results of a subroutine which has the function, say, of picking out the orientation of edges. Imagine the subroutine is 'tunable' by inputs requiring it to be particularly sensitive to, to continue with the example, a particular orientation in a particular part of the visual field. It has these among its local parameters. Then the command might be 'GOSUB (edges in S, orientation o)'. That seems the natural way to describe what seems to be the inevitable routine.[3]

But how are we to interpret the name of the subroutine, for example, the edge-finding subroutine in the example? One possibility is that there is a single specification of the subroutine, that instead of the abbreviation 'edges in S, orientation o' we could just write out the whole subroutine, which would take the same form in all people. But this is very doubtful. For, as stated above, the natural assumption to make is that there will be individual variation on such matters. That is, the exact segment of the bottom-up program which is accessed by the top-down program will vary from one person to another. And thus while there may be a universal program-sketch involving the line 'GOSUB (edges in S, orientation o)', this specification of the subroutine will pick out slightly different subroutines in the psychologies of different people.

There is in fact some evidence for something closely related to this. Jerome Kagan (1971) has argued fairly convincingly that one difference between quite young children lies in their ability to focus their attention. The difference manifests itself in children only a few months old in what Kagan calls 'conceptual tempo', the amount of time the child invests in a given motor or perceptual task, in relation to the amount of immediate satisfaction it gives. At a later age slow conceptual tempo develops into an ability to tell oneself what to attend to, what aspects of the perceptual environment to separate out from the rest. It follows that, among the older children of Kagan's studies, at least, bottom-up visual processing is affected more intimately by cognitive and motivational inputs in some than in others. One would expect some of these individual differences to persist into later life.

Now the connection with Stich's ideas is just this: if when we write out the program for vision we find allusions to subroutines whose exact specification cannot be given, then our use of symbols is not purely syntactical. There is a relevant *semantics* to subroutine specification. 'GOSUB (edges in S, orientation o)' means 'go to that subroutine which you – the organism in question – are capable of, or used to, accessing efficiently, and which gives information about edges and their orientations'. Even this is not a full explanation, for the phrase 'information about edges and their orientations' needs to be explained. And there are two ways of doing it. One is in terms of edges and orientations in the environment, and the other is in terms of the subject's conceptual representations of 'edge' and 'orientation' at the higher level which is accessing the lower level. Presumably both are relevant. But the point is that both are intrinsically semantical.

This may be called 'inner semantics', because the immediate reference of a symbol in a program is taken to be another bit of psychology, another stretch of program, a symbol elsewhere in the program, or some other aspect of the individual's psychology at some level of abstraction. The variety of objects of reference could be quite great; sometimes the best that a psychological theory will be able to specify will be that at some point a program should refer to the result of some neural process, not itself representable in computational terms. In that case the 'inner reference' will be to something physiologically specifiable. But the *easiest* way to specify inner semantics is in terms of conventional outer semantics: one refers to the individual's environment and says, as in the last paragraph, 'the subroutine that picks out edges and orientations'. But it may be that this is just a heuristic, and I do not want to assume that this will always be the way in which semantical connections between computational elements are to be explained. What I do want to claim comes in two parts

1   When we see the variation in psychological structure between individuals as consisting largely in the different improvised connections they make between routines which are universals of human psychology – which may usually be represented computationally and interpreted purely syntactically – then one of our main tools for explaining individual variation, and hence much of mental development, will inevitably be inner semantics – meaning relations between different elements within an individual's mental organization.

2   When common sense identifies mental states in terms of the objects and facts in the world to which they refer it is doing something which cannot be replaced by a purely syntactical characterization of these states, since one function of this common-sensical strategy is to use the environment common to different agents to identify their particular psychological processes, whose exact nature will vary from individual to individual.

It is by virtue of 2 that inner semantics is semantics.

FACTS AND METHODS

To end this chapter I should be clear about the form of my argument. It is an argument from ignorance: I claim that we do not know various facts which would enable us to arrive at firm conclusions about what is likely to pay off in psychology. (Sometimes discovery precedes method.) It is therefore enough for my purposes that the various psychological theories and conjectures I have appealed to are live ideas, not obviously refuted or unprofitable. I have used Marr's theory of vision, in its very general outline; a conjecture arising out of it about the relation between bottom-up and top-down processing; some work of Kagan, Willats, and Freeman on children's perception. All of these are good live theories, though it would be extraordinary if all of them were true. But that is not what I need.

The factual uncertainty which underlies these methodological questions can be seen schematically. There are two extremes. At one end we have the possibility that human individuals are, in Quine's metaphor, like so many trees shaped by careful topiary to similar shapes which bely the utterly different patterns of branches beneath their surfaces. If this is right, the only laws are purely behaviourial and neurological, common sense psychology is intrinsically shallow, and Churchland is right. At the other end we have the possibility that there is a single abstract formula relating states defined in a purely abstract manner, *the* program of human psychology, which can account for everything in human thought or action that any psychological theory can. If this is right psychological reality is essentially syntactic, semantics is irrelevant, and Stich is right. (Note how both possibilities are intrinsically connected with developmental psychology: the first says that only conditioning makes us develop into the similar creatures we eventually are, and the second entails there being a fixed universal formula for human development.) I do not think we can completely rule out either of these extremes. But I do not see much reason to have much faith in either of them. My expectation, which I suspect is that of most psychologists, is that the truth is somewhere in between. And if it is comfortably in between the extremes, psychological states will have to be described in terms of propositions which have both syntactical and semantical features.[4]

NOTES

1   The idea of folk psychology is due to D. C. Dennett, though premonitions of it can be found in Ryle and Strawson and Sellars. See Dennett (1971) and Morton (1979).
2   One counterexample to this derives from 'deviant causal chains'. See Peacocke (1979).
3   In a more sophisticated programming language this might involve the definition of a function or a procedure, but the point would be the same.
4   I have had helpful criticism from Norman Freeman, Kathy Wilkes, and Andrew Woodfield.

REFERENCES

Churchland, P. 1979: *Scientific Realism and the Plasticity of Mind*. Cambridge: Cambridge University Press.
Dennett, D. C. 1971: Intentional systems. *Journal of Philosophy*, 68, 87–106.
Kagan, J. 1971: *Change and Continuity in Infancy*. New York: John Wiley.
Kitcher, P. 1984: In defense of intentional psychology. *Journal of Philosophy*, 81, 65–86.
Marr, D. 1982: *Vision*. San Francisco, Calif.: W. H. Freeman.
Morton, A. 1979: *Frames of Mind*. Oxford: Oxford University Press.

5

Reasons for retaining the view that there is perceptual development in childhood

James Russell

Whether some developmental change or developmental incapacity should be characterized as a *perceptual* change or a *perceptual* incapacity is not, of course, a purely empirical matter. It all depends on what you want to mean by the term 'perception'.

The concern here is with the extent to which perception can be said to develop during childhood. Now, if by 'perception' you mean something as basic as 'the sense organs being responsive to stimuli' then 'perceptual development' hardly exists. In this sense, babies 'see' at birth. But if, at the other extreme, you take the term to mean something like 'way of experiencing the world' or even 'being in the world' then the case for there actually being perceptual development throughout the *lifespan* looks strong. Can you remember what it was like to see the world as a 4-year-old, indeed, as a 16-year-old?

The starting point is the claim that developmental psychologists have been too narrow in their interpretation of the term 'perception'. They have tended towards the first extreme. Because of this they have found it natural to deny that there is any significant perceptual development after infancy. (An external examiner once queried an examination question of mine because it asked about 'perceptual development in childhood'.)

The intention is to analyse in some detail the notion of 'perception' and to produce, on this basis, a taxonomy of interpretations of the term. The psychological reality of these usages will be discussed. The argument will then be that cognitive growth in late infancy and in early childhood is easier to understand when we try to do justice to the perceptual features of these developments through the adoption of a suitably enriched view of perception. This 'suitably enriched view' will be, very roughly, viewing perception as the ability to locate fields of experience within the web of intention and relative to the knowledge base.

As a first step the three main considerations (often tacitly held) that have lead people to be sceptical about the existence of perceptual development after infancy will be summarized.

The first reason for believing that there is no significant perceptual development in childhood is that numerous experiments with infants have shown up a far greater degree of innate organization in the perceptual system than was dreamt of in the old associationist psychologies. The first and largest wave of data broke in the mid-1960s with T. G. R. Bower's (1966) demonstration that babies of only a few weeks old are responsive to size and shape constancies. It has been objected that Bower's data are overinterpreted (see, for example, Russell, 1978), but he was certainly not the only worker to have produced such results (e.g. McKenzie and Day, 1972). The idea that constancy is something that continues to develop through to mid or late childhood (e.g. Seigler and Leibowitz, 1957) was washed away, and in 1974 Bower was able to write that 'During infancy . . . perceptual development is virtually completed' (p. vii).

Most textbooks now tell us that the perceptual systems of tiny babies possess the basic structural properties that the Gestaltists regarded as the 'laws' of perception. And as it is the structure that interests developmental psychologists there does not seem to be very much left to study after infancy. More recently, data from A. Meltzoff (e.g. Meltzoff and Moore, 1977) on the precocious cross-model capacities of neonates and of very young infants persuaded many (though see Kaye, 1984) that the links between kinaesthetic feedback and vision, and between tactile exploration and vision are not dependent on learning during development. Finally, we can place in this category experimental work influenced by James Gibson's (1979) theory of 'direct perception': Lee and Aronson's (1974), and Butterworth and Hick's (1977) studies of 'visual proprioception' which are interpreted as showing that information contained in the light rays defines self-movement versus world-movement and that the perceptual system is innately primed to pick up this information. Moreover, G. E. Butterworth's (Butterworth and Cochran, 1980) studies of babies' abilities in following the direction of the mother's gaze are interpreted by him as showing that the infant's capacity for acting on the basis of *possible sensation* is something primitively present in the perceptual system, not the result of overcoming a primordial solipsism via motor experience, as in Piaget's theory.

The second reason for scepticism is not so easy to pin-point. In the late 1950s and early 1960s a lot of experiments were published on children's susceptibility to visual illusions and on their constancy abilities. The picture that they produced was a confusing one. Susceptibility to some illusions increased with age and to other illusions decreased with age (e.g. Wong, 1979). Sometimes children showed overconstancy and sometimes underconstancy (Seigler and Leibowitz, 1957). But there was a much deeper problem: there was no sure way of telling whether the age-related changes were due to changing perceptions of the world or due to changing interpretations of the instructions (e.g. does the experimenter mean the real size or the apparent size?). This is, of course, one of the central theoretical problems in psychology itself, not just in mental development, and it runs like a geological fault beneath whole edifices of data. It is certainly a major problem in neuropsychology and has been brought to our minds forcefully in recent years through the 'blindsight' controversy (where patients who lack a visual cortex and report themselves to be 'blind' nevertheless show capacities for locating targets visually – see Weiskrantz et al., 1974): how do we know that blindsight is not the result of patients having more stringent criteria for verbally judging something to be present, when asked so to judge, than when told to point as best they can (Campion et al., 1983)? Perhaps there is a logical barrier against using verbal reports – especially the reports of children, the brain-damaged and the mentally ill – as data about 'perception'.

Whilst developmental psychologists became sensitized to the problem of verbal misinterpretation as it bears on Piagetian research (on conservation principally) and came to put down many kinds of 'cognitive' failure to failures of verbal understanding, it became even easier to dismiss studies of perceptual development in childhood as not being about 'perceptual development' at all. Consider the work of E. Vurpillot (1968) on the eye movements that children at different ages make when told to decide whether drawings of two houses are the same. The basic finding is that younger children only scan a portion of each drawing and say 'same' when only a subset of the features have been checked. But, the argument runs, the younger and the older children are probably operating with two different criteria for sameness; for the younger children 'same' means something like 'alike in most respects' rather as we judge a 1950s and a 1970s VW Beetle to be the same kind of car despite the design having changed considerably over the years. Only the most cursory visual inspection is needed to tell us that the two cars are 'the same'.

Similar remarks can be made about Piaget's (1969) work on eye movements. Because of his notoriously strong distinction between perception and intelligence, the experiments which he performed on 'perceptual transport' showing that younger children do not change their point of fixation as often as do older children (cf. Vurpillot) and therefore overestimate the relative size of fixated portions, were interpreted by him as showing the underdeveloped state of a specifically perceptual 'autoregulatory' system. However it is possible to argue that the results of many of these studies are better interpreted as reflecting failures of strategy – a cognitive failure. Learning to look back and forth between two figures whose relative sizes we are trying to estimate ('reciprocal transport' – Piaget) may be better regarded as the perceptual *result* of knowledge development (see Elkind, 1975, for discussion).

One can detect a similar reluctance to explain the results of perception experiments in terms of more central processes in the work on perceptual matching carried out by E. J. Gibson and her associates. In particular, P. E. Bryant (1971) has argued that perceptual matching skills are confounded with memory factors in Gibson's experiments. This does not mean that when memory factors are hived off nothing of perceptual development remains. But if we look carefully at the perceptual matching itself – with memory controlled for – we may find that it is skill that is decomposable into a number of subskills (e.g. the control of eye movements by some central, strategy-generating mechanism) with the result that the hoped-for data on perceptual development, as opposed to cognitive development, has evaporated. At least this is one way of seeing the issue.

Suggestions of this kind are somewhat in the spirit of D. W. Hamlyn's (1957) early writings on perception. For essentially Wittgensteinian reasons, Hamlyn argued that there can be no psychology of veridical perception, only a psychology of susceptibility to illusion and a neuro-physiology of perception. There is no 'purely psychological' process that makes perception veridical. Hamlyn also made the related point that studies of perceptual capacity are also, perforce, studies of dis-crimination, and discrimination is conceptually distinct from perception, in so far as it is related to the *utilization* of experience. Clearly, if this is so we are never going to achieve a psychology of the normal course of 'perceptual development' as distinct from the development of learning capacities.

So, in a nutshell, the second reason for being sceptical about perceptual development in childhood is that any data produced in this area are probably better explained as the result of cognitive or linguistic processes. And it may finally be noted here that the almost exclusive concern with the development of *visual* perception in childhood seems to imply that vision is the primary modality and that therefore lack of visual development must cause dramatic impairments in cognition. This does not seem to be the case, as experimental studies of blind children's cognitive capacities have shown (Cromer, 1973).

The third reason for scepticism is still more difficult to place and much less traceable to evidence. It also seems to reflect the converse view of perception to that just sketched. It is the view that the basic perceptual mechanisms form a 'module', to the extent of being distinct from higher cognitive influence. This module has its *sui generis* principles of operation (cf. the *Gestalt* 'laws') which can be studied with little or no regard to 'top-down' (i.e. cognitive) factors. This view has recently gained ascendancy through the late David Marr's (1982) work on vision.

What was distinctive about Marr's work on vision was not its 'computational' nature; there were numerous computational theories of vision before Marr's appeared. It was that Marr was able to provide an account of the visual mechanisms which was not only mathematically rigorous and tightly constrained by the neurological evidence (for the early stages of vision) but also strikingly independent of the knowledge system. Its computational predecessors were excessively top-down. A guiding principle was to only resort to high-level knowledge in cases of ambiguity. Indeed even in explaining a capacity as high-level as object recognition Marr and Nishihara's (1978) model works in terms of a finite set of descriptive primitives (e.g. describing objects as 'generalized cones'). The perception of something as ambiguous as a silhouette is handled by sets of contour generators with *sui generis* rules of application.

Need this have any implications for perceptual development? It *need* not. But there are some theorists, most notably J. A. Fodor (1983), who would claim that there is a strong conceptual bond between a capacity's being modular, its having a fixed neural architecture (some of Marr's ideas imply this) and its having, in Fodor's words, 'a characteristic pace and sequence of development'. Carefully avoiding the term 'innate', one might say that these features add up to the claim that the development of the (visual at least) perceptual system is not determined by interaction between subject and world to anything like the extent to which cognitive development is determined. It therefore bears more resemblance to the development of a function like locomotion than to cognitive development – which of course makes it a rather unpromising area in which to ask important questions about mental development. In short, accepting a modular view of perception can carry with it the assumption (putting this weakly) that perceptual development is the predictable unfolding of a quite particular mechanism; that it is not developmental changes in the quality of sensory access to the world determining, and being determined by, the central cognitive mechanisms.

This reason for scepticism may appear to be incompatible with the second reason, but in fact it is not. For it is perfectly possible to hold both that the experiments which some think are informative about perceptual development really concern cognitive strategies and linguistic interpretation, and that the study of perceptual development is not informative about cognitive development, and vice versa.

A TAXONOMY: WHAT WE CAN MEAN BY 'PERCEPTION'

The argument which will be advanced here is that the climate of sceptical opinion about perceptual development in childhood is the outcome of an excessively restrictive view of the nature of perception. To anticipate: perception is, from the sceptical position, something like 'appropriate responsivity to stimulation'. I will argue, against this, that we have to enrich our concept of perception to do justice to the facts and to make cognitive development intelligible. The view that cognitive development could take place independently of perceptual development rests on a mistake. The first, and rather drawn-out, stage of the argument is the construction of a taxonomy of ways of regarding perception. These are not intended to be types of perceptual *process* or ways of perceiving. However, the line between how we regard mental processes and mental processes them-selves is often difficult to draw because in regarding mental processes in a certain light we can be, in effect, establishing types of process for our consideration. It is a four-way taxonomy based on two intersecting distinctions.

The first distinction is one that has been most clearly made by G. E. M. Anscombe (1965). It is the distinction between perception in extension (perception$_e$) and perception in intention (perception$_i$) and it grows out of the ambiguity in perception verbs such as *see* and *hear*. To take the case of vision, seeing$_e$ is relative to the object that reflects light-rays to our eyes. So long as these reflected light-rays are recorded/coded/responded to in *some* way we can give any characterization of the object of perception and it will be true. Perception$_e$ is 'referentially transparent'. Here are some examples, the first being Anscombe's.

1a　The hunter saw$_e$ his father in the bushes, though he did not know it was his father.
2a　The hamster saw$_e$ the electron microscope.
3a　The police inspector saw$_e$ the murderer, though he did not know that he was looking at the murderer.

In these cases little if any cognitive appreciation of the nature of the perceived object as described in the complement is assumed: *whatever* mental event occurred at the time it was not the recording of the object as expressed in the sentence. Unlike purely extensional verbal expressions, however, such as *walk past*, *stand behind* or *live near*, we do assume some kind of mental recording of the event.[1] Let us consider parallel examples of seeing in intention.

1b　The hunter saw$_i$ a stag in the bushes and shot; thus shooting his father.

2b   The hamster saw$_i$ an obstacle/place to sleep/big thing (which was in fact an electron microscope).

3b   The police inspector saw$_i$ the vicar who, unbeknownst to him, was the murderer.

Because of this divergence we naturally feel that reference to 'mental representations' in perception is in order. In perceiving we do not simply 'record a stimulus' but make some account of it to ourselves – 'seeing-as' this is sometimes called.

So far this is quite uncontroversial; but I want to take it a little further and suggest that we can distinguish between extensional properties (properties$_e$) and intentional properties (properties$_i$) as objects of perceptual acts. When organisms perceive$_e$ properties$_e$ we can say that the perception is either true or false, because the nature of the property$_e$ is as it is quite independently of any organism's 'representation' of it. The clearest case here is that of the so-called primary qualities – solidity, extension, shape, motion or rest, and number, in Locke's listing. But we must immediately be careful to avoid a confusion here. Primary qualities are taken to be the qualities of objects that they have in themselves and which every object must possess. For example every object must have a degree of solidity, and an extension, but need not have a smell, nor make a sound, nor have a taste. A property$_e$, on the other hand, is not *the fact that* an object has *an* extension: it is the particular extension that it has (e.g. two-dimensional versus three-dimensional). Similarly, solidity itself is a primary quality, but a particular object's being solid or liquid is a property$_e$.

The perception$_e$ of an object as solid, or three-dimensional, or cuboid, or moving relative to a fixed point, or a singleton, is something that must be right or wrong. This is not taken to mean that in all such cases the organism can easily be seen to be wrong on the basis of its perception-guided behaviour (e.g. trying to drink the set-solid 'liquid' in the jar). This is correctness or incorrectness of the perception *whatever* the organism does on its basis. (This distinction will, it is hoped, become clearer when we come to properties$_i$.)

However, properties$_e$ are not exclusively derived from primary qualities. For X to be on top of Y is a property$_e$, and for X to be behind Y is a property$_e$ (note the spatial-relation nature of the 'purely extensional verbs' mentioned above). The division between such, as we may call them, 'relational properties$_e$' and the non-relational variety (e.g. solidity) is made in terms of the fact that in the former case the position of the viewer is taken into account. But this does not rob properties$_e$ of the objectivity that delineates them from properties$_i$ because the location of the *viewer* is itself a property$_e$.

There can be perception$_i$ of properties$_e$. For example we either succeed or fail to perceive$_e$ the fact that something is square or is liquid; but it is possible to bracket off the validity of the perception and yet have properties$_e$ as perceptual$_i$ objects. We can, after all, form mental images of properties$_e$. Furthermore, humans at least can see something *as* solid that they know to be liquid, something as a unity that they know to be a collection, and so forth. But perception of properties$_e$ that is 'in earnest' is perception$_e$.[2]

Properties$_i$, unlike properties$_e$, only exist as expressions of an organism's cognitive constitution, and must therefore be described in relation to: the interests of the organism (fight, flight, feeding, and finding a mate); the organism's conceptual system (leaving open the question of whether we should say that non-verbal or pre-verbal creatures have such); and the behavioural capacities of the organism (for example, being able to jump 2 ft.). Some examples of properties$_i$ are: being edible, being throwable, being a hiding place, being currency, being a place to sleep, being Monty's double.

The question of whether an organism is right about property$_i$ of an object must be assessed relative to its interests, conceptual system and behavioural capacities. Contrast this with the case of properties$_e$. As stated earlier, when properties$_e$ are perceived$_e$ the perception is right or wrong whether or not action is taken on that basis, because the correctness or otherwise is an objective property of the world. When properties$_i$ are perceived$_i$, however, there is nothing correct or incorrect about the perception itself. Using the 'perception-as'[3] terminology may help to clarify matters here. There is nothing inherently wrong in seeing ball-bearings as edible, grass-seeds as currency, or the Chrysler Building as something that one could throw like a spear. The incorrectness, in cases like this, is *post hoc* in the sense that such seeings-as imply that certain courses of action will be successful. (In the conceptual system case, for example, we would have to succeed in using the grass seed as currency.) Cases of perception$_i$ rarely, if ever, fall neatly into one of the three categories. Seeing$_i$ a chair, for instance implies interests (what fulfils one's need for a chair), a conceptual system (verbal judgements derived from this perception$_i$ are corrigible) and a behavioural capacity (somebody more or less human being able to sit on it).

Another way of drawing the line between perception$_e$ and perception$_i$ is by appeal to the fact that only in the former case is the perception explicable by physical causal chains (see Searle, 1984, chap. 5). There is no place for interests, conceptual systems, and (contingent) behavioural capacities in physics.

The perception$_e$/perception$_i$ distinction is essentially linguistic because it is surely possible that languages might exist in which all perception verbs are intentional or all extensional. In this sense, then, the ambiguity is a feature of a particular conceptual system. The second distinction, on the other hand, is epistemological rather than linguistic, because it concerns

the way in which perceptual experience relates to knowledge. Traditionally, it has been made in terms of 'sensation' versus 'perception'; but
present ends are better served by using a modern version of the distinction
set out by C. Peacocke (1983).

A perception, says Peacocke, has *representational content* (and thus
representational properties) and a *sensational character* (and thus sensational properties). To put it loosely, the first is objective in that it points
outwards to the object being perceived whilst the second is subjective,
pointing inwards to the character of the experience enjoyed in the act of
perception. In seeing a tree, for example, the representational content is
that of a tree; so a second person would usually only need to follow our
line of visual regard to find the representational content of our visual
perception. But the perception which the person undergoes is also an
experience with an intrinsic, sensational character – the character that a
painter might try to capture and that may be referred to as the state of the
person's visual field at a particular time.

Many theorists of perception would mistrust this distinction. But before
considering Peacocke's defence of it mention should be made of two
things that representational content is *not*. It is not a perceptual belief; for,
to illustrate, a subject in a visual illusion experiment, presented with the
Muller–Leyer illusion, may have the representational *content* of two
parallel lines one *longer* than the other, whilst correctly believing that the
two lines are really equal. Neither is representational content equatable
with the objective 'informational content'. To take the Muller–Leyer
example again, the informational content of the perception is that the two
lines are *equal*, and this informational content (cf. properties$_e$) is a
determinant of the sensational character of the perception. Therefore the
representational content may succeed or fail to capture the informational
content of a perception – which is to say that it can be true or false. Also,
content is *intrinsic to* the perceptual experience – entailing that two
identical experiences cannot produce different representational contents,
which in turn means that representational content is not something
inferred or abstracted away from the phenomenology, nor a matter of
judgement over and above the perceptual experience, and certainly not
(cf. the visual illusions) a matter of choice or interpretation.

Now it is possible to reject this distinction by saying that a description of
the representational content of a perception exhausts what we need to say
about it: talk about an intrinsic sensational character is redundant. This is
equivalent to the claim that all we need to do to capture the intrinsic nature
of (say) a visual experience is to use the preface 'it visually appears to the
subject that . . .' before a description of the physical object to which the
eyes are directed. Peacocke calls this the Adequacy Thesis and argues
against it by fielding three counter-examples. First, in perspectival vision,
objects are at once larger than others (retinally) and the same size

(veridically). We need the sensation/representational content distinction to make sense of this paradox; on the Adequacy Thesis it remains a paradox. Second, in monocular versus binocular vision we encounter a case of two perceptions having the same representational content (i.e. some objects being in front of others) but quite different intrinsic sensational properties. Third, when presented with an ambiguous figure such as the Necker cube we can have perceptions with two different representational contents (e.g face ABCD towards me versus face EFGH towards me). But we additionally perceive non-representational *similarities* between the representations – we literally 'see that it has not changed' (Wittgenstein, 1958, p. 193). We therefore – at least according to Peacocke – require another means of regarding perception in addition to the representational in order to explain this seeing that nothing has changed, because this cannot be tied down to any particular representational content.

Whether or not we happen to agree that these examples are sufficiently clear to refute the Adequacy Thesis[4] it is surely the case that the thesis is wrong in so far as it implies that the relation between a physical object and the content of a perception is a relation of causal necessity. *All things being equal* a tilted circular plate should give rise to the perception of an ellipse, but it does not *have* to do so. To think that it does is to make the classic error of interpreting visual perception on the model of the formation of an image on the back of a camera. Quite apart from its invitation to an infinite regress, such a conception ignores the role of the perceiver (his biochemical state, 'set' and so forth[5]) in the perceptual act.

Neither of these distinctions (intentional/extensional and representational content/sensational character) is satisfactory by itself. The first is essentially linguistic and the second is excessively difficult to state and defend because of the deeply ambiguous nature of the terms which have to be employed. Combining the distinctions into a four-way taxonomy will help to remove some of these ambiguities and give us a framework within which to contrast different perceptual phenomena.

This is the taxonomy:

1   Sensational perception in extension (Sen.per$_e$)
2   Sensational perception in intention (Sen.per$_i$)
3   Representational perception in extension (Rep.per$_e$)
4   Representational perception in intention (Rep.per$_i$).

Sen.per$_e$

This is what the phenomenologist Husserl thought would be the result of *epoche* – the process of bracketing off all epistemic content from a perceptual experience. In the case of vision this might result in something like a visual field consisting a flat mosaic of colour. Perception regarded in this way is extensional because it is causally determined by whatever the proximal stimulation happens to be, and should thus be strictly explicable as the result of a series of causal chains 'upwards' from stimulus to percept. It is also extensional in that it is capable of assessment as true or false, but only in the sense that a photograph can be true or false, i.e. accurate or inaccurate.

Is this way of regarding perception coherent and useful? Such a notion closely parallels some recent claims made by F. Dretske (1983). I suspect that Dretske's account is flawed, but in discussing it we should become clearer about how to locate Sen.per$_e$.

Dretske also distinguishes between 'extensional' and 'intentional' perception, but, unlike the present distinction, extensional perception is exclusively a processing *stage*. The extensional, for Dretske, is pre-selective, photographic, and, in his terminology, an 'analog' – a 'sensory representation' coded 'in preparation for its selective utilization by the cognitive centres (where the *belief* that it is a duck may be generated)' (p. 60). The extensional stage of sensory representation is rich in redundant information, and cognitive processes will select in the second stage what is needed for the belief-infused perception – intentional perception. He gives the example of glancing round a room in which there are 28 people. This information is 'contained in the sensory representation without receiving the kind of cognitive transformation . . . associated with conceptualisation (belief)' (p. 61). This is not, Dretske insists, a stage of awareness, 'on the contrary', he says, 'what we perceive (what we are aware of) are the things represented by these internal representations (not the representations themselves), the things *about which* they carry information' (p. 61).

Psychologists will immediately be reminded of the 'icon' here. This is the processing stage, suggested initially to account for G. Sperling's (1960) data, in which something like a snapshot of an array (usually a row of letters) is briefly (about a quarter of a second) available, and decays rapidly as cognitive operations pick out elements of it for short-term memory retention. It may be objected that in this lies the vulnerability of Dretske's notion of extensional perception; that because Dretske regards it as a stage in the perceptual process he is in fact making a speculative empirical claim not a conceptual claim. There is no conceptual necessity for there being 'a sensory representation' of the kind that he imagines. We certainly do not need to posit it to explain the undoubted fact that more perceptual information 'gets in' than we process in current awareness. For this reason the category is only as strong as the evidence for the iconic stage of processing, and this is not strong (see Haber, 1983).

There is something in this complaint, but it rests on a rather priggishly clean division between empirical and conceptual questions. Moreover, although the claim that we potentially have access to a kind of 100 per cent accurate 'representation' is not empirically attractive and exploits a very strange use of the term 'representation', we surely do need some concept of perception (this is where Dretske's 'extensional perception' and our Sen.per$_e$ overlap) which accounts for the possibility that we *register* in *some* way the impinging light-rays without *perceiving* anything. What makes the claim difficult, however, is the question of whether and when we are going to talk about 'experience'. As was the case for Peacocke, this leads to confusion.[6] On the one hand he writes of 'our experience of the world being rich in information in a way that our consequent beliefs (if any) are not' (1983, p. 60), implying that extensional perception is, as it was for Husserl, a possible level of awareness. On the other hand – as has been mentioned already – he explicitly denies that we are aware of the 'sensory representation', implying, perhaps, that extensional perception does not have a phenomenology. Or does it imply that we cannot reflect on it?

Within the current taxonomy, Sen.per$_e$ is presented as a possible kind of phenomenology. Bearing this in mind, let us turn to Dretske on development.

He writes: 'A normal child of two can *see* as well as I can (probably better). This child's experience of the world is (I rashly conjecture) as rich and as variegated as that of the most knowledgeable adult. What is lacking is the capacity to exploit these experiences in the generation of reliable belief (knowledge) about what the child sees' (1983, p. 60). Dretske's picture is, therefore, that of Sen.per$_e$ not developing and maybe even deteriorating from infancy to adulthood. Perceptual development is the cognitive process of belief extraction from the extensional array.

This conception is flawed. First, it contains the assumption that the sensory registering of a pattern of light (at the retina?) implies experience when, of course, it should imply nothing mental at all. To become something mental (on the simple assumption that the brain is more than a camera) this pattern has to be processed into something similar, at least, to Marr's 'raw primal sketch' in which information about surfaces, edges, and textures is registered. This is a form of extensional perception. Indeed we may also regard Marr's 2½D sketch (viewer-centred or projective) and even possibly the 3D model (object-centred) as extensional (see below for more on this question). But what we seek is a way of regarding perception in which there is *no* representational content and yet there is sensory experience. Given the necessity for processing *at the outset* that Marr's work amply demonstrates it seems that such a neutral mosaic of experience is an impossibility, at least as a primitive 'early' form of perception. Significantly Marr employs the term 'representation' even for the earliest state of visual information processing – a usage justified by the fact that registering (say) an edge as an edge has representational content. It is surely a myth that children are little phenomenologists with perceptual fields which, as yet, lack representational content. If an organism has awareness *of* anything then there is representational content. This makes Dretske's apparent claim that (extensional) 'experience' remains constant through development similarly mythological.

The suggestion that adults have, we may call them, 'unbelieved experiences' lasting about as long as an icon lasts is also untenable. If we did have them then our visual perception would be a hopeless jumble of overlapping pictures produced each time we change fixation. Certainly we require the notion that more information may enter the system than is believed; this is an argument for *un*conscious processes in visual perception. But these unconscious processes seem, on the present state of the evidence, to be semantic in nature (see Marcel, 1983), not the mere registering of blobs of colour.

May Sen.per$_e$ then have psychological reality?[7] If it does have developmental reality then it should be regarded as the *product* of perceptual development. A highly sophisticated perceiver *may* be able deliberately to bracket off representational content *in* experience. But this is indeed a remote possibility given that the perceptual system appears to have an essentially mandatory nature. One should not, however, assume that we cannot bracket off representational content *from* experience *post hoc*: we do this in drawing and painting. Sen.per$_e$ becomes on this view an imagined possibility on which we can act, rather than a mode of experience. But the acting on the possibility – i.e. the appreciation of the possibility of regarding our phenomenal field as a mosaic – must be the *result* of perceptual development; it depends upon the existence of a representational content with a degree of elaboration *sufficient for the deliberate subtraction of this content.*

Sen.per$_i$

This is perhaps the best candidate for designation as 'perceptual experience' and is best understood in terms of the paradoxes which it invites. It has just been said that any kind of perceptual experience, no matter how primitive, must be representational in the sense that it must be the result of processing. What we do not need to say, however, is that *the representational level* is a sensory experience. This would have absurd consequences: that we actually *see* the world as blurred for a brief while as our primal sketch is computed, and that a computer running a primal sketch program has similar experiences. This kind of representation will be called here 'computational' – it being one of the difficulties with Dretske's notion of 'sensory representation' that this representation is regarded as something immediate and uncomputed. Thus, Sen.per$_i$ *is the result of computational representations* produced within the nervous system, but it has no 'representational content' in the sense in which the term has been used here.

The next paradox concerns this very absence of representational content. Such an absence does not mean that the perception does not have meaning for the subject; rather the perception does not have a *truth value*. Now to explain what this means.

What it means to say that Sen.per$_i$ has no representational content is that we can regard any perceptual experience as a *possible hallucination*, just as we can (see above) regard (though probably not *experience*) our visual field as a two-dimensional mosaic of colour. This is not just a question of disbelieving individual percepts – as might a sophisticated subject in a visual illusion experiment – but of bracketing off the truth or falsehood of the phenomenal field. Consider, in illustration, what introspection shows us about the relation between a sensory memory of a scene and the imaginative construction of a scene: whatever the difference is, there is some commonality of sensory content. What the memory of seeing a black dog jump into a khaki-coloured canal to fetch a stick and imagining seeing the event *have in common* is, perhaps, the essence of Sen.per$_i$.[8]

Sen.per$_i$ can be regarded as the object of perceptual introspection. We cannot, in contrast, say that the representational content is the object of perceptual introspection for this is what the subject succeeds or fails to perceive (e.g. he fails to see two equal lines in the Muller–Leyer illusion and succeeds in seeing two parallel lines). It is because the subject can regard perception as Sen.per$_i$ that instructions such as 'Just tell me what you now have in your visual field/how this changes what you can see/how this looks now' are intelligible to him. We can also say that Sen.per$_i$ is reflected in our capacity for 'lifting' perceptual experience free of its engagement with the world, of treating our perceptual experiences as if they were merely *in the running* for truth and representing them in paintings and drawings. There is, in short, a significant gap in human perception between sensational character and the truth- or falsity-giving conditions in the world. There is nothing illogical in a statement of the kind 'I now have the visual experience as of a red triangle although I haven't a clue about what is really there'.[9] But does this not thereby become representational content itself? It does not, because on Peacocke's terms representational content has to be something *either believed or not believed*. My claim is that we have the appropriate view of perceptual experience if we leave beliefs about veridicality altogether out of account.

Another difference between Sen.per$_i$ and representational content is that the former has to be modality specific (that is, visual, auditory, or . . .). However, representational content, so far as I understand what Peacocke intends, can be supra-modal.

However, it is not simply a desire for conceptual refinement that motivates this category of intentional perception without representational content. For the bracketing off of representation enables us to avoid one of the classic pitfalls in perceptual theory. It takes this form: 'perceptual-experience-as-representation' is seen as a kind of middle term in the three-term relation 'subject–experience–object'. The representational experience is thus 'between' the subject and the object, which suggests the view that perception is successful *by virtue of* the experience accurately representing the object and illusory in so far as it does not resemble the object. There are a host of problems with this, not the least of which is that it invites an infinite regress. On this view perception is picture-like experience on a kind of mental back-projection screen – a picture that is more or less vivid, more or less detailed. But if so we need another agency or 'homunculus' in the brain to perceive our internal picture and a further homunculus to perceive his, and so on. It is like saying that perceptual representations are the experiences that *enable* us to perceive; put like this the absurdity is clear.

A second problem with running perceptual representations into perceptual experience is how we are to deal with perceptions that have representational content but which do not have a sensory character. Whatever procedural faults may be found with the studies of blindsight (see above) and with demonstrations of unconscious extraction of meaning from single words (Marcel, 1983), we should not try to rule out perceptions with representational content but without a phenomenology as impossible.

What we have to do in order to avoid these two consequences is to hive off perceptual experience from perception *qua* the veridical or non-veridical mental representation of things in the world. The category of Sen.per$_i$ achieves this.

Although the developmental implications of the category will be spelt out in the final section, it would be well to give a brief trailer for what will be said there about Sen.per$_i$. There are two kinds of advantage to be gained from using this notion in developmental theory. First, it enables us to at least consider the possibility that although a child at a certain age may succeed on perceptual tasks just as we do, he may live in a quite different kind of perceptual world; the quality of his perceptual experiences may be different from ours if not the accuracy of his perceptual acts. This may influence the way in which perception informs his verbal judgements. Second, the conceptual separation of semantically rich sensational character from perception as representation, may be psychologically manifested in the process through which perceptual experiences in childhood become, in J. M. Baldwin's (1906) phrase, 'liftable' in imagery-guided imitation and fantasy. We may be able to regard the sensory quality of some of our representations (recalling or imagining tunes, tasks, scenes for example) as a kind of 'spin off' from the making of the sensory meaning/representational content division in development.

Rep.per$_e$

To view a perception representationally does not mean denying that it has a sensory character. Rather, we treat the question of sensory character as irrelevant just as we treated the question of the veridicality of the perception as irrelevant within the two sensational categories. Perhaps the best way of understanding Rep.per$_e$ is in terms of the extreme liberality of its criteria for whether or not a 'perception' has taken place. What may be called 'the bare registering of proximal stimulation defining an extensional property' is sufficient for Rep.per$_e$.

It is within this category that we can place the precocious perceptual capacities of human infants that were mentioned at the beginning. For example, Bower's (1967) demonstration that infants of a few days or weeks old are sensitive to the properties of visual input that define 'existence constancy' versus those which do not, does not require that we attribute to them any awareness of the existence of objects in the third dimension. All we need to say is that the input is coded appropriately. Similarly the supra-modal translation of visual input from a facial gesture (Meltzoff and Moore, 1977) into whatever kinaesthetic coding is necessary for the imitation of that gesture is not a process that we have to regard either in terms of the particular sensory character of the visual input and the kinaesthetic feedback or in terms of an achieved division between self and other (see Rep.per$_i$).

In fact the distinction between bare coding and awareness in perception is one that has been quite widely discussed in the literature, having been made initially by Irving Rock (1968), and then later by Bower (1975). In Bower's terminology, and terminology is all-important here, the distinction is between 'discriminating between values on all the proximal variables that specify position in the third dimension' and being 'aware of position in the third dimension per se'.

The Rep.per$_e$ view is not only necessitated by the perceptual successes of primitive or undeveloped creatures. Much of adults' perceptual engagement with the world is through the agency of what Fodor (1983) has called 'input processes' that are, at least, mandatory, very fast, non-conscious, and informationally encapsulated. In spatial perception, for example, the perceptual judgements that result are not founded on anything like *estimation*. As Gareth Evans (1983) expressed it: 'When we hear a sound as coming from a certain direction, we do not have to *think* or *calculate* which way to turn our heads (say) in order to look for the source of the sound' (p. 155). In this case – and in the case of any organism moving about – sensory inputs acquire, in Evans's words again, 'a (non-conceptual) spatial *content* for an organism by being linked with behavioural output' (p. 156). Always bearing in mind that 'the non-conceptual contents of perceptual informational states [roughly, Rep.per$_e$] . . . are not

ipso facto perceptual *experiences* – that is, states of a conscious subject'
(p. 159). He continues, with Fodor's language-of-thought thesis clearly in
mind: 'However addicted we may be to thinking of the links between
auditory input in information-processing terms – in terms of computing
the solution to simultaneous equations – it seems absolutely clear that
evolution could throw up an organism in which such advantageous links
were established, long before it had provided us with a conscious subject
of experience' (pp. 157–8). He adds in a footnote: 'One of the dis-
advantages of this addiction is that it tends to blur the distinction I am
trying to explain'.

Rep.per$_i$

Here we have success or failure in perceiving objects, properties and
events that are relative to the organism's interests, conceptual system, and
physical capacities, without prejudice to the sensory character of the
perceptual experiences, or indeed to whether experiences of any kind are
undergone.[10]

We need this category in order to encompass successful and unsuccessful semantic perception (note that the truth and falsity of such intentional
perception is always *post hoc*) in such a way that no assumptions need to
be made about consciousness. Many of the phenomena discussed by
James Gibson under the heading of the perception of *affordances* are
relevant here: an animal's perception of something as edible or as a hiding
place, for example. Although Gibson's notion of affordance can be
criticized for its awkward straddling of the intentional/extensional distinction (see Russell, 1984, chap. 5) it is useful in that it frees us from the language of sensory character, perceptual experience, and visual fields in
explaining how an organism perceives the meaning of objects.

Let us consider some human examples of Rep.per$_i$ – of semantic
perception without sensory character. If we perceive an individual to be a
threat, or a dolt, or a sage this need involve no consciousness of the
individual as being such; certainly it need involve no alteration of the
sensory field. (Note how this is sometimes achieved via the alteration of
sensory fields in cartoons: an ill-intentioned character grows horns, hoofs
and develops a twisted leer, for example.) We may simply feel, respectively, threatened, contemptuous, or shallow in his presence; we may
indeed be aware of feeling none of these things but simply behave in a
defensive, condescending, or tentative manner in the presence of such
persons. With the result that others may be in a better position to record
our successful Rep.per$_i$ than ourselves.

By way of rounding off the discussion of Rep.per$_e$ and Rep.per$_i$, and as a
bridge to the discussion of how all this distinction-breeding is supposed to
bear on cognitive-developmental psychology, some more brief points

about the term 'representation' will be made, and the importance of distinguishing clearly between representation and experience will be elaborated on.

We have already discussed how the view that we perceive by constructing a phenomenal 'representation' of the object leads to an infinite regress. Does not this regress loom over *any* account of perception in terms of 'representations' – phenomenal or otherwise? It does not, so long as we regard *the representations in virtue of which perception succeeds* as being constructs or necessary fictions (cf. Dennett, 1982, on conscious representation) that have more reality 'in the head' of the student of perception than 'in the head' of the subject. On this view there are not, strictly representations in the brain, but neural states and processes that have the status of representations *in our theories*. Explanation in terms of what we referred to earlier as computational representations – *à la* Marr – form a subset of these; but only a subset because there is no need for any *a priori* restriction on the mode of expression of such theories. A computational mode of expression may indeed be necessary for the earlier stages of perceptual information-processing, but it could well turn out to be an inappropriately fine grain for the higher, semantic levels.

But representational accounts of perception need not necessarily be theories of brain processes. It may prove a fruitful research strategy in perception to describe rigorously (perhaps in computational language) perceptual experience at the level of Sen.per$_i$. These 'representations' would be, as before, theoretical constructs [in Winston's (1984) textbook of artificial intelligence a representation is defined as 'a set of conventions about how to describe a class of things'] which would result in theories of the semantic perceptual field or *Umwelt* (Uexhull, 1957) of the organism, without prejudice to the brain processes responsible for these fields. One of the reasons for undertaking such description – one supposes – would be to make *learning* more intelligible.[11]

This is what is meant here, then, by saying that the representations in perceptual theories are a kind of necessary fiction: 'necessary' because they make neural processes intelligible and the semantic field in perception describable – but 'fictions' because no matter how long you search in the brain you will never find them. In contrast *perceptual experiences* are not constructs. They have a reality for the subject and do not, *pace* Dennett (1981), rely for their reality upon interpretation by others who take up 'intentional stances' to the subject – to think this is to confuse them with representations.

PERCEPTION AND THE STUDY OF MENTAL DEVELOPMENT

Armed with this taxonomy we can now reconsider the three sceptical cases against the existence of perceptual development in childhood. The rejection of these will mean viewing developmental changes which are normally regarded as being *cognitive* changes as also being expressions of perceptual development – on an enriched view of perception.

The first reason discussed above for distrusting the notion of perceptual development in childhood was grounded in the belief that young babies already possess the basic structural capacities for veridical perception. In the present terms what this boils down to is that they perceive sufficiently well for us to view these capacities as Rep.per$_e$. This immediately implies that nothing can necessarily be concluded about their awareness of the world nor about their perception as the acquisition of knowledge. My argument will be that when we place infants' successes at perceptual (e.g. constancy) tasks alongside their failures at 'cognitive' (e.g. object concept) tasks we see that perceptual development is such a fundamental feature of the infant's mental development that continuities become apparent between perceptual development in infancy and something that we would want to call perceptual development in childhood.

The way to approach the matter is by reference to 'utilizing one's perceptual field'. The 6-week-old babies in Bower's (1966) well-known size constancy experiments did not need to utilize their visual fields in order to respond on the basis of real rather than phenomenal size. They needed, rather, to utilize the cue or cues (probably 'cue'-motion parallax) that defined invariant size and invariant distance. Now this is remarkable enough, but still more remarkable would have been their responding on the basis of the *phenomenal* size given that this would have involved the filtering out of cues to three-dimensionality. To regard a two-dimensional perception of the world as somehow more *primitive* here is a mistake traceable to the belief, noted above, that perception begins (in development or in processing) with a coloured mosaic. Why should two-dimensional size invariance be more easily extractable than three-dimensional size invariance when the latter has more informational support?

If infants did respond in terms of phenomenal size in this kind of experiment we could regard it as a first step towards the utilization of their visual fields; but it would only be a first step. It would not be full utilization because what we have in such paradigms is the calling out of a response under conditions of highly stage-managed visual input. What is intended by the 'utilization of one's visual field', in contrast, is spontaneous behaviour towards objects that is informed by their appearance to oneself. What hinges on the difference between an evoked response and spontaneous behaviour here is the fact that in the latter case sensory input is governed by the organism as well as being world-governed.[12] So the visual field is, to that extent, distinguished from states of the world. However, when captive infants are presented with experimenter-governed displays the infants have merely to respond to the input. They need only be, in Evans's terminology, in an appropriate 'informational state'.

Peacocke's (1983) terminology will be borrowed once more to call the ability to guide behaviour in terms of the nature of one's visual field 'perspectival sensitivity'. As an organism moves about the world the actions it takes are informed by changes in the way the world appears to it: 'his intentional web must be recentred on the place determined in normal circumstances by the change in the sensational properties of his experience' (p. 69). There are two principal advantages of concentrating on perspectival change and movement. The first is that it forces us to attend to the organism's capacities for knitting sets of perspectival information together rather than producing the appropriate behaviour in a particular circumstance presented to it. Our visual field is usually only informative to us in terms of a history of linked fields and an evolving web of expectations about future experiences. And to the extent that the organism–environment relation inherent in a visual field is not *unique*, that relation is *structured*. 'For instance,' writes Evans, 'the subject must be able to think of the relation in which he stands to a tree that he can see as an instance of the relation in which (say) the Albert Hall stands to the Albert Memorial' (1983, p. 163).

The second advantage of focusing on perspectival sensitivity is that locating the successions of visual fields within a motoric, physical web enables us to see how an organism might come to *disbelieve* its visual experience (Sen.per$_i$, recall, was neither true nor false, but a candidate for belief or disbelief). Indeed one might disbelieve one's auditory, haptic of kinaesthetic input on the basis of the visual. Although this way of putting things ignores the complexities in Peacocke's treatment, we can imagine a case where a person's visual experiences do not match with his tactual and kinaesthetic experiences so that he may do one of two things: either utilize the anomalous visual experiences at the outset, later ignoring them as they come to produce errors; or reflect upon them, *withholding assent* (as it is possible to do with Sen.per$_i$), and monitor future results of action. Responding in the *second* way would be a clear indication of – and perhaps even a sufficient condition for – guiding one's intentions in accordance with one's visual field. (There will no doubt be readers who have been subjects in displacing-goggles experiments who will recognize the experience of this second way. Although the brain eventually changes the visual field the initial experience is of refusing to believe that the world is as we see it.) What perspectival sensitivity boils down to here is the ability to take a perceptual field as *interpretable in the light of information from other sources*. This may be information from other modalities or it may not (for example, information in memory or motor habits).

Can infants' failures on object concept tasks be made intelligible in terms of their problems with perspectival sensitivity – as failures to regard (in this case) visual fields as being *interpretable*? I believe they can if we attend to two possible consequences of such a failure. First, an infant who lacks perspectival sensitivity will tend to assume that there is a one-to-one relationship between what is seen and what is in the world. There will be a kind of naïve 'trusting' of visual experience. Second, the failure to regard the visual field as interpretable in the light of other information (e.g. resulting from past actions or observations) may cause him to fail to appreciate that when there is a *conflict* between sources of information or when one source of information shows that another source of information is now unreliable or in need of updating there will be no attempt to relate one source of information to another. What may happen in this case is that visual information will simply be ignored and the other source of information relied on entirely. The result is that an infant who lacks perspectival sensitivity will sometimes naïvely trust a field of perceptual information and sometimes naïvely ignore it.

The failure to retrieve completely occluded objects before 8 months of age is easily regarded in the light of the first kind of ('naïve trusting') difficulty. When the object has been occluded, the visual field defines absence of the occluded object. If there is no rattle to be seen then there simply *is* no rattle. It is not just that the infant allows visual information to override current tactual information (although he may do this[13]) but that each visual impression is regarded ahistorically – that is, as decoupled from the impressions which preceded it. Thus, the visual field t_2 seems to be treated as an infallible guide to reality at t_2 despite what was witnessed at t_1. We have then an underdeveloped notion of Sen.per$_i$ – the knowledge that (in this case) visual experience is only in the running for truth.

The almost glaringly obvious objection to this thesis is that it is a mere rhapsodizing on a failure that is simply a failure of *memory*[14] – the baby forgets the occlusion. Now in considering data which refute the memory failure explanation we also find examples of the second kind of failure in which a field of perceptual experience is naïvely ignored. If we place an object inside a transparent cup that a 6-month-old baby badly wants, the baby will often stare helplessly at the cup and fail just as if it were opaque (Neilson, 1977). So it cannot be simply that he forgets that the object was put there. *What* is happening here? The traditional view that this is simply a question about Rep.per$_e$ and, assuming that this kind of perceptual development is well advanced at 6 months of age, further assumes that the difficulty is not perceptual. I would suggest that the problem is with failing to believe what is seen. To explain: if lack of perspectival sensitivity can involve ignoring one source of perceptual information as soon as it conflicts with another source there should be particular difficulty with understanding transparency because here the conflict is quite dramatic. In the present experiment the object is visible and yet something is covering it, and a baby of 6 months probably knows enough about cups to guess that covering something with a cup prevents its being touched. When faced with the conflict the infant fails to utilize his visual experience, 'seeing' what is there but not allowing this to guide the search. This implies that if the cup occluded the object in such a way that the object *remained touchable* then there would be less conflict and therefore more likelihood of the baby retrieving it. This would be the case if the object were placed inside an *upright* transparent cup rather than the cup being placed over the object – the baby probably knows how to touch things inside cups. In fact, Bower's observations (1974, chap. 7) confirm that object is much more likely to be retrieved in the upright-cup case.

The making of the so-called 'perseveration' error is also intelligible in terms of inappropriately ignoring visual experience. In this error, which continues until about 12 months of age, an object is hidden behind occluder *A*, retrieved a few times, then with the infant attentive, hidden behind another occluder *B* within easy reaching distance. The baby 'sees' the occlusion at *B* but searches at *A*. Again we have a conflict of information from two sources: the infant's stored record that the object is at *A* and the visual information about placement at *B*. We have again the inappropriate neglect of visual information. This is a failure of perspectival sensitivity in that no attempt is made to relate what is seen to the recent history of experience – if visual information implies the need to update other information then it is disregarded.

Again, the objection runs that this could just be due to a failure to remember the recent placement, because the memory of placement at *A* is more deeply ingrained. And again, experiments with transparent containers both refute the memory-failure explanation and give further evidence of ignoring visual information. The evidence is provided in an experiment by Paul Harris (1974). In this, occluders *A* and *B* were boxes with transparent, lockable doors – 'garages' into which a toy car could be put. Having retrieved the car at *A* a few times it was placed at *B* and the doors locked. The majority of the 10- to 12-month-old subjects went straight to *B* and when they failed to gain entry they *returned to A* to search at the visibly empty space. The minority actually went to *A first*, ignoring *B* in which they could 'see' the car. Finally, the intensity of the search (there were pressure transducers on the doors) increased with the age of the subject. This is surely a case of ignoring visual input. Indeed this study shows in a particularly clear way that there is no room for the view that there is *nothing perceptual* in infants' failures of such tasks. Such a view reflects the prejudice that perceptual development is the development of Rep.per$_e$ and that as this is more or less complete by 6 months, failures on object-permanence tasks cannot be perceptual failures. But if so, how on earth *are* we to characterize the 10-month-old's perception? – 'The baby sees the car in three dimensions complete with its properties$_e$ but, well ... it's not actually *there* for her. Also, she sees an empty box perfectly well but she represents it as having a toy car in it.'

This problem with transparency may continue into the second year of life. In infants as old as 13 months [and in monkeys with lesions of the parietal cortex (Moll and Kupers, 1977)] Butterworth and his colleagues (to be published) found failure to reach round a transparent screen to retrieve an object – often shaking the screen in frustration – when they could easily manage the same kind of detour when the screen was *opaque*. The infants seem to be again refusing to believe that what they see is a guide to where they should reach – a clear failure of perspectival sensitivity.[15] What is certainly not being claimed here is that the problem is *exclusively* perceptual because of course there must be a whole nest of skills involved in the acquisition of object permanence: memorial, attentional, spatial, and so forth. But the problem certainly is perceptual in so far as it involves the locating of kinds of perceptual experience in relation to other kinds of perceptual experience and in relation to stored information.

So my answer to a holder of the first sceptical position on perceptual development in childhood is as follows. Your concept of 'perception' is a very restricted one – Rep.per$_e$. The experimental performances sufficient for perceptual success on this view need take no account of perception as the utilization of perceptual fields. The results of object permanence studies throughout infancy can only be made intelligible if we attend to the perceptual failures that they suggest, failures which imply an inability to utilize and locate within the current intentional web a field of perceptual experience that is 'in the running for' truth and falsity – Sen.per$_i$. The baby veers between naïvely trusting and naïvely ignoring its (say) visual field. I am not claiming that this is a *kind* of perception that develops in infancy; rather that taking the perspective of Sen.per$_i$ enables us to give the perceptual contribution to cognitive change its full due. Everyone accepts that some form of cognitive change continues from infancy to adolescence. Given this, and given that it is possible to place perceptual processes more centrally in theories of cognitive change in infancy by taking a less representational and extensional view of 'perception', we should expect that some aspects of cognitive development in *childhood* should be similarly amenable to a perceptual reinterpretation.

On the second sceptical view, the studies of children – as opposed to infants – which purport to show development in perceptual capacities are really showing changes in verbal interpretation or in purely cognitive processing. It will be argued here that when we examine some experimental work we see that it concerns, as do the infancy experiments, the development of Sen.per$_i$ – the perceptual appreciation of fields of experience. In other cases we can refer to the influence of Rep.per$_i$. We will first consider some studies of drawing.

Perhaps some of the very early developmental psychologists believed that how a child draws pictures is a direct reflection of the way he sees the world; though it is doubtful that anyone believed that young children see people with limbs sprouting from their heads. Certainly in the early history of the discipline, and of course in psychoanalytical work, there was a tendency to think that drawings 'tell us' something about thought and perception. Now there has been a swing in the opposite direction – to the view that drawings represent little more than biases in modes of graphic production and cognitive biases in interpretation (see Freeman, 1980, for discussion). Perhaps the pendulum has swung too far.

Consider, for instance, 'intellectual realism' – the tendency of younger children to draw what they *know* to be in a display rather than what they can see in it, so producing a 'good' (*qua* revealing) view (for example, from above), not their own perspective on the array. This is not, studies have shown, merely the product of graphic incompetence (Light and Mackintosh, 1980) nor of a belief that 'this is what the experimenter wants' (Light and Simmons, 1983). Now this is exactly what we should expect from subjects who lack the appropriate notion of a visual field and who therefore find themselves unable to reflect on the nature of their visual field at a particular time. Put this way, in terms of 'notions' and 'reflection' the failure sounds cognitive, but (and this is the main message of this section) cognitive capacities of this kind may well be grounded in qualities of perception. I am suggesting that the capacity to reflect upon one's sensory field is unlikely to exist independently from the quality of the sensory field itself. What may be responsible for the lack of reflective capacity is the underdeveloped state of the *object* of reflection. Of course this does not *have* to be so because there is no logical barrier against the view that reflective capacities develop *sui generis* apart from the domains in which they are expressed. The claim is, then, an empirical one: intellectual realism in drawing results from the difficulty that children have in reflecting on their fields of visual experience because perception in early childhood is less a matter of experiencing a sensory field set off from an object-centred reality as a perspective than it is in adulthood. Of course it is no easy matter to devise experiments to decide whether the difficulty is with reflection *per se* or with an undifferentiated object of reflection – but it is not impossible. Training studies would seem to be one method.[16] In any event, the aim of this chapter is to say why we need the notion of perceptual development in childhood, and without such a notion this question could not even be *posed*. The question about the object of reflection arises from taking a Sen.per$_i$ view of perception.

But what happened to Rep.per$_i$? Taking this perspective on perceptual development encourages us to consider – leaving aside the question about modes of perceptual experience – how modes of perception are influenced by *conceptual* factors. Thus in the context of drawing we can consider whether or not the child's representational content is of a particular cultural object. Take the case of a child seeing a wooden brick and being told to draw it. At the very least this 'perception' can be regarded both as a field of semantic experience (Sen.per$_i$) and as (interest-, concept- and behaviour-driven) acquaintance with a kind of object (Rep.per$_i$). Successful drawing relies on the right kind of *reflection* in the former case, but it also relies on the right kind of *suppression* in the latter case. For example, a study by Phillips et al (1978) showed that children's copying of a line-drawing of a cube is much better if the to-be-copied drawing is tilted through 90° so that it does *not look like a cube* but like an abstract figure. The idea is that our verbal–conceptual knowledge of the object *interferes* with our representation of it as a figure. Adults have similar, though far less dramatic, problems with drawing what they see. Indeed a popular book on drawing by Betty Edwards (1979) tells us that if we, like the children in Phillips et al.'s experiment, copy *inverted* pictures, our drawings are far more successful than if we copy the right way up. This seems to be the case (at least in my experience); and it is a success caused by *suppressing* 'perception' *qua* Rep.per$_i$.

We now turn to a verbal manifestation of intellectual realism. A preschooler is shown a stone, formed and painted so that it looks like an egg. We ensure that he knows that it is a stone. He is asked what the thing 'looks like to your eyes'. He answers 'a stone' – thus evincing intellectual realism. The same child is then shown a white index card placed behind a sheet of blue perspex in such a way that it is clear to him that the change in colour is only apparent. With the card behind the plastic we ask 'What colour is the card really, really?'. The child says 'blue' – evincing what Flavell (Flavell et al., 1983), the author of the studies, calls, after Piaget, 'phenomenism'. Once again this is just what we would expect from a child who lacks the adult notion of a visual field.

It is possible to regard phenomenism and intellectual realism as products of the same kind of perceptual difficulty that may be (at least partly) responsible for infants' problems with object permanence tasks. To put the suggestion in Piagetian terms, we may be finding a replication of a developmental problem on the verbal–conceptual plane that was initially solved on the sensorimotor plane. Thus, phenomenism results from naïvely trusting the visual field to yield the answer (cf. the infant younger than 8 months who fails to search because the visual field does not contain the desired object), and intellectual realism results from naïvely ignoring information in the visual field when it should be acted on (cf. the transparent garages experiment). In infants this was regarded as a failure to locate visual experiences within an intentional web. In the experiments by Flavell et al. we find a parallel problem: that of locating visual experiences within a verbal–interpretive or *intensional* web.

This is not, however, the only way of regarding intellectual realism. Intellectual realism in answer to questions of the 'Looks like?' kind may be explicable in the same way as the difficulties with cube-drawing in the Phillips et al. (1978) study – as due to the inability to suppress the top-down influence of Rep.per$_i$. But, as before, the question of what particular aspect we wish to stress is less important, for present purposes, than the fact of accepting the possibility that *some* kind of failure to locate perceptual experiences within a web of intention and interpretation may be responsible for the difficulty.[17]

Let us now return to phenomenism and question a child in the early school years. Martin Braine (Braine and Shanks, 1965) has shown that children of 5 years are normally quite capable of discriminating 'Looks X' from 'Is really X' questions. However, when they are presented with a neutral question ('Is it X?') and when the display is a visual illusion (e.g. a stick apparently 'bent' by light refraction in a tank of water) they answer in phenomenal terms ('Yes the stick is bent'). They will probably continue to do this until they are about 7 years old. The kind of explanation for this failure often encountered in contemporary developmental psychology is in terms of a 'this is what the experimenter wants me to say' kind of pragmatic failure. Psychologists may even say that the tendency to answer phenomenally is due to features of the social relation or the 'negotiation of meanings' between experimenter and child. But to say that the child gives phenomenist answers because this is what he thinks is expected of him is only the *first* step towards an explanation. *Why*, in the child's semantic system, does 'is bent = looks bent'? Saying that the experimental set-up somehow 'makes the stick's bent appearance more salient than its real straightness' through instructions and by non-verbal cues is no help *because adults are not similarly influenced*. Social events only affect cognition via a perceiving mental system; psychological tendencies at different ages cannot be reduced to social influences.[18]

Now nothing terribly original is being proposed in the claim that the verbal misinterpretation in such experiments is the result of taking one's perception *qua* Sen.per$_i$, at face value. It is, in fact, a relative of Piaget's claim that 4- to 7-year-old children inhabit an 'intuitive' substage in which their judgements are dominated by unidimensional snapshots that they regard as 'irreversible' or frozen in time; and it is a closer relative to Jerome Bruner's (1966) idea that such children's mode of mental representation is iconic in nature. But, as with the drawing research, it can be put forward as a serious, testable, empirical hypothesis that verbal interpretation is phenomenal in such cases because of the nature of childish perception. To put the matter with a necessarily large degree of looseness and metaphor, subjects who do not, in their perceptual life, 'carry round with them' the notion of a perceptual field are going to be prey to the influence of any event that is perceptually striking. They will be prey to these events because a perceptual experience *qua* Sen.per$_i$ is not regarded as being *merely in the running* for truth or falsity. Having the concept of a perceptual field breeds a principled scepticism and makes possible a whole range of discriminations between appearance and reality. Such an oversusceptibilty to perceptual change will reveal itself in the way young children interpret the language of appearance and reality – *looks*, *is really*, *more*, *less*, *same*, and so forth (see Pillow and Flavell, 1985, for data on this).

Once again, a caveat must be entered here about what is being attempted: the aim is not to *deduce* developmental processes from conceptual distinctions, but to liberalize our notion of what is the 'perception' that might develop and to liberalize it sufficiently well for us to do justice to the perceptual face of mental development after the first few months or so of life. It may well be that too elaborate a justice has been done to the perceptual face – that is an empirical question. The main conceptual point here, though, is that the dangers of *contracting* our notion of perceptual development so that the features of the child's perceptual life *cannot* be appealed to in explaining cognitive change (substituting 'social', 'verbal', 'information-processing', 'metacognitive', 'pragmatic', and so on) are far worse. The danger is, in a nutshell, that of uncoupling cognition from experience. Without some guiding theory of experiential development or the development of awareness[19] (of which regarding perception as Sen.per$_i$ is a part) references to linguistic factors, metacognition, and so forth will always *float free*. Why, for example, are *more*, and *same* and *looks like* difficult words for the child to use properly? There is no such thing as an *inherently* difficult word. A sensible way of explaining why some words are difficult is by reference to how they make contact with experience.

Finally, we re-encounter the third proposed reason for scepticism about the notion of 'perceptual development'. Can perception be regarded primarily as a *sui generis* input system, with no significant influence from top-down central systems? Might its development be analogous to that of a bodily organ or a distinct behavioural capacity such as locomotion? The success achieved by the late David Marr (see Morgan, 1984, for some sceptical remarks) in his attempt to describe how levels of 'representation' are built up through computations, based on vision-specific rules, on the information carried in the light rays, has encouraged many computationally minded people towards the view that explaining vision in particular, and therefore perception and perceptual development in general, is solely a matter of providing the right kind of computational models.

Predictably, my answer is that it is one thing to produce computational models of how the brain processes visual information and quite another to study the place of perceptual experience in mental development. Conclusions about the former need not determine ideas about the latter. This is not to say that the points made by Marr about the nature of perception are irrelevant to the latter interest. Far from it: recall the discussion of Sen.per$_e$ in which it was argued that Marr's demonstration that processing – *qua* representation construction – is present even in the earliest stages of vision is a major reason for abandoning the view that we have primitive acquaintance with non-intentional fields of experience from which the processing is done *post hoc*. Of course James Gibson also argued against this view, though for quite different reasons.

What we are in fact facing here is one of the most difficult problems in theoretical psychology: how to divide up the explanatory labour between fine-grain, low level, computational theories and holistic, high-level theorizing.

A supporter of the computational approach would probably dismiss the use that has been made here of Sen.per$_i$ on the grounds that it is a theoretical construct pitched at too high a level. He would perhaps use the term 'folk psychological' to describe it. ['Folk psychology' means the system of ideas that we all use informally to predict and explain human behaviour; for example, 'John did X because he believed p and wanted q'. The folk psychological notion of 'belief' has come under attack recently from S. P. Stich (1983).] From such a perspective, deriving 'views' about perception from consideration of what people *say* and *believe* about perception and from the contingencies of linguistic usage is founding one's theorizing on the marshy soil of folk psychology. This view is highly questionable. For the onus is upon those who believe that all theories of perceptual development must be presented in fine-grain computational terms to show why the attempt to describe the nature and consequences of developmental changes in perceptual experience is based on a folk psychological *illusion* (see Russell, in press, for elaboration). We should ask why it is that we talk about perception in terms of such notions as consciousness and its cognates – perhaps we do so because perceptions do *in fact* have a quality that other kinds of mental function (for example, the automatic aspects of recognition memory) lack. And we do not find in the other sciences such a *principled* dismissal of 'pre-theoretical' notions. Physicists did not feel that they had to eradicate terms such as 'weight' or 'force' from their theoretical vocabulary, but rather modified them when necessary. So objectors must say *in the light of what* our folk psychological notions require revision. It is not sufficient merely to present the computational metatheory as the preferred alternative.

The obvious counterobjection is that this view entails a denial that perceptual experiences are *in fact* computational processes in the brain, and the assertion that they are Cartesian ghosts. It entails no such thing. The denial is rather that we can retain, let alone increase, intelligibility in trying to decompose such high-level theories (for example, about the introspectability of visual fields) into the kind of detail that Marr employed in describing how zero-crossings are computed. The case of Piaget certainly shows us that high-level theories do not inhibit the collection of data.

NOTES

1 Though young children often interpret these verbal expressions *intentionally*. See J. Russell (1987).

2 This does not mean that properties$_i$ are the same as Locke's secondary qualities (colours, smells, sounds, felt qualities, tastes). Although Locke defined them as sensation dependent they must be accommodated under properties$_e$ without actually *being* properties$_e$. My suggestion is that we adopt, for the sake of the distinction, what has been called the 'medium theory' of secondary qualities – a theory proposed most explicitly by C. Hooker (1978). This is the view that the perception of primary qualities is made up of the perception of secondary qualities. (It seems that in order for this to work there has to be a further distinction within secondary qualities between those that are mandatory and those that are not. For example, 3D shape must have some felt quality to be perceived by touch and some colour to be perceived by sight – even transparent objects like glass cubes have dark-coloured lines round them.) So the perception of a primary quality can be decomposed into that of secondary qualities.

McGinn (1983) has objected against the medium theory that it commits us to a 'very radical error theory of sensory experience' (p. 97). Thus it is, an illusion on the medium theory, that secondary qualities are properties of the same things to which primary qualities are ascribed; it is a confusion of medium and message and makes primary qualities just what we take them *not* to be – mind dependent. But it is, I think, a degree of *contingency* in the primary qualities to which the medium theory commits us, not illusion. To illustrate: we see a square made up of red lines a, b, c, d. Given that line c, the right-hand line, is tilting at 70° to the horizontal, line d, the bottom line *had* to tilt 20° from the horizontal. Thus the *disposition* of line d is entirely determined; but it's colour is not. It might just as well have been green. The objectivity derives from the determination of the line's disposition, a determination that is not present in secondary qualities. The primary quality in our example is not therefore dependent on any *particular* secondary medium, and therefore on any particular secondary representation. However, for a mind-independent quality to be represented in a mind (as primary qualities can be although they do not *need* to be) they are going to require some, essentially arbitrary, mode of sensory presentation. (The idealist philosopher F. H. Bradley wrote that 'Extension cannot be presented, or thought of, except as one with quality that is secondary.' McGinn calls this the 'inseparability thesis'.)

There is an additional reason for accommodating secondary qualities under properties$_e$. Take the example of colour. Hardin (1981) has recently pointed out that neither the properties of light nor the properties of objects correlate well with the properties of perceived colours. Blue things, for example, have nothing physical in common. He argues: 'objectivism [that is, about colour] fails ... because nothing in the domain of objects properties and processes beyond our skins is both causally connected with our colour experiences and models the essential characteristics of colours' (p. 496). But this does not mean that the stimulation that gave rise to the sensation was mind independent. The particular perceptual experiences of colours, smells, tastes, and so forth possess a subjectivity and an area of incorrigibiilty, but the causes of these sensations are objective in so far as they are *describable* in entirely physical terms. The same is not true, as we shall see, for intentional properties.

3 As Dunlop (1984) has pointed out, we must be very wary of using this terminology. There is a sense, for example, in which we do not see a face *as* a face. We see a face.

4 In the first case one may object that there is no 'paradox' because the Adequacy Thesis could expand the characterization of the object to include a statement about the visual angle subtended by the object. This is no more 'subjective' or 'sensational' – the argument could run – than a mirror's reflection of the scene. In the second case, perhaps some would deny that monocular and binocular vision *do* have the same representational content. Third, one may deny that the 'neutral' construal (nothing has changed) is sensational – it is a *post hoc* inference not a perception.

5 Could Peacocke not have made much the same point merely by citing some clear cases of where the perceiver's state 'contributes' to the perception – for example the visual field is often yellowish in people with jaundice?

6 This distinction is easier to grasp intuitively than to express through criteria. For example, on the one hand Peacocke (1983) says that the 'content is something intrinsic to the experience itself' (p. 9) (which seems to suggest that it is not dissociable from the sensational raw material), yet at the same time he holds that the 'cases of change of aspect (Necker cube) show that sensational properties [=visual experience] do not determine representational content, while the case of the binocular vision of depth shows that representational content in a given sense modality does not determine sensational properties' (p. 23). The paradox is that one is supposed to be intrinsic to the other and yet they are causally independent. This confusing complexity (or actual inconsistency) results, perhaps, from the difficulty of knowing how to regard the perceptual 'experience'. The representational content has just as much claim to be called the 'experience' as the subjective sensational character, given that 'experience' implies intentionality, or 'directedness' in this context. One of the things that I hope my combining of these two distinctions will achieve is the removal of this ambiguity.

7 But this is not the only psychological area in which we may make use of the notion as Sen.per$_e$. It could prove useful in explaining certain kinds of pathology. Consider the question of the extent to which visual agnosia may be the result of a 'sensory' as opposed to a 'perceptual' deficit. John Campion (1986) has recently proposed that some kind of so-called agnosia may be due

to a sensory deficit (agnosia is usually defined as being a perceptual deficit *without* a sensory deficit). Campion claims that the visual field of some agnosics may be 'peppered' with small blind areas. This is visual field *qua* Sen.per$_e$.

8 After completing this chapter I encountered Alan Leslie's (1986) ideas about the development significance of pretend play. Leslie refers to a process of 'decoupling' a perceptual representation in such a way that it can be treated by the child as neither true nor false, but as a 'formal object' within mental quotation marks that the child can then manipulate in fantasy. There are some similarities here to Sen.per$_i$ – but also some differences.

9 Peacocke (1983) draws a parallel in this context with Kripke's theory of reference: just as we can correctly say of whoever it was invented the wheel (call him 'Bright') 'It might have been that Bright never invented the wheel' so 'we can conceive of cirucmstances in which, for example, a tilted plate does not produce an elliptical region of the visual field' (p. 21). I am going a little further here to say that the same holds for the sensational character of perceptions with rich intentional content – i.e. not only 'elliptical regions of the visual field' but elephants and gimlets.

10 This is not, in fact, a parallel to Evans's (1983) distinction between non-conceptual and conceptual informational states in spatial perception because what is essential to the conceptual for Evans is consciousness. And what makes any such parallel impossible is that we are here concerned with ways of regarding perception – whereas Evans was concerned with types of perception, as we shall be in the final section of the chapter.

11 For example, David Hamlyn (1972) has emphasized the importance of perceptual theory in explaining the results of animal learning experiments.

12 This is Kant's distinction (made in the Second Analogy Section of the *Critique of Pure Reason*) between world-given perceptual sequences (e.g watching a ship sail upstream) and self-generated perceptual sequences (e.g. scanning the front of a house). Kant regarded the drawing of such a distinction as a necessary condition for objective experience. Piaget did not in fact use Kant's argument, but it certainly has a Piagetian ring to it.

13 Sometimes the infant will not retrieve the object even when she has already grasped it; for example, in cases where the experimenter covers both the grasping hand and the object with a cloth. See Gratch and Landers (1971).

14 In Piaget's original account of the study, he answers this memory objection on conceptual grounds (1954, pp. 64–5). His answer was essentially that a memory as bad as *this* would *itself* imply a lack of object concept. One could not have 'object concept plus bad memory' in this case. See J. Russell (1978, p. 133) for a brief discussion of this important point.

15 Butterworth's own interpretation of the data is as follows: 'it is as if the transparency encourages the use of a direct perceptual solution when a representational one would have been more appropriate though the object is in full view' (personal communication, August 1985).

16 Typically (e.g. Edwards, 1979) programmes of drawing instruction teach us to *see* rather than to reflect on what we see – for example, to look more at the object and less at the drawing.

17 Flavell's (1986) account of children's difficulty with appearance–reality tasks

is not very different from the present account. The argument is that children below about 4 years of age are, what Flavell calls, 'Level 1 thinkers'. This means that they are incapable of appreciating that one object (state of affairs, situation) can give rise to more than one kind of 'representation'. Thus the stone 'egg' and the 'blue' card can only be represented in one way. What then determines the particular representation that the child adopts is 'cognitive salience', that which is 'most "up front" in consciousness at a given moment' (Flavell et al., 1983, p. 99). In the 'egg' case the fact that it has turned out to really be a stone is arresting, as is the card's change from white to blue. This is not a million miles away from the present claim that children's judgements are being determined by the tendency to believe that a perceptual experience is either a 1:1 representation of reality or it does not represent reality at all – there is no capacity to reflect on and assess perceptual experience as a *contender* for truth, so the child tends to flip from one kind of judgement to another. The trick is to hold both $Sen.per_i$ and $Rep.per_i$ in mind at one time – hold seemingly incompatible representations in Flavell's terms.

18   For a critique of the neo-Piagetian social causation view see Russell (1982). For an expression of a non-Piagetian version of the view see Walkerdine and Sinha (1978).

19   For a challenging reappraisal of the role of 'awareness' *vis-à-vis* 'processing' in cognitive phenomena see J. Yates (1985).

REFERENCES

Anscombe, G. E. M. 1965: The intentionality of perception: a grammatical feature. In R. J. Butler (ed.), *Analytical Philosophy*. Oxford: Basil Blackwell.

Atkinson, J. 1984: Human visual development over the first 6 months of life. A review and a hypothesis. *Human Neurobiology*, 3, 61–74.

Baldwin, J. M. 1906. *Thought and Things*, vol. 1. London: Swann and Sonnenschein.

Bower, T. G. R. 1966: The visual world of the infant. *Scientific American*, 215, 80–92.

   1967: The development of object permanence: some studies of existence constancy. *Perception and Psychophysics*, 2, 411–18.

   1974: *Development in Infancy*. San Francisco, Calif.: W. H. Freeman.

   1975: Infant perception of the third dimension and object concept development. In L. B. Cohen and P. Salapatek (eds), *Infant Perception: From Sensation to Cognition*, vol. 2. New York: Academic Press.

Braine, M. D. S. and Shanks, B. L. 1965: The development of the conservation of size. *Journal of Verbal Learning and Verbal Behaviour*, 4, 227–42.

Bruce, V. and Green, P. 1985: *Visual Perception: Physiology, Psychology and Ecology*. Hillsdale, NJ: Lawrence Erlbaum.

Bruner, J. S. 1966: On the conservation of liquids. In J. S. Bruner, R. R. Olver, and P. M. Greenfield (eds), *Studies in Cognitive Growth*. Chichester: John Wiley.

Bryant, P. E. 1971: Cognitive development. *British Medical Bulletin*, 27, 200–5.

Butterworth, G. E. and Cochran, E. 1980: Towards a mechanism of joint visual attention. *International Journal of Behavioural Development*, 3, 253–72.

Butterworth, G. E. and Hicks, L. 1977: Visual proprioception and postural stability: a developmental study. *Perception*, 6, 255–62.
Butterworth, G. E., Jarrett, N. and Hicks, L. 1982: Spatiotemporal identity in infancy: perceptual competence and conceptual deficit. *Developmental Psychology*, 18, 435–49.
Campion, J. 1986: Apperceptive agnosia: frameworks, models, and paradigms. In G. Humphreys and J. Riddock (eds), *Visual Object Processing: A Cognitive Neuropsychological Approach*. London: Academic Press.
Campion, J., Latto, R. M. and Smith, E. M. 1983: Is blindsight an effect of scattered light, spared cortex, and near-threshold vision? *Behavioural and Brain Sciences*, 6, 623–50.
Cromer, R. 1973: Conservation in the congenitally blind. *British Journal of Psychology*, 64, 241–50.
Dennett, D. C. 1981: Three kinds of intentional psychology. In R. Healey (ed.), *Reductionism, Time, and Reality*. Cambridge: Cambridge University Press.
 1982: How to study human consciousness empirically, or 'Nothing comes to mind'. *Synthèse*, 53, 159–80.
Dretske, F. 1983: Précis of 'Knowledge and the flow of information'. *Behavioural and Brain Sciences*, 6, 55–90.
Edwards, B. 1979: *Drawing on the Right Hand Side of the Brain*. London: Souvenir Press.
Elkind, D. 1975: Perceptual development in children. *American Scientist*, 10, 533–41.
Evans, G. 1983: *The Varieties of Reference*. Oxford: Oxford University Press.
Flavell, J. H. 1986: The development of children's knowledge about the appearance–reality distinction. *American Psychologist*, 41, 418–25.
Flavell, J. H., Flavell, E. R. and Green, F. L. 1983: Development of the appearance–reality distinction. *Cognitive Psychology*, 15, 95–120.
Fodor, J. A. 1983: *The Modularity of Mind: An Essay in Faculty Psychology*. Cambridge, Mass.: MIT Press.
Freeman, N. H. 1980: *Strategies of Representation: Analysis of Spatial Skills and Drawing Processes*. London: Academic Press.
Gibson, J. J. 1979: *The Ecological Approach to Visual Perception*. boston: Houghton Mifflin.
Gibson, E. J., Gibson, J. J., Pick, A. and Osser, H. A. 1962: A developmental study of the discrimination of letter-like forms. *Journal of Comparative and Physiological Psychology*, 55, 897–905.
Gratch, G. and Landers, W. T. 1971: Stage IV of Piaget's theory of infant's object concepts: a longtitudinal study. *Child Development*, 42, 359–72.
Haber, R. N. 1983: The impending demise of the icon: a critique of the concept of iconic storage in visual information processing. *Behavioural and Brain Sciences*, 6, 1–54.
Hamlyn, D. W. 1957: *The Psychology of Perception*. London: Routledge and Kegan Paul.
 1972: Conditioning and learning. In R. Borger and F. Cioffi (eds), *Explanation in the Behavioural Sciences*. Cambridge: Cambridge University Press.
Hardin, C. L. 1981: Are 'scientific' objects coloured? *Mind*, XCIII, 491–501.

Harris, P. L. 1974: Perseveration at a visibly empty space by young infants. *Journal of Experimental Child Psychology*, 18, 535–42.

Hoften, C. and Spelke, E. S. 1985: Object perception and object-directed reach in infancy. *Journal of Experimental Psychology: General*, 114, 198–212.

Hooker, C. 1978: An evolutionary naturalistic realist doctrine of perception and secondary qualities. In W. Savage (ed.), *Perception and Cognition: Issues in the Foundations of Psychology*. Minneapolis, Minn.: University of Minnesota Press.

Kaye, K. 1984: *The Mental Life and Social Life of Babies*. London: Methuen.

Lee, D. N. and Aronson, E. 1974: Visual proprioceptive control of standing in human infants. *Perception and Psychophysics*, 15, 529–32.

Leslie, A. M. 1986: Pretence and representation in infancy: the origins of a theory of mind. Manuscript available from MRC Cognitive Development Unit, 17 Gordon Street, London WC1.

Light, P. and Mackintosh, E. 1980: Depth relations in young children's drawings. *Journal of Experimental Child Psychology*, 30, 79–87.

Light, P. and Simmons, B. 1983: The effect of a communication task upon the representation of depth relations in young children's drawings. *Journal of Experimental Child Psychology*, 35, 81–92.

Marcel, A. J. 1983: Conscious and unconscious perception: Experiments on visual masking and word recognition. *Cognitive Psychology*, 15, 197–237.

Marr, D. 1982: *Vision: A Computational Investigation into the Human Representation and Processing of Visual Information*. San Francisco, Calif.: W. H. Freeman.

Marr, D. and Nishihara, N. K. 1978: Representation and recognition of the spatial organisation of three-dimensional shapes. *Proceedings of the Royal Society of London, Series B*, 200, 269–94.

McGinn, C. 1983: *The Subjective View: Secondary Qualities and Indexical Thoughts*. Oxford: Clarendon Press.

McKenzie, N. B. E. and Day, R. H. 1972: Objective distance as a determinant of visual fixation in early infancy. *Science*, 178, 1108–10.

Meltzoff, A. N. and Moore, M. K. 1977: Imitation of facial and manual gestures by human neonates. *Science*, 198, 75–8.

Moll, L. and Kupers, H. 1977: Premotor cortical ablations in monkeys: contralateral changes in visually guided reaching behaviour. *Science*, 198, 317–19.

Morgan, M. J. 1984: Computational theories of vision (a critical review of *Vision* by D. Marr). *Quarterly Journal of Experimental Psychology*, 36, 157–66.

Neilson, I. E. 1977: A reinterpretation of the development of the object concept. Unpublished Ph.D. thesis, University of Edinburgh.

Peacocke, C. 1983: *Sense and Content: Experience, Thought, and their Relations*. Oxford: Oxford University Press.

Phillips, W. A., Hobbs, S. B. and Pratt, F. R. 1978: Intellectual realism in children's drawings of cubes. *Cognition*, 6, 15–33.

Piaget, J. 1954: *The Child's Construction of Reality*. London: Routledge and Kegan Paul.

—— 1969: *The Mechanisms of Perception*. London: Routledge and Kegan Paul.

Pillow, B. H. and Flavell, J. H. 1985: Intellectual realism: the role of children's interpretation of pictures and perceptual verbs. *Child Development*, 56, 664–70.

Rock, I. 1968: When the world is tilt. *Psychology Today*, 1, 211–31.

Russell, J. 1978: *The Acquisition of Knowledge*. London: Macmillan.

1982: Propositional attitudes. In M. Beveridge (ed.), *Children Thinking through Language*. London: Edward Arnold.

1984: *Explaining Mental Life: Some Philosophical Issues in Psychology*. London: Macmillan.

1987: Can we say. . .? Children's understanding of intensionality. *Cognition*, 25, 105–25.

in press: Cognizance and intelligence. In M. Khalfa (ed.), *Can Intelligence be Explained?* Oxford: Oxford University Press.

Searle, J. 1984: *Minds, Brains and Programs*. London: BBC Publications.

Seigler, H. P. and Leibowitz, H. 1957: The development of constancy. *American Journal of Psychology*, 70, 106–9.

Sperling, G. 1960: The information available in brief presentations. *Psychological Monographs*, 74, no. 498.

Stich, S. P. 1983: *From Folkpsychology to Cognitive Science*. Cambridge, Mass.: MIT Press.

Uexhull, J. 1957: A stroll through the world of animals and men. In C. H. Schiller (ed.), *Instinctive Behaviour*. London: Methuen.

Vurpillot, E. 1968: The development of scanning strategies and their relation to visual differentiation. *Journal of Experimental Child Psychology*, 6, 632–50.

Walkerdine, V. and Sinha, C. 1978: The internal triangle: language, reasoning and social context. In I. Markova (ed.), *The Social Context of Language*. Chichester: Wiley.

Weiskrantz, L., Warrington, E. K., Sanders, M. D. and Marshall, J. 1974: Visual capacity of the hemianopic field following a restricted occipital ablation. *Brain*, 97, 709–28.

Wittgenstein, L. 1958: *Philosophical Investigations*. Oxford: Basil Blackwell.

Winston, P. H. 1984: *Artificial Intelligence*. New York: Addison-Wesley.

Wong, T. S. 1979: Developmental study of a haptic illusion in relation to Piaget's centration theory. *Journal of Experimental Child Psychology*, 27, 489–500.

Yates, J. 1985: The content of awareness is a model of the world. *Psychological Review*, 92, 249–84.

PART III

Ego Development

6

A dualist perspective on psychological development

Howard Robinson

I

Talk of mental development implies that there is a change from a state of relative psychological immaturity to a state of relative maturity. This naturally prompts one to ask about the nature of the mentally immature person, the nature of the mature person, and of what has been acquired in the move from being a person of the former sort to being one of the latter. Some of the answers to such an inquiry will be philosophically un-controversial. For example, there has undoubtedly been what is known as 'cognitive development'; that is the person has learnt to exercise capacities for perception, memory and conceptualized and linguistic thought which, at birth he could not exercise. Much of what is generally known as 'developmental psychology' is concerned with such cognitive develop-ment. But it is not obvious that all forms of mental development can be captured within the cognitive net. It does not seem natural to regard emotional development and growth of personality simply as forms of cognitive development. Furthermore, one's philosophical position con-cerning the human mind may affect what one regards as mental develop-ment. Someone who believes in the immortality of the human mind may think of psychological development as having a religious dimension and culminating, not in one's ability to perceive, remember, manage and talk to objects in the mundane environment, but in being of such a mind that one can face the beatific vision, or recognize one's affinity with the Absolute. Developmental psychology, being a mundane science, rightly does not concern itself directly with these latter issues, but the fact that the methods of natural science more easily accommodate investigation of our developing ability to cope with the commonplace does not of itself legitimize a theory of mind which presupposes that this is the only form of mental development of which we are capable.

I make these rather pompous cautionary remarks because my principal purpose here is not to discuss the concepts, methodology, or conclusions generally associated with developmental psychology, but to investigate what psychological development might consist in for someone who believes that the mind is an immaterial substance. This raises metaphysical problems concerning the nature of such a substance and what it is for it to be embodied. This latter question is the one which raises developmental issues, for it seems natural, from a dualist perspective, to regard mental development as the process by which the immaterial element comes to express itself as an embodied conscious intelligence.

A concern with such problems as these is nowadays regarded as bizarre and eccentric, because the adoption of substance dualism is thought to be quaint – especially by those who have fallen under the influence of contemporary cognitive psychology, which is peculiarly committed to a physicalist theory of the mind. The dualist's predicament is aggravated by the problem of development. As will be explained more fully in section V, substance dualists have tended to treat the immaterial substance as being pure thought, or a pure conscious ego: but if it is essentially a pure active intellect what possible need or scope could there be for its development? Development and growth are most naturally regarded as features of the body, but for the classical Aristotelian and neo-Platonist dualist, the active intellect thinks unhindered by the body, and this view passed into modern dualism through Descartes, who affirmed that 'the brain can be of no use in pure thought' (Haldane and Ross, 1968, p. 212). In the most recent extended defence of dualism, Sir John Eccles (1984, p. 228) treats the immaterial mind as, in itself and without the help of the body, a self-conscious unity. In all these theories, no development would seem to be required to give a complete inner life of the mind. This problem which the apparent fact of development presents for dualism is, of course, just a special case of the more general difficulty that all our intellectual activities and even our capacity for a unified perceptual world (as attested by split-brain patients) depend on the properly unified working of the central nervous system (see Nagel, 1971, for discussion). For those modern cognitive scientists who take a computational cum functionalist view of the mind, on the other hand, mental development brings no essential problems. Physical growth develops the hardware and experience fills the memory-banks and modifies the program(s). How physical growth, experimental growth, and reprogramming interact is, no doubt, a very difficult problem, but the computational picture is vague and comprehensive enough to allow such difficulties to be deferred for later empirical investigation without the general philosophy being challenged.

The current credibility of dualism is, therefore, so bad, and its main rival stands so high that before looking more deeply into how a dualist can approach development it is necessary to give some reasons for treating substance dualism as a live option. I shall, therefore, try to indicate the inadequacies of the fashionable physicalist theories that are favoured by psychologists, so that the reader will think it worthwhile to consider the dualist account.

II

For most modern theorists of psychology, functionalism, augmented by the computational theory of mind is the beginning of wisdom. It has been described by Fodor (1981) as 'the best – indeed the only – psychology that we've got'. In this section reasons for thinking that all such theories of psychology and their more radical offshoots are false are presented.

The most fundamental problem facing functionalism of all sorts is the *quale* problem, for, if that problem is insoluble, functionalism cannot cope with ordinary sensory consciousness, and that is about as comprehensive a sort of failure as any to which an overall theory of mind could be subject.

There are at least two current responses to the claim that no functional or computational account can be given of the content of consciousness. Johnson-Laird (1983, pp. 453ff) suggests that though nothing we have at present instantiates the right model, parallel-processing machines could solve the problem. A particularly interesting version of this is the prospect of the quantum computer, which combines with parallel processing the features of quantum indeterminancy which philosophers of various colours have felt might be connected with human freedom. Unfortunately, I cannot see how such developments could assist with the problem of subjective content. Some opponents of the cybernetic view of mind have argued that a machine could never be inventive, imaginative, and the like. More sophisticated forms of processing might help to tackle this problem, but it seems simply irrelevant to the problem of subjectivity as expressed in the qualia problem.[1] Directly relevant, on the other hand, is Shoemaker's (1984) claim that qualia, if there are any, cannot pose a threat to functionalism.[2] As will be shown, Shoemaker's argument is mistaken but is an instructive one.

Shoemaker argues that it would not be possible to fault the best functional definition of (for example) pain by claiming that someone might be in that functional state and yet not be in pain because he lacked the appropriate qualitative state. His reason is as follows. A functional definition does not only make reference to ultimate behavioural consequences, but also to any further mental state to which the one being defined necessarily gives rise. Now pains standardly give rise to beliefs that there is a pain (or 'that one is in pain'). If we take the case of the creature in the appropriate functional state, but supposedly not in real pain, we can ask whether it believes it is in pain. If the answer is 'no', then it is not going to satisfy the functional process specified, for this does involve such a belief. If the answer is 'yes', then this creature judges it to be in pain just as we do and there can be no subjective difference between it and us. This is assuming that its belief is deemed a real belief, and this is permitted because the objection to functionalism was that it could not accommodate qualia, not that it could not cope with belief.

The argument is sound, interpreted as a proof that it is not possible to combine an insistence on the existence of irreducible qualia with an acceptance of a reductive treatment of belief (see also Robinson, 1982, pp. 105–7). This does not show, however, that the qualia objection is mistaken, or that an independent objection to the functionalist treatment of belief is also in play. It demonstrates two things. First, it shows that if functionalism cannot capture the qualitative content of experience it also fails to capture the recognitional states which are immediately directed at those experiences. Second, and consequent on the first point, it shows that the relationship between qualia and the recognitional states directed onto them is not a simple causal one, for if it were then the recognitional state could exist without the qualia and the qualia would not enter into the subject's judgemental state. This is not a surprising conclusion. The recognition that I have a bright red sense-content, or that I feel a burning pain is not simply some propositional or linguistic belief which follows upon the experience, but a conceptual mode of focusing on or attending to the experience itself. The quale is part of the content of the cognitive state, not just its cause. The qualia objection, therefore, does subvert the reductive treatment of at least some beliefs, but this is a consequence of the force of the qualia objection, and is not derived from some independent objection to the functionalist treatment of belief.

It is interesting that the failure of the computer model to cope with qualia shows that it also cannot cope with certain fundamental cognitive states, namely such recognitional states. But, quite apart from this spin-off from the qualia problems, how plausible is the computational treatment of cognitive states? In other words, how convincing is its treatment of intentionality and of the semantic properties of signs?

The answer is that it has made no serious progress on this point. Common sense rejects behaviourism because it denies the interiority of thought and experience. But psychologists and philosophers of the more formal sort reject it because it requires that there be laws connecting stimulus and response directly, and such laws are supposedly not forth-coming except in very simple situations. In a normal mature human being, the response to most stimuli depends on a great number of already present psychological states, which are connected via various processes and operations, and differences in these states make great differences to the response. Constructing a behaviourist psychology would be like trying to develop a physics in which the laws related observations directly, without postulating theoretical entities and unobserved events. Because of the hopelessness of such enterprises, the mind ceased to be represented by the behaviourist's black box, which was replaced by the flow charts and functional models of cognitive psychology.

Given that the connections between stimulus and response are too subtle and remote to allow direct nomic connection, and that the postulation of mediating mechanisms is required, what constraints are there on the sorts of mechanisms that would fit the bill? The question suggests two more. First, was the failure of behaviourism purely third-personal and technical; that is, did it fail to deal with our cognitive psychology *just* because it would have required laws that were too rebarbitively complex? The reply to Shoemaker suggests that it did not fail only for that reason, but that it failed to capture certain cognitive states of which we were directly aware. Second, given the need for a mechanism, why should 'folk psychology' have come up with one which involved intentional states and semantic properties rather than some sort of plainly physical hypothetical mechanism?

There are a variety of possible answers to this second question, some of which are *prima facie* acceptable to the physicalistic cognitive psychologist and others which are not.

1 The first is not acceptable to such physicalists, and it is the reply suggested by my response to the first question. It might be claimed that the reason why we postulate a mechanism involving intentional states is that we are directly aware of such states in some *sui generis* and irreducible form. As well as being available to dualists, this answer is open to dual aspects theorists and it is, indeed, a position adopted by Searle (1983, pp. 262–72).

If one rejects the claim that intentional states must be postulated because we experience them, then there remain two other explanations of why they are postulated for the mechanism.

2 According to the second theory, there is no need for the internal mechanisms to include any intentional states. The final correct theory will belong to neurology or some other pure science, free of intentional concepts. There is no deep reason for the inclusion of intentional states in the explanation of the connection between stimulus and response. It just so happens that the primitive theory nowadays called 'folk psychology' contained such entities. We can replace this mechanism by a wholly non-intentional one as soon as science gives us some idea of what the probable mechanism is. This is a version of eliminative or 'disappearance' materialism.

3   It might be argued that, by definition, anything which explained the relation of stimulus and response would be intentional, for intentionality can be defined by reference to such functions. On this view, intentional explanation is as physicalistic as any functional explanation. It simply involves picking out the more behaviourably relevant causal tendencies of the organism, and treating the inner states responsible for those tendencies as thereby possessed of the corresponding intentionality.

Given that 1 is not compatible with functionalist or computational theories, 2 and 3 will be considered. Explanation 2 is firmly espoused by Stich (1983, pp. 228–42) and by Churchland (1981). At first sight, the disappearance theory appears to be self-refuting. Its adherents seem to *believe* that there are no such things as *beliefs*. Clearly no one could admit to being in such a state. 'That there are no such things as beliefs' expresses an essential part of the theory, so no objection can be made to this component in what is attributed here to the disappearance theorist. He must, therefore, deny that he *believes* this. Nothing will be achieved by a mere verbal manœuvre, such as claiming to *hold* or *assent to*, rather than *believe* the proposition, for if respectability could be given to these formulae, then an account of belief in terms of holding or assenting could be presented, so that one would have a reductive, and not a disappearance, account of this piece of folk psychology. An alternative defence might be to admit that, speaking within the idiom of folk psychology, the disappearance theorist does believe that there are no beliefs, but that this idiom is not basic: fundamentally there are neither believings nor propositions to be believed. This brings home even more dramatically the paradoxical nature of the eliminative approach to cognitive states, for the very heart of the theory – the proposition that there are no beliefs – is itself part of what is to be eliminated. This position is totally self-destructive, because it denies the existence of all theories and systems of belief, which all consist of propositions, including that which contains the eliminative theory. It is necessary to preserve the intelligibility of the theory whilst eliminating belief. Churchland (1984) says that this is possible provided that one adopts a theory of meaning which does not invoke the notion of belief: in particular, one must avoid the Gricean intention – (or belief) – communication theory of meaning. Churchland says that '[i]f eliminative materialism is true, then meaningfulness must have some other source' (p. 48). It is not enough, however, to avoid the Gricean theory. The only available theory of meaning which makes no direct reference to the thoughts of speakers is the Davidsonian truth-conditions theory. But, according to that account, we can only select the correct theory of meaning for a language if we choose that theory which, charitably, attributes to speakers the maximum number of true *beliefs* (Davidson,

1984, pp. 125–39). Therefore, although it does not invoke belief at the initial stage, the truth-conditions theory does require it, or some equivalent notion, at a slightly higher level. The eliminative theory, therefore, depends on the development of a new theory of meaning which is independent of any psychological constraints, at any level, and it is speculative, if not positively unreasonable, to expect such a theory to be forthcoming.

The accusation that the eliminative theory of folk-psychology is self-refuting is justified, therefore, on two grounds. First, even supposing that we could give meaning to what is being asserted without invoking beliefs, we would have no account of the holder (or negator) of that theory's relation to it without invoking a relation equivalent to belief. Second, it is extremely doubtful whether we can have an account of the meaning of what is asserted (for this assertion or any other) without bringing belief or an equivalent notion into play.

Option 3 is no better than 2. According to 3, states of the brain acquire intentionality only from their causal relations to stimulus and response: intrinsically, internal states are purely 'syntactic', not 'semantic', that is, they consist only of ordinary physical properties and have no intrinsic intentionality (Dennett, 1981, pp. 37–61). The internal workings that determine the person's behaviour are, therefore, in Dennett's phrase, 'sub-personal', which means that they do not possess the intentionality which we usually assume belongs to those inner states which influence our behaviour (p. 53). The person conceived of as a physical system (which, for the physicalist, is all he actually is) is not a 'semantic engine' (pp. 53–4). This raises a very serious difficulty. If no one in his inner workings – that is, in his psychology – really possesses any semantic or intentional states, then no one possesses thoughts with content. It will not do to say that inner states possess them by virtue of their causal relations to other things, for these relations do not transform the inner states from syntactic to semantic states.[3] In their own intrinsic nature, the psychological (that is, inner causal) states of the person are bereft of intentionality. They possess it only seen in the light of their causal relations. It is one thing to allow that some thoughts have a *de re* component so that they are not 'in the head', and quite another to locate *all* thought content outside the subject's mind. Introspection could not reveal any thought content, and this includes the informational content of perceptual states, which must be equally syntactic, for introspection cannot reveal the remote causal relations of our inner states.

Dennett tries to save the situation by treating the attribution of intentional states as a matter of interpretation; but this only emphasizes the hopelessness of the predicament, for the suggestion that a creature which possesses no intentional states in its own right can interpret another creature as possessing them is doubly contradictory (see Dennett, 1981, pp. 59–60). First, it attributes to the interpreter an understanding of the intentional idiom, which itself presupposes that the interpreter has a capacity for belief and a grasp of concepts, which are themselves intentional capacities. Second, the very act of *interpreting* something presupposes the possession of an intentional psychology, for it involves making a hypothesis about the *meaning* and *significance* of what is being interpreted. The picture which Dennett's theory summons up and trades on is of a human being interpreting a robot or an animal anthropomorphically, thus applying a mode of explanation which roughly works, but is not actually true of its object. The human interpreter is, of course, in this picture the genuine possessor of an intrinsic intentional psychology. But Dennett's actual theory modifies this picture by denying that psychology to the interpreter himself, for he is of the same species as those he is interpreting. We supposedly attribute intentional states to each other without any of us really possessing them ourselves: an impossibility, because even to make such an attribution presupposes a grasp on intentional concepts and hence the genuine possession of intentional states.

The physicalist who wishes to avoid the disappearance theory is caught in an insoluble problem because he needs to combine three ideas that are together not consistent with his physicalism. He claims (a) that intentionality is not genuinely emergent, in the way Searle, for example, believes it to be; (b) that intentionality is not present in any physical organism as such; and (c) that intentional states really do exist as part of the inner workings and psychology of humans.

The disappearance theorist denies (c), but we have seen that his theory is self-refuting. Another theory denies (b) by attributing intentionality to quite ordinary causal physical processes. This is the information theoretic approach, which sees all physical mechanisms as transmitting information, quite independently of any interpretation. This theory cannot be discussed here, but it seems to have been shown elsewhere to fail to develop a conception of information which is independent of human interpetation and purposes.[4] Another doctrine which appears at first sight to deny (b) is the doctrine of mental representation. Calling certain inner structures 'representations' appears to imply that they possess semantic properties. Fodor, for example, sometimes appears to be attributing descriptive content to some form of 'brain writing', and hence giving semantic properties to purely physical processes.[5] But this impression is misleading. Fodor (e.g. 1981, pp. 204–24) is, in the end, as clear as Dennett that any 'mental representation' has purely syntactic properties – the semantic ones must come from elsewhere. (Quite from where, he admits he does not know – which, considering that the problem of intentionality is the main philosophical problem in this area, and one to which it appeared *at first sight* the doctrine of mental representation was a proposed solution, is a serious admission. In fact, the current discussions of mental representation do not concern the major philosophical topic of intentionality, but constitute a much more parochial argument amongst protagonists of the computational theory of mind concerning whether the inner machinery that is required by that theory need or need not possess certain language-like features.)

III

The fact that the forms of physicalism adopted by cognitive scientists face apparently insuperable problems does not force one immediately to accept substance dualism. Searle (1983, chap. 10) would be in agreement with much of what precedes, I think, but adopts a dual-aspected physicalism, in which mental states are emergent intentional states. Emergent materialism is rendered more plausible if it is claimed that such emergence is a common feature of nature and not unique to mentality. It if were unique then the claim that mind was simply a part of physical nature would look like special pleading, designed simply to avoid dualism at all costs. Searle (1983, pp. 265–6) does not think it is unique – indeed he thinks that emergence is a common phenomenon. Such properties as liquidity and transparency are emergent with respect to the properties of the particles that constitute liquid and transparent objects in much the same way as mind is emergent with respect to the physical properties of neurons. This comparison of mentality with liquidity and transparency is misconceived. Liquidity and transparency describe the behaviour of objects, and, although the molecules of water are not themselves liquid or those of glass transparent, the liquid behaviour of water follows necessarily from the behavioural properties of water molecules, and the capacity of glass to let light waves pass through can be deduced from the properties of its constituent molecules. By contrast, in the opinion of any non-reductionist, such as Searle or any defender of the dual aspect theory, the unique feature of consciousness is that neither its existence nor its quality can be deduced from the physical properties of the body. We cannot know what it is like to be a bat just by examining the bat's nervous system. Nor, if reductionism is false, can a congenitally deaf man learn what it is like to hear by studying the neurology of hearing.

The sense in which mentality is emergent is, therefore, much stronger than for anything else. The mind is a singularity in nature in a way which makes implausible the claim that these non-physical states are simply aspects of a physical organism. There appears to be no significant difference between such a theory and the weak bundle dualist claim that mental events are non-physical, but are causally dependent on the body and are not associated with any immaterial substance.

IV

Even if, as has been argued here, all physicalist theories are very problematic, any cautious person or reader of Hume will opt for bundle dualism in preference to substance dualism. Nevertheless, despite the disdain with which substance dualism has been treated, at least since Ryle's polemic in *The Concept of Mind* (1949), there is a good *prima facie* case for preferring it to the bundle theory. As the present task is only to justify treating substance dualism as a live option and not to prove it, the argument will only be sketched. The argument appeals to the often-repeated claim that identity, as it relates to people, matters in a way that it does not for non-conscious beings. It appeals to this intention not as it applies to identity thorough time, but to certain counterfactual cases. If it is asked whether a particular table (for example) would or would not have been the same object if it had been manufactured with, say, 20 per cent different matter, one might be inclined to answer one way or the other, or not to know how to answer. But whatever the initial inclination, we would not think that there was a real matter of fact of whether it would really have been the same table, over and above the fact that it would have had so much the same matter and so much different. It does not seem possible to think that there is no further matter of fact in the case of conscious subjects. Imagine some change in the matter of the sperm or egg from which you were produced and then ask the question whether, in that case, you would or would not have existed. Even if one does not know how to decide whether one would or not, the answer that one neither would nor would not seems to make no sense. We understand what it is for ourselves to exist, and what it is not to exist (a hundred years ago one did not exist) but one cannot imagine what it would be for oneself as a subject neither to exist nor not exist; nor what it would be to partially exist, as one might say the table with some different matter would have partially existed. There is a material overlap in the case of the table which tells all of the story, but the notion of a mental overlap across possibilities (so that a counterpart person who is, perhaps, *qualitatively* just as you are, possessing some, but not all, of your mental states) makes no sense.

There are, of course, many further moves that can be made for and against the above argument, but the summary gives the general drift.[6] Assuming that the argument cannot be convincingly refuted, what are its consequences? Simply that the element of vagueness in the case of the identity of the physical object arises directly from the fact that it is a composite entity, and that if a similar vagueness is not possible for the mind it must, therefore, be a logically simple object. It is not logically simple on the bundle theory, but is according to substance dualism. In so far as the argument presented in this section has any plausibility, it is, therefore, an argument for the plausibility of substance dualism.

V

I shall assume that I have shown that there are reasons for being a substance dualist and that, therefore, it is not an eccentric activity to consider the problems that mental development might present for someone of that point of view.

The substance dualist immediately runs up against a major problem when he tries to relate it to any doctrine of mental development, namely that substance dualism appears to deny the existence of such development. According to standard dualist theories, the immaterial substance is a mental substance and its essence is intellectual. Because pure thought (or consciousness) is its essence it has no need or possibilty of *developing* intellectually, for pure intellectual activity is what it already is. It might be objected that, through time, it becomes more intellectual than it was originally and hence does develop. But this is incompatible with its simplicity, which we have already accepted as part of the argument for substance dualism. Development and growth are features of complex objects and hence do not apply to the immaterial mind or self. The reintroduction of self, however, when talking about the mind suggests a further line of argument. It was the self which was proved to be simple, not the intellect, and the identification of the self with the intellect is, perhaps, precipitate. Perhaps the intellect is the product of the interaction of self and body. (It could hardly be a feature of body alone, given the arguments in section II to show that physicalists cannot cope with intentionality.)

There are at least three sources for the view that mind is complete in itself and does not depend on the body for its actualization. First there is an historical reason, namely the belief that the intellect does not and cannot depend on a physical organ. The classical reasons for thinking this are given by Aristotle, but it was believed by Descartes also.[7] If the mind is not realized in an organ then its own growth cannot be dependent on the growth of the body. We now believe that thought depends on the brain and hence has an organ: even if the mind can exist without the brain, it cannot (in our embodied state at least) operate without it. The beginnings of a theory of how the immaterial mind can be embodied within the brain will be presented below.

Second there is an argument from innateness. Both Plato and Descartes believed that the mind could not acquire concepts, and so must possess them innately.[8] Their reason was that in order to acquire a concept one must possess it already. For example, one cannot acquire the concept 'red' by observing red things because unless one already possess that concept one will not be able to see that the red things are similar to each other – a capacity to recognize a universal was taken, very plausibly, to be an exercise of that universal and hence to presuppose the possession of it. The mistake here is to confuse a general capacity to recognize universals – which is a defining property of intellect – with the possession of all those universals.[9] This, however, leads to the third reason for the traditional theory. Aristotle, Plotinus, and Descartes all claimed that the mind thought at all times when it existed.[10] One very plausible reason for thinking this is that any object must be actually something whenever it exists, for the only sort of real existence (at least for a substance) is actual existence. As the mind possesses no physical properties it must always possess some mental property and 'thought' stands generically for mental properties. As we shall see, this is a serious point, because the natural responses to the first and second reasons lead one towards characterizing the mind as a capacity for thought and consciousness, and to be merely a capacity does not seem to amount to being an actual substance.

The dualist requires a more sophisticated doctrine of embodiment than he has so far possessed. Such an account must accommodate the fact that intellect does not depend on the body simply to provide the information which informs its thought, but depends on it also for the operation of thought itself. If this can be done then the development of our mental life can partake in the development of the body, and the mind of embodied creatures need not be thought of as complete from the start.

Traditional dualists, both classical and modern, have agreed that the articulation – including the private articulation – of human thinking requires embodiment in some medium. The natural candidate for the role was mental images. If the inclusion of verbal images is allowed this is a plausible requirement, because, though we often feel we have a thought prior to its internal articulation in some verbal or other representational form, we cannot make clear – even to ourselves – what the content of the thought is until we have expressed it in such a way. If we think of the production of images as somehow dependent on the body, then this will produce some form of dependence of intellect upon the body. But this is not enough. Someone who has suffered a stroke and cannot find the right word seems to fit exactly the case of not being able to develop one's thoughts because the body can no longer produce the appropriate image. But someone who lacks the ability to solve a problem in logic, mathematics, or ordinary analytical thought is not someone who 'knows what he wants to say' but cannot make it come out. What he lacks is not merely the ability to articulate the thought, but the ability to carry through the activities of thinking required to reach the conclusion. Physical damage can restrict such activities as well as restrict their expression. This shows that the activity of thought is embodied as well as its expression.

A way of understanding these two forms of embodiment can be provided by means of an analogy. Imagine someone, S, preparing to work a computer with a keyboard and a visual display unit. S cannot perceive any other part of the computer than the VDU screen. He can touch type, but this is not by distinct sensations in the fingers – only a vague kinaesthetic sense of what he seems to be trying to do. He judges what he has actually done by what appears on the screen. So far the operation corresponds to the production of verbal and other images in the process of thought. But the machine is a computer, not just a word-processor, and S wishes to solve a problem which he could not do without the machine, and which breaks down into several parts, so that one derives an answer displayed on the screen to each part which one uses in the next; thus some of the things the computer computes go on silently in the machinery, but some of the results are displayed. Next imagine that S does not know what the problem is that he needs to solve. He knows, from previous thought, its general area and he has a feeling that he knows what he is after. He needs to play around with the keyboard, like someone thinking with a pencil and pad, until he has for himself a clear formulation of what it is he wishes to calculate. A limiting case would be if S, when he first became attached to the machine possessed no articulated thoughts at all, but only an innate ability to understand English sentences when visually presented to him and an innate inclination to try to solve certain specific problems. S is unaware of the nature of those inclinations, but he is naturally active and derives some sort of positive feeling whenever he does anything which contributes to solving those problems. S's development would consist both of coming to realize what it was he was naturally disposed to do, and doing it. He would experiment with producing sentences on the screen and gradually find his way to the articulation of the problems which he was innately disposed to try to solve. Then he could begin the task of devising the answers. S is much more limited in his purposes and solipsistic than we are, but it is clear how the example could be extended. For example, we can add a screen, loud-speakers, and so on carrying information about the external world, and an ability to move. With such extras S could learn from and about his environment and we could attribute more practical and less purely calculative dispositions than those imagined above. The original version of the analogy is, however, sufficient to illustrate the principles of the deeper form of embodiment that is involved in rejecting Descartes's view that 'the brain can be of no use in pure thought'. S's ability to make connections in thought depends upon the working of the computer which he operates blindly, judging such thought by the satis-factoriness of the results to be seen on the VDU. It is a necessary condition for S's making the moves in thought that he does, that there be the hardware required to execute them; otherwise there would be no more than an inarticulate feeling that he wants to say something, without being able to see clearly what.

On this conception of the self, all that we can say about it is that it is a logically simple entity with the *capacity* for discursive thought and consciousness. This suggestion runs immediately into the objection that it cannot be a real individual if it is simply a capacity or set of capacities.

There are at least two replies to this objection. First, physical science seems to be perfectly satisfied with basic entities which are only capacities or powers; for elementary particles are treated as point sources of influence. If such individuals are respectable in the physical domain, why not in the mental? Second, although the self possesses no actual empirical properties it does possess an individuating metaphysical property. The argument against bundle dualism, if sound, showed that the mind or self is a genuine individual in a way that no physical object could be. It possesses this simplicity because of the counterfactual properties of the consciousness which is its natural expression. A self-conscious being is, therefore, a pure individual in a way which nothing else could be. As being a pure individual is tied to being self-conscious in this unique way it might be thought that pure individuality is a sufficiently categorical property to characterize the mind when it is not exercising its capacity for thought or consciousness.

If we accept that the immaterial self is a simple substance with a capacity for (at least) consciousness and thought, then the framework for development is established, for none of these capacities are realized except through the body and learning how to realize these capacities is from scratch, as it was for S in our analogy above. The fact that the self's nature is not immediately wholly expressed establishes a distinction between the self and its conscious understanding or articulation of itself. S sees and recognizes his own thoughts only as they appear on the VDU and therefore has a conscious appreciation of himself only in the form of the persona that they build up. Of himself as a further agent his complete nature is never open to his gaze, although he can tell that he, as an agent, is something more than the thoughts of which he is aware. This establishes a distinction between the self and the ego, if the latter is construed as the conscious personality; and in so far as we think of ourselves as our conscious ego, it leaves scope for development first in the process of the formation of the ego, then in the task of making the ego an accurate basic representation of the self. This picture of the framework of development is satisfactory only if we can think of the self as having a character which can be realized, or fail to be realized, in the ego. Unfortunately, the properties we have attributed to the self so far are sparse and formal; namely of being logically simple and possessing a capacity for thought, consciousness and self-consciousness. This characterization does not, of itself, entail any particular purposes, desires or personality.

The difficulty of ascribing a particular character to the immaterial self is a serious one. We can, however, make some progress if we think of the character of the embodied self. Whatever may be the case with the immaterial self, once embodied the conscious (or potentially conscious) being has various desires and purposes. In the discussion of consciousness it was argued that thoughts could only become conscious if they were

A dualist perspective   133

embodied in an image – verbal or otherwise. It follows that if we are to become conscious of these desires and purposes they must achieve some sort of representation. Their form of representation will be somewhat different from that of the images representing objects of perception and words. Images of sensible objects are, roughly, pictorial representations of them. Simple desires and affective states come before consciousness in a hardly more complicated way. For example, a simple image of water can take on an intense feeling-tone of desirability when one is thirsty and the simple felt desirability of the water is sufficient to represent that desire to consciousness. But if more complex desires are to present themselves to consciousness in a unified way they cannot be so simply or so literally represented. Suppose that people have, from an early age, such desires as a desire for security, for coherence of personality, for certain sorts of relationships with their parents, or for power over others. If such desires were to present themselves to consciousness they could not be represented by a 'photographic' image, for nothing of that sort would contain their whole content. Such complex inclinations contain behavioural elements which can be represented in an ordinary perceptual mode, feelings of desire attaching to simple states (for example, the desire to be held or comforted) and less tangible states, such as the desire to be valued or made to feel important. These will be brought together in the desire or instinct as a whole, and this complex could only be represented symbolically, by something which somehow represented by association the complex features of such desires, and thereby allowed the feeling of that desire to coalesce around a particular representation. This picture of symbolic representations of fundamental or 'archetypal' instincts is, roughly, Jungian and therefore unlikely to commend itself to many academic psychologists. It rests, however, on a single very plausible assumption, namely that our more complex and long-term desires do, or can, find their way into consciousness in something other than a discursive verbal form. Only something which was symbolic, rather than directly or 'photographically' representational could do this, for the reasons given above.

The suggestion that mental development involves learning to understand representations of both external and internal reality should not sound too implausible. A note of disclaimer is however required in this context because of the wild ideas which have found their way into Jungian theories of child development. Some Jungian thought on early development has been baroque and speculative in the role it has assigned to archetypal symbols. For example, the impression has sometimes been given that the dreams of young children consist very largely of archetypal material, rather than of material from everyday life. There seems to be no reasons to believe that this is true.[11] More importantly, even the mainstream Jungian developmentalists treat the life of the small child, prior to the formation of the ego, as a sort of perpetual psychic storm, in which the defenceless baby is at the mercy of untrammelled archetypal forces which are calmed only by the presence of a 'good breast'.[12] None of these excesses is required by the sober claim that it is an important part of development to come to some sort of conscious apprehension of deep and complicated archetypal drives, and that the symbols of the sort to be found in certain literary, mythopaeic and religious forms are, not unusually, connected with this enterprise. As is well known, Jung himself was more concerned with the development of the adult psyche than with children. This is because the process by which the self finds its most complete expression in consciousness (called by Jung 'individuation') takes place in middle and later life and under the critical gaze of the intelligence. For Jung, mental development is not founded on unconscious reactions to repressed traumas, but is a natural process of growth and the extension of knowledge of one's own nature, as well as of the external world. Similarly, Jung's conception of the unconscious was not of it as a sewer of shameful material repressed from out of consciousness, but as the vast resources of the self which have not yet been discovered. His theory fits well with the model of the relation of the self, embodiment and the ego developed above. But into the lacuna that Jung left on the subject of early development, others have inserted theories which are more Freudian or Kleinian, invoking supposed traumas, of birth or 'the bad breast', from which the psychology of the child develops. Such theories, like most of the remainder of psychoanalysis, rests on evidence which is discernible only to analysts of the right school. The broadly Jungian picture I have so far developed, far from resting on some pessimistic modern mythology, is required by the straightforward doctrines of the self and its relation to the body which I have explained above, plus the premise that there are complex drives which can be given imaginative representation.

The distinction between the more literal or 'photographic' representations of the external world, and symbolic representations of the inner world constitutes a foundation for that aspect of Jung's psychology which has found most favour with experimentalists, namely the distinction between extroversion and introversion.[13] The extrovert learns to think in a way which duplicates the observed patterns of behaviour of the world; the introvert incorporates his experience into the system of subjective meanings that are represented by the symbols of the inner life. In so far as the initial stages of development concern learning to adapt to an external world and to recognize both how it works and the fact that it operates independently of us, we begin by by learning to be more extroverted. Our initial attitudes are what Piaget calls 'animistic', and Jung compares to the participation mystique of primitive peoples with their environment; namely that we see the world as run-through with the personal forces that characterize our own inner life (see Fordham, 1969, p. 126). Most developmental cognitive psychology is concerned with how we achieve this grasp on external reality.

The need for development from this 'animistic' phase is clear enough; it is part of coming to recognize the real nature of the external physical world. But in terms of the introvert and extrovert psychological tendencies that we all possess, it raises problems as well as solves them. It is a commonplace that the mark of the modern age is the move towards a quantitative and scientific understanding of the world and the abandonment of a qualitative and teleological conception of the cosmos. We used to believe that the universe as a whole shared the purposive nature of man: now we think of man as of a piece with the mechanical and purposeless processes which our struggle to come to terms with external reality has led us to believe is the nature of the external world. The extrovert paradigm has become dominant and left the introvert factor with no obvious legitimate sphere of activity, confining it to the realm of subjective fantasy. The phenomenon of cultural development has its parallel in the mental growth of the individual. Although we have to begin by learning how to cope with the physical world and with what is expected of us socially – that is, by conforming our minds to the external and social reality – we also need to attend to the inner promptings of a more personal and possibly more disruptive kind; we need to decide what life *means* for us in the reality we have accepted. The cultural and individual problems with the introvert function are not entirely separate. A milieu which rejects purpose metaphysically threatens the individual's search for meaning in his life.

There have been serious thinkers – usually poets and novelists – who have tried to solve this problem by defending the animistic theory of the external world, though there is often some doubt about whether they wish to be taken entirely literally.[14] Others try to re-establish a more orthodox kind of religious or metaphysical purpose. Nevertheless, for all but a few modern would-be pagans, it is uncontroversial that the acquisition of those concepts and capacities which make possible what is now called 'cognitive development' and which concerns our ability to cope with the external world, is an appropriate subject for the psychologist's investigation. Almost no one would claim that serious questions are being begged in calling this process 'development'. But the question of the proper role of the introvert factor is not separable from philosophical problems concerning whether man has a purpose and whether anything in reality corresponds to his aspirations. Attempts to produce a theory of psychological harmony – such as Jung's theory of the process of individuation – in abstraction from the question of the truth of religious and metaphysical claims run the risk of being intellectually disingenuous. As sympathetic but religiously more orthodox critics have pointed out, Jung himself is at least ambiguous on this question.[15] Some of his followers seek to treat the metaphysical and religious issues as mere historical adjuncts to the psychological process. Fordham (1973), the most prominent of British Jungians, for example, has said:

> it is important to keep in mind that the concept of 'self', as well as that of individuation, is born out of a psychological need and not in the first place out of a religious one, where the imagery is embodied in and is interpreted in terms of metaphysics. (p. 22)

> In short, modern consciousness leads to historical metaphysical experience being expressed more and more in terms of interpersonal relations. (p. 23)

It cannot be legitimate to respond to the observation that man requires a purpose and perhaps a religion by making such purposes and beliefs an issue of mental health, as if the psychologist can abstract from the question of truth because it is beyond his competence to solve these metaphysical questions.

It is in this area – that is, the higher forms of development, rather than questions of early learning – that the dualist has a specific contribution. If he can justify the philosophical doctrine that man is essentially a non-physical substance, he is justifying an essential element of a world view which allows for the reality of the purposes which are foreshadowed in our inner life. But not only can dualism underpin a fuller conception of development, a traditional approach to development can also support dualism. This approach is again one adopted by Jung and concerns the role of the mandala as a symbol of the self. Traditional dualism, mandala theory and Jungian psychology are essentially in harmony in their conceptions both of the structure of the psyche and of the proper path for psychic growth. What one might call the traditional conception of the self contains two poles which are apparently in tension. On the one hand, the self is, as the argument of section IV requires, absolutely simple. On the other, as it expresses itself in embodied activity, it is diverse in its character and capacities. It is precisely this duality in the self which the mandala represents. The leading western scholar of the mandala (Tucci, 1948) explains its purpose as representing a process of reintegration, whereby the adept can 'bring back the plurality into which our psyche is shattered to ... the One, Luminous, Undifferentiated Source'. Jung (1968, vol. 9, part i) casts it in this role in his theory of individuation. Not surprisingly, therefore, the same duality is to be found in Jung's conception of the self. On the one hand, the self includes everything in the psyche, including the conscious ego; on the other, it is the central point of the psyche – it is, that is, both the psychic totality and the archetype which is 'the real organizing principle' of the totality, the controlling centre, not the whole (Fordham, 1969, p. 28; Jung, 1968, vol. 9, part ii, p. 204). Some Jungians have feared that this dual conception is inconsistent (Fordham, 1969, pp. 24ff), but the argument in section IV which shows the simplicity of the self, together with the fact that sensible and embodied articulation requires diversity, shows that analytically Jung is quite correct. Indeed, that our articulate thoughts are complex is strictly required by the move from the un-articulated feeling that one has something to say, to any surveyable expression of the thought. It is striking that this combination of simplicity and complexity are ubiquitous in traditional theories of consciousness, both eastern and western. Plotinus (*Ennead V*, Book 4) for example, adopts a theory very similar to the Indian, with the One producing as emanation Intellect, which is, so to speak, the sum of all intelligibly expressed possibilities. (Emanation is a relation which causes philo-sophers great trouble. But, for the present purposes, it can be thought of as that form of production whereby something originally taken as a unit or whole is spelled out and articulated by a more complex structure of simpler parts. It parallels, that is, the relation between an unarticulated thought one feels one has, and its worked-out verbal expression.)

It appears, therefore, to be a conceptual requirement of the existence of self-conscious and hence intelligent beings that they be logically simple entities; and to be a conceptual requirement that if the self-conscious intelligence be expressed in an embodied form that there flow from the simplicity a complex form of expression.

We can conclude, therefore, that the message of mandala symbolism, of Jung's theory of individuation, and, hence, of a non-reductive account of psychological development is to remind us of what conceptual analysis has already indicated, namely that the fall into embodiment and com-plexity should not cut us off from our nature as indivisible and immaterial selves.

NOTES

1 On the other hand, following Gödel, J. R. Lucas (1961) has argued that no machine could be creative. His argument is one of those with which almost everyone feels obliged to disagree, though no two critics can agree on the reason.

2 This argument is to be found in two essays in Shoemaker's *Identity, Cause and Mind* (1984). They are 'Functionalism and qualia', pp. 184–205 and 'Absent qualia are impossible: a reply to Ned Block', pp. 309–26.

3 I am not saying that brain state *plus* causal relation could not be a composite semantic state, only that the causal relations do not make the brain state itself into a semantic state.

4 See the discussions of Fred Dretske's target article (1983) especially the comments by Kenneth Sayre and Ernest Sosa.

5 This appears to be suggested in 'Methodological solipsism', reprinted in Fodor (1981, pp. 225–53). At one point (p. 245) Fodor appears to suggest

that the absence of semantic properties just means the absence of the ability to distinguish between H_2O on earth and its counterpart XY on twin-earth; that is, it is only the *de re* element which is missing, the descriptive content is safe and non-semantic. Fodor is taken to task for this by Kent Bach (1982).

6   For a defence of this conception of the self see Geoffrey Madell (1981).

7   For a discussion of Aristotle's reasons, see Robinson (1983).

8   For Plato, see *The Meno*; for Descartes, see 'Notes against a Programme', in Haldane and Ross (1968, vol. 1, p. 443).

9   Which is not to say that Fodor is wrong to deny that new logics can be learnt – this is another issue. See Fodor (1976, pp. 88–95).

10 In the case of Aristotle it follows from the doctrine of the active intellect found in *De Anima III*, 5. For Plotinus see, for example, *Ennead I*, 4, chaps 9 and 10. For Descartes, see, for example, 'Discourse on method' in Haldane and Ross (1968, vol. I, p. 101) or 'Principles of philosophy', Part I Principle L111 in Haldane and Ross (1968, vol. I, p. 240). See also A. Kenny (1968).

11 For a moderating emphasis, see Michael Fordham (1969).

12 For example, M. Sidoli (1983).

13 *Psychological Types*, C. G. Jung, vol. 6 of Jung's collected works; pp. 330–407 give the best general account.

14 D. H. Lawrence certainly meant it seriously, and, in a slightly less violent way, so did Yeats.

15 For example, Kathleen Raine (1983).

REFERENCES

Bach, K. 1982: *De re* belief and methodological solipsism. In A. Woodfield (ed.), *Thought and Object*. Oxford: Clarendon Press.

Churchland, P. 1981: Eliminative materialism and propositional attitudes. *Journal of Philosophy*, 78, 22–36.

1984: *Matter and Consciousness*. Cambridge, Mass.: MIT Press.

Davidson, D. 1984: Radical interpretation. In *Truth and Interpretation*. Oxford: Clarendon Press.

Dennett, D. 1981: Three kinds of intentional psychology. In R. Healey (ed.), *Reductionism, Time, and Reality*. Cambridge: Cambridge University Press.

Dretske, F. 1983: Precis of 'Knowledge and the Flow of Information'. *The Behavioural and Brain Sciences*, 6, 55–90.

Eccles, J. C. 1984: *The Human Mystery*. London: Routledge and Kegan Paul.

Fordham, M. 1969: *Children as Individuals*. London: Hodder and Stoughton.

1973: The empirical foundation and theories of the self in Jung's works. In M. Fordham (ed.), *Analytical Psychology: A Modern Science*. London: Heineman.

Fodor, J. A. 1976: *The Language of Thought*. Brighton, Sussex: Harvester Press.

1981: *Representations*. Brighton, Sussex: Harvester Press.

Haldane, E. S. and Ross, G. R. T. 1968: *The Philosophical Works of Descartes*, 2 vols. Cambridge: Cambridge University Press.

Johnson-Laird, P. N. 1983: *Mental Models*. Cambridge: Cambridge University Press.

Jung, C. G. 1968: *Collected Works*. London: Routledge and Kegan Paul.

Kenny, A. 1968: *Descartes*. London: Random House.

Lucas, J. R. 1961: Minds, machines and Gödel. *Philosophy*, 36, 112–27.

Madell, G. 1981: *The Identity of the Self*. Edinburgh: Edinburgh University Press.

Nagel, T. 1971: Brain bisection and the unity of consciousness. *Synthèse*, 22, 396–413.

Robinson, H. 1982: *Matter and Sense*. Cambridge: Cambridge University Press.
    1983: Aristotelian dualism. *Oxford Studies in Ancient Philosophy*, 1, 55–61.

Raine, K. 1983: The inner journey of the poet. In M. Tudy (ed.), *In the Wake of Jung*. New York: Coventure Press.

Ryle, G. 1949: *The Concept of Mind*. London: Hutchinson.

Searle, J. R. 1983: *Intentionality*. Cambridge: Cambridge University Press.

Sidoli, M. 1983: De-integration and re-integration in the first two weeks of life. *Journal of Analytical Psychology*, 28, 201–12.

Shoemaker, S. 1984: *Identity, Cause, and Mind*. Cambridge: Cambridge University Press.

Stich, S. P. 1983: *From Folk Psychology to Cognitive Science*. Cambridge, Mass.: MIT Press.

Tucci, G. 1948: *Theory and Practice of the Mandala*. London: Rider.

7

Synthesis in the imagination: psychoanalysis, infantile experience and the concept of an object

James Hopkins

In recent decades infancy has been the subject of two quite different kinds of psychological research. In experimental psychology the observations and theories of Piaget have been the main stimulus and organizing focus for a large and rapidly growing body of work on children and babies. And a striking development in psychoanalysis since Freud has been the analysis, by methods closely related to his, of very young children. As Freud had put forward new descriptions of childhood to explain what he had found in analysing adults, so Melanie Klein, one of the first and most influential child analysts, advanced new and detailed hypotheses about early infancy to account for the further data which emerged in treating children.[1]

Although very different, and based on different observations, Klein's and Piaget's accounts of infantile development share a central idea which is plausible and powerful. This is, that the infant's use of the concept of identity – the application of the idea of a single, enduring object of perception, emotion and action – plays a pivotal role in both cognitive and emotional development. In what follows both theories will be discussed in light of this, and an attempt made to show that both philosophical arguments and experimental results indicate that they should be regarded as complementary. Although these considerations are not conclusive, it is hoped they suggest that concentration on the concept of identity may help in understanding issues in development in infancy.

The discussion falls into three main parts. Familiarity with Klein's work has not been assumed, so in the first section some relevant aspects of this will be sketched, with a brief attempt at indicating some relations of her concepts to Freud's, and to analytic data. The second section considers Piaget's account of infantile conceptions of self and object, and argues for an alternative which, although somewhat different, is still close to the original. The third relates this, via the concept of identity, to the aspects of Kleinian theory under discussion, and also to some results of experiment.

Obviously both analysts and experimental psychologists will know their literature, concepts, and procedures better than I do. Still I hope that a philosophically informed comparative discussion may be useful, and that the overall line of argument will remain intact despite errors in under-standing.

I

Psychoanalytic theory is continuous with the common-sense psychology in terms of which we understand one another in daily life. In this we constantly interpret behaviour as action derived from motives. Although such interpretations are intuitive, they cohere in a system of explanation for behaviour which we take to be, in the main, cogent. This is partly because the way we fit individual interpretations with one another into our overall account of motive ensures that that they are continually cross-checked and revised in light of one another, and so can be seen to form a mutually interlocking and confirming group[2] (see Wilkes, this volume).

Freud discovered that many things persons do – including many dreams, symptoms, and slips – could be understood not (or not only) as actions, but also as wish-fulfilments. Such events in behaviour could be seen to involve imaginative *representations*, with content which was sensitive to underlying motive. In these the motives were not realistically acted on, but rather – as in the day-dreaming or wishful thinking – merely imagined or represented as fulfilled.

This greatly enlarged the field of data which could be seen as relevant to framing and checking accounts of motive, and hence enabled Freud to extend radically common-sense psychology itself. By interpreting dreams and symptoms together with free association, memory, and transference, he was able to see much of the mental life of his analysands as derived from motives which had originated in early childhood.

Now of course children, and especially very young ones, cannot put into words the kind of material connected with their symptoms and difficulties which Freud had used. They do, however, constantly and spontaneously represent things – with dolls, toys, clay, paints, games of make-believe – in play. Klein (1975) realized that these representations too could be seen as constantly reflecting motive and mental state, and as embodying wish-fulfilling fantasy. To take some examples from a girl of six:

Erna began her play by taking a small carriage which stood on the table among the other toys and letting it run towards me. She declared she had come to fetch me. But she put a toy woman in the carriage instead and added a toy man. The two loved and kissed one another and drove up and down all the time. Then a toy man in another carriage collided with them, ran over them and killed them, and then roasted them and ate them up. (vol. II, p. 40)

Here the toy couple killed and eaten, apparently for loving one another and driving up and down all the time, could be taken as representing the parents, and the third figure as Erna herself. Closely related motives came out quite explicitly in other play, which worked over themes introduced in the first. Thus when Erna

as queen, had celebrated her marriage to the king, she lay down on the sofa and wanted me, as the king, to lie down beside her. As I refused to do this I had to sit on a little chair by her side and knock at the sofa with my fist. This she called 'churning' . . . immediately after this she announced that a child was creeping out of her, and she represented the scene in a quite realistic way, writhing about and groaning. Her imaginary child then had to share its parents' bedroom and had to be a spectator of sexual intercourse between them. If it interrupted, it was beaten. . . . If she, as the mother, put the child to bed, it was only in order to get rid of it and to be able to be united with the father all the sooner. (vol. II, p. 40)

Both these games apparently concerned the child's feelings about her parents loving each other. The representations of their relations – as one of loving and kissing, and driving up and down all the time, or again as lying together with something knocking something, 'churning' – have elements which could be taken as sexual symbolism in adult dreams. There such elements could be connected by association to articulate adult sexual thoughts, which could in turn be seen to have influenced other features of the dream. Here the referent of a representation was shown by the structure of the play (e.g. the fact that the knocking or 'churning' took place after the couple lay down together, and was followed by the birth of the child).

Matters might, however, be shown more explicitly, or in ways which combined modes of representation. When Erna masturbated (as she did both at home and in her sessions) she would play what she called 'the cupboard game' in which she pulled at her clitoris, saying she 'wanted to pull out something very long'. She also played that a small piece of paper in a basin was a sea-captain, whose ship had gone down. He was able to save himself because he had something 'long and golden' which held him in the water. She then tore off his head and announced 'His head's gone, now he's drowned' (vol. II, pp. 50, 38).[3]

Children played out many fantasies related to their psychological problems or conditions particularly clearly. For example,

Erna often made me be a child, while she was the mother or a teacher. I then had to undergo fantastic tortures and humiliations. If in the game anyone treated me kindly, it generally turned out that the kindness was only simulated. The paranoic traits showed in the fact that I was constantly spied upon, people divined my thoughts, and the father or teacher allied with the mother against me – in fact, I was always surrounded by persecutors. I myself, in the role of the child, had constantly to spy on and torment the others. Often Erna herself played the child. Then the game generally ended in her escaping the persecutions (on these occasions the 'child' was good), becoming rich and powerful, being made a queen and taking a cruel revenge on her persecutors. (vol. I, p. 200)

Sometimes the emnity and persecution was particularly secret and insidious, and disguised as love. The mother and father in Erna's fantasies ate marvellous foods made of whipped cream or a special milk, but gave the child semolina which made it sick. In other games Erna would sell fish, which were clearly connected in her mind with faeces, since she called them 'Kakelfish' – 'Kaki' being her word for faeces – and would have an urge to defecate when playing at cutting them up. In other games she and Klein would exchange such goods, apparently with love; but her depression afterwards showed that these 'good' anal presents were actually felt as poisonous. So the deep content of the representations was that figures representing her mother and herself were constantly poisoning one another (vol. II, p. 46).

In general the child's play could be seen to involve very persecuting 'bad' figures, very idealized 'good' ones, and others, such as that of the queen, or again the poisoning mother, in which very good or bad features seemed confusedly combined. These could be seen as images which reflected and governed many of the child's feelings and fantasies about the parents, although of course they were very different from those consciously held. (Erna regarded her real mother as fond of her, never criticized her, and was, if anything, overly affectionate to her.)

Sometimes the 'bad' parents seemed the result of various sorts of projections of the child's own feelings; and sometimes they were made bad by envious or jealous attacks. For example a little boy of 3 years 9 months

phantisized that he cut off papa's 'popochen' (his word for penis) with a knife, and that the latter sawed his off with a saw. The outcome, however, was that he had his papa's. Then he cut off his father's head, after which the latter could do no more to him because he could not see – but the eyes in the head saw him, nevertheless. (vol. I, p. 65)

Again, a little girl of just under 4 years would play make-believe that it was night-time and she and the analyst were asleep. She would then come from her own bedroom and attack the analyst in bed in various ways. In one episode she

> wanted to hit me in the stomach and declared that she was taking out my 'A – A's (stool) and was making me poor. She then seized the cushions, which she repeatedly called children, and hid herself with them behind the sofa. There she crouched in the corner with an intense expression of fear, covered herself up, sucked her fingers, and wetted herself ... [This behaviour] corresponded in every detail with the way she had behaved when, at a time she was not yet two, she had begun to have night terrors. (vol. II, p. 5)

Erna, similarly, had fears of a 'robber woman' who would 'take out everything inside her', and she could not sleep at night for fear of burglars (vol. II, pp. 39, 214).

Now these observations both fit with, and extend, Freud's theories of illness and personality, and the account of childhood mental life he had reconstructed. Freud had understood his patients' symptoms as largely determined by fantastic childhood hostilities and fears, focused on the parents, and had uncovered both childhood neuroses such as Klein's patients had and unconscious childhood images and fantasies such as they displayed in play and transference.[4] Thus Klein's patients showed such Freudian phenomena as childhood preoccupation with sexual rivalry, castration, and so on; and they did so in accord with what Freud had described as the sexual theories of children, as seen, for example, in the equations made in play above, between faeces and babies, faeces and food, and so on.

Also, Klein saw that the roles which the children assigned to different figures in play could be taken as personifying the agencies which Freud had described in terms of the ego, super-ego, and id (Klein, 1975, vol. I, pp. 199ff). Thus one figure would have as its purpose to satisfy some repressed or split-off desire, while another would serve to prevent this, so that a compromise was reached; or the other would punish the first, cause him anxiety, and so forth (the eyes that see none the less, above). This meant that in their play the children could be seen as externalizing the working of these agencies, or projecting the images of figures involved in them on to figures in the outside world, and this could be studied further.

Klein found such representations in the play of even the smallest children, which indicated that such fantasies and images were well established by the time a child could speak, and had a history before that. This meant that they could not be accounted for by frustrations, threats, or punishments in childhood. So the sorts of sexual and aggressive feelings which Freud had assigned to childhood, as well as the development of agencies like the punishing super-ego, had to be seen as originating even earlier than he had been willing to suppose, and indeed as being rooted in infancy. Such conclusions were of course very controversial; in one way they may be less so now, since psychologists are more willing to take things shown in early childhood as having a prior or innate basis.

Klein found many additional fantasies and preoccupations concerning for example devouring and being devoured, robbing the mother's body and being robbed oneself, and poisoning and being poisoned. This went with the fact that the main themes of the children's fantasies seemed to turn on activities involving bodily parts and substances – breasts, genitals, milk, urine, faeces – which could, like the figures in the child's world, be very good or very bad.

Such significant bodily parts or substances were themselves repre-sented as animate creatures, which played attacking or avenging roles comparable to those assigned to whole persons. Thus one little girl had ritually to be tucked up at bedtime, lest a 'mouse or a Butzen' [her word for genitals] would get in and bite off her own 'Butzen'. In analysis her doll was likewise tucked up, and she had her toy elephant to keep it from getting out of bed, lest it get into the parents' bedroom and 'do something to them or take something away from them'. Again, Erna had fantasies of 'a flea which was "black and yellow mixed", and which she herself at once recognized as a bit of faeces – dangerous, poisoned faeces ... [which] came out of [Klein's] anus and forced its way into hers and injured her' (vol. II, pp. 6, 44).

This meant that such partial or incomplete figures also played roles analogous to those of the super-ego, ego and id, as described above. They could serve as imaginary embodiments of unacknowledged or disowned aggressive impulses, and so as split-off, 'bad' parts of the self;[5] or again as other selves, which were vengeful, controlling, or whatever. Klein also found that parts of one self were fantasized not only to enter another, but also to do various things inside – take the other over, control it, become a parasite,and so on.[6] And since such a role could be played by something as primitive as a piece of faeces, a representation of a faecal attack could at the same time be that of a projective one, in which a bad part of one self was put into another, as in the example of the faecal flea above.

Freud had taken a person's image of himself and others as built up through both projection and introjection. In projection, roughly speaking, a person alters his representation of someone else by putting into it something which originates from himself. In introjection, by contrast, a person changes his representation of himself, by putting into it something originating from another.

Freud had described these mechanisms as interacting, on roughly the following lines. A person built up his self-image, and so his ego and super-ego, by modelling himself on others, and by representing himself as in relation to them. A boy, for example, both identified with his father, and also felt himself to be set standards and criticized by an internal agency derived from his parents. The images set up in introjection would, however, depend upon what had been projected. So the punishing severity of the super-ego, for example, was usually not to be explained by the actual severity of the parents, but rather by the child's own perception of them, which was distorted by projection.

Klein found introjective representations which paralleled the projective ones already described. Just as projective fantasies could be effected by the explusion of something from the body, so introjective ones could be implemented by taking something into it. Thus if, as frequently happened, a child enacted the eating of some figure in play, this could result in his feeling that he had inside him a presence related to that figure. The internal figure might help him or be assimilated to himself, so that he could in fact do things better; or the figure might condemn, attack him, and so forth, and so inhibit or disable him. This extended to part as well as whole objects, so that a child might represent the eating of a penis or breast as creating an internal source of fullness or potency, faeces as making something horrible inside, and so on. The nature of the internal figure or presence depended upon the fantasy in which it was taken in. So, for example, the sort of aggressive eating of the parental couple which Erna played out in the instance quoted above would not have enabled her to feel she had taken in the desirable qualities she envied, but rather only things which were bad.[7]

In this also Klein was extending Freud's observations. He had held that introjection and identification, and the formation of the ego and super-ego, were bound up with bodily images. Thus Freud said that the ego was 'first and foremost a bodily Ego' (vol. XIX. pp. 25–6), involving an image of the body surface, as felt from inside. And he linked introjection itself with fantasies of taking the introjected object into the body, connecting the origin of the super-ego, for example, with innate fantasies of devouring a punitive father.

Abraham (1973) has carried Freud's work on this topic further, and distinguished between relations to a whole object and what he called 'partial object relations'. Abraham had noticed how frequently patients represented others by parts of the body, and in doing so adopted correspondingly primitive ways of relating to them. A mother, for example, could be represented only by a breast, which would be eaten up; or again a persecuting enemy by a bit of faeces, which the patient would try to expel (pp. 418ff). Abraham took these partial relations to originate in an early stage of life, in which particular parts or products of the bodies of others, or its own, were especially salient to the child, and in which introjection and projection operated on such part-objects.

Klein's account of early introjective and projective representations thus enabled her to consolidate Freud's and Abraham's descriptions of these matters. The earliest projective and introjective fantasies could simply be taken as those which arose while the infant did not yet think of its mother or itself in terms of whole bodies, and also while it represented things most concretely, and hence in terms of bodily takings in and puttings out. This seemed to correspond with a layering which emerged in the analysis of a given image of an object. Conscious and relatively realistic images seemed underpinned and shaped by others which were progressively less realistic, less anatomically and psychologically complete, more concrete and physical, and more sharply divided as between good and bad. So the infant's construction of his own image by introjection, and his alteration of his image of the object of his experience and action by projection, could be taken as starting in his first relation with the mother, and in particular with her breast.

Klein took projection and introjection to operate together with another mechanism, which she called 'splitting'. It was this which accounted for the division between 'bad' and 'good' images so marked in the children's fantasies. The working of this, and its hypothesized role in development, can be illustrated by reference to some further material.

It could be observed that children were commonly faced with deep uncertainty about someone with whom they had a relationship. In such a case, a child was liable to split the figure concerned – that is, to form or keep one representation of the figure as good and in close relation to itself, and at the same time to form another representation, also derived from the uncertain figure, of someone bad and to be kept away.

For example many of the difficulties of Klein's patient Richard could be traced to paranoid fears, which he first expressed as relating to two figures in his household, the cook and the maid.

> Suddenly and with determination he said that he wanted to tell Mrs. K. something which was worrying him very much. He was afraid of being poisoned by Cook or Bessie. They would do this because he was often horrid or cheeky to them. From time to time he had a good look at the food, to find out whether it was poisoned. He looked into bottles in the kitchen to see what they contained: they might have poison in them which Cook would mix with his food. Sometimes he thought that Bessie, the maid, was a German spy. He occasionally listened at the key-hole to find out whether Cook and Bessie were speaking German together. (Both Cook and Bessie were British and did not know a word of German, as I subsequently ascertained.) ... He obviously forced himself to tell all this, looking tortured and worried. He said that these fears made him very unhappy and asked if Mrs. K. could help him with them. (vol. IV, p. 128)

Klein took these fears to originate in the child's relation to his mother. They also showed in a number of ways in his transference to her. Among other things, he felt what she said to him as both good and giving him the sort of help he needed, and also as bad and making him sick. He seemed to maintain his good relation with her by repeatedly splitting off what he felt to be bad into images of others.

Thus at one point, when it seemed his fears were rising, he began behaving with particular fondness towards Mrs Klein, singing to her, telling her about a sweet little puppy, and so on. He put his arm around her, saying 'I am very happy and I am very fond of you'. But his attention was attracted by an old, neglected-looking woman passing by, who he said was horrid, and spat awful yellow stuff out of her mouth. Here, apparently, was an alternative, split-off image of Mrs Klein, and perhaps of her analysis as awful stuff, like urine, which had to be spat out. Thus, it seems, he kept his anxieties about being poisoned out of his image of his relations with Mrs Klein, but not entirely out of his mind. And by the next session he was physically ill, and worried that mucous behind his nose was poison, and that Bessie and Cook had actually poisoned him.[8]

Now the mechanism thus illustrated as operating in a session could be hypothesized to play a similar role in development. The conscious images which Richard had built up included an unambiguously good one of his mother, but others of figures who fed and looked after him, and might well be persecutors. His unconscious images of his mother, as shown in his drawings and other play, seemed to contain all these elements. So the various images he had could be explained on the supposition that he had early on been inclined to feel uncertain about his mother, particularly with respect to feeding, and that when he felt this he had split her into good and bad feeding figures, with the former kept close and in good relation with him and the latter at greater distance. The former images were more salient in his conscious representation of his mother, and the latter were, so to speak, now inherited by Cook and Bessie.

Klein took Richard's uncertainty towards his mother as a feeding figure to be rooted in attacks on his mother, or his mother's breasts, which he also played out in analysis. In these, as Klein interpreted them, he put faeces and urine into his mother, and also the bad parts of himself, which he characteristically represented in terms of Hitler and the Germans. By doing this he made his mother bad and poisonous. The same structure can perhaps be seen in the example of Erna's fantasies above, where the parent-figure and child are exchanging bad substances, and thereby making one another bad.

In general, the images which Klein's patients produced in analysis could be understood as built up in this way, through the systemtic use of projection, introjection, and splitting. The mechanisms could, in fact, be seen as integral to one another. Thus if a bad part of one self was represented as put in another, as in projection, this would result on a further representation of the other, as with the bad part inside. So the other was now split, and partly bad. The original self, however, would now be represented as lacking the part; so it too was split (and diminished) but good. Good parts could also be split off and projected, thus creating good or idealized objects. The representations of figures and relations partly determined by projection would be introjected, so that a new layer was acquired in the representation of the self and its inner world. This would form the basis for new projections, and so on.

The overall effect of such interacting fantasies was to build up a picture of the world as divided into good and bad figures, in contrasting relations with the self. The 'good' figures were closely identified with the self, shared its perspective, and were in helpful and co-operative relations with it. The 'bad' figures were kept out of consciousness, or in one way or another represented as distanced or alien. So the pattern was in effect that of good us/bad them. But since the bad figures contained what the self felt as most intimately bad or threatening, they could seem to confront, impinge upon, or invade it with mirroring directness.

Very roughly, the symptoms of the children Klein analysed could be seen as arising because they had early 'bad' images of their parents which were so divorced from the 'good' ones that the parents had constantly to be feared, and attacked in the imagination, as extremely bad. But since these fears and attacks were also, at another level, felt as affecting the parents the patients loved and depended upon, such imaginings miscarried, or were distressing, in a variety of ways.

It could, therefore, be supposed that at an early or primitive level the child took differing images derived from experience with the same person as if they corresponded to distinct objects. Such early images were overlain by others, which served progressively to integrate them into representations of whole persons, and one person. But if this process were only partly successful – if some images, as it were, failed to dovetail fully with their successors – various sorts of disfunction, including the sort of misdirected fear and aggression described above, could result.

These were the images which emerged in analysis and became focused on the analyst, and so could be worked through in light of more mature ones, and better connected with them. In dealing with them, the analysand would attempt to identify with the good figures and obliterate the bad or keep them away. However, as it became clearer that diverse images in fact related to single objects, and in particular the mother, a number of connected and far-reaching changes could be observed, and could be hypothesized to occur in normal development.

Grasping that apparently incompatible good and bad images related to one object accompanied recognition that the good might be harmed by measures taken against what was felt to be bad. This was all the more serious, because it also went with realizing that there were not many 'good' mother-figures but only one; who was, therefore, unique and irreplaceable. Hence the mother was now pictured not only as good, but also as indispensible and under threat from a self which might misconceive and harm or lose her. So there arose feelings of concern for this mother, pining for her, desires to make good damage done to her, and so on. A whole new range of feelings, that is, seemed to be consequent on recognizing that the object was a whole, single, and correspondingly complex.

Synthesizing the disparate images of the object required working through these feelings, and this was in turn required for introjecting a whole object and forming a coherent self-image as well. This process could, however, be impeded by various defences against the painful feelings of dependency, depression, and so forth, which were involved. These included: the 'manic' defences of exerting imaginary control over the object; denying its uniqueness or complexity by re-splitting it; denying that any damage had been done in the imagination, or alternatively, that everything could be put right magically; and so on.

Since Klein held that responding to depression was one of the most important aspects of this phase, and that the constellation of feelings, problems, defences, and so on in it were of importance throughout life, she called it the depressive position.[9] She hypothesized that the infant began to take its mother as a whole person, and so to enter this position, in the fourth or fifth month of life (vol. I, pp. 285–6; cf., however, the modification in vol. III, p. 35).

In the previous phase, apparently, the infant started from relations to parts of the mother's body and worked up representations of these, with 'bad' and 'good' aspects sharply separated, until he began to unite the aspects and then the parts. The conception of the depressive position enabled Klein to distinguish the depressive anxieties consequent on unification from those endemic to relations with such incomplete objects. Since the latter anxieties were of a paranoid nature, and the earliest representations of self and objects both ununified and liable to radical distortion by splitting and projection, she called this first phase the 'paranoid–schizoid position'.

Working through the depressive position meant a dimunition in splitting and projection, which served to maintain the division between good and bad. It seemed, however, that the unification of these aspects could not take place unless the person already possessed the requisite images of good and bad objects in contrasting relations to the self. In many instances, however, these were unavailable. If the most basic good or idealized figures were felt to contain too much that was bad – if, say, the mother or breast represented as feeding was also inevitably represented as poisoning – they could not be represented as in a stable good relation to the self, but had rather to be subjected to repeated splitting and projection to keep the bad out and away.

This was itself a source of instability, and the process had to be carried on until a more realistic and lasting division between good and bad was finally achieved. This, however, meant that making a proper division between good and bad was itself to be taken as an early accomplishment, effected mainly by splitting and projection. So Klein was able to see the mechanisms of splitting and projection as serving to organize the first phase of mental life in such a way that it, and their use, could be partly superseded.

Finally, Klein concluded that a main cause of the failure to form a stable representation of a good object was the use of projective identification, which both eroded the primitive distinction between self and object and made the object bad. She took this to be the expression of a primitive form of envy, which, as it were, would not tolerate anything to be both good and distinct from the self. This emotion she took as one of the fundamental causes of pathology.

Having before us this sketch of some of Klein's ideas, let us now turn to the work of Piaget.

II

As is well known, Piaget's account of cognitive and emotional development turns on the concept of an enduring object. To describe the world-picture of the infant who has yet to use this concept, Piaget (Piaget and Inhelder, 1969) introduces the term 'tableau':

> The universe of the young baby is a world without objects, consisting only of shifting and unsubstantial 'tableaux' which appear and are then reabsorbed, either without returning, or reappearing in a modified or analogous form. (p. 25)

Piaget's account of the infant's coming to understand his experience is thus one of progress from representation in terms of such tableaux, or episodic objects, to representations in terms of enduring ones. As he summarizes

> When the little child ceases to relate everything to his states and to his own action, and begins to substitute for a world of fluctuating tableaux without spatio-temporal consistency or external physical causality a universe of permanent objects structured according to its own groups of spatio-temporal displacements and according to an objectified and spatialized causality, then his affectivity will also be attached to these localizable permanent objects and sources of causality which persons come to be. Whence the formation of 'object relations' [marking the double formation of a self differentiated from other people and other people becoming objects of affectivity] in close connection with the scheme of permanent objects. (pp. 25–6)

Piaget's use of 'object relations' here – and his definition in terms of a 'double formation' – is an explicit reference to Freudian theory, acknowledging coincidence of explanatory aims. But it is plain that there is also a clear comparison to be made with the work of Klein – hers is, precisely, a theory of the mental development of the infant as it moves from the world of the partial and episodic objects of the paranoid–schizoid position to that of the enduring and whole objects of the depressive position.

Klein's attention, of course, is not so much focused upon the conception of a physical object as that of an enduring unified object of emotion, and a counterpart unified self, and the emotional changes in the development of these. Nevertheless, in her account, as in Piaget's, development of physical and psychological representation go together. So let us consider what Piaget says about psychological development, to see how his treatment of this matter can be related to Klein's.

One part of Piaget's account is readily understandable. This concerns the links among the concept of an enduring object, the distinction between subjective experiences and objective external objects, and the location of these latter in space. These show most clearly if we consider the role of the concept of identity.

The concept of identity is part of that of an enduring object, since this is, precisely, an object which retains its identity over time. One relation of this to our concepts of subjective and objective shows in the case where we perceive an object, cease to perceive it, and later do so again, taking the object seen on the first occasion to be (identical with) that seen on the second. Here the judgement of identity implies that the twice-perceived object existed unperceived – endured – in the interval. This entails that it exists independently of our subjective perceptions or experiences of it, which did not likewise endure.

We employ this same concept of identity when we distinguish between encountering an object which resembles one previously perceived from meeting the very same object again. Our grounds for holding that we have met the same object may be that what is now perceived has an appropriate resemblance to something perceived before. In judging identity, however, we go beyond this, since such grounds are consistent with the hypothesis that we have met distinct but resembling objects, while the judgement of identity is not.

We could not oppose likeness and identity in this way if we thought of objects as episodic, as coming into or going out of existence with perception, rather than as persisting in space over time. For we could not identify an object with one previously met without holding that it had kept on being the same, while yet it had not kept on being; and this is close to contradiction. If, however, we assume that something keeps on being, we must envisage its continued existence. And if the kind of objects we are concerned with are those which can be seen, touched, or acted upon, this means understanding them as continuing to exist in the space to which we have access in perception and action, and hence in which we ourselves are.

Thus the connection between our concept of a single (identical) enduring object of perception and action and that of the place in which it endures unperceived is intrinsic; and this extends to the conception of events or episodes involving such objects. Where concepts are connected in this way, one cannot be fully employed in the absence of others. So we can see that Piaget's investigations, which trace the co-ordinated emergence of the use of these connected concepts, have, at least in part, a clear philosophical basis.[10]

So far, as we are concerned with the infant's transition from episodic to enduring objects, we are, therefore, concerned with the notion of identity, upon which a particular differentiation of subjective and objective turns. Further, it is clear that we regard one another both as enduring physical objects and also as persons in relation; so we can take such a representation as the terminus of what Piaget describes as the 'decentering' from initial episodic subjectivity.

What is not marked in our common-sense concepts, however, is any line of development of concepts of self and other from the episodic state to this terminus. Piaget clearly holds that there is such a development; but he does not, so far as I can see, describe how it takes place. And in relation to this topic the remarks he does offer seem unsatisfactory in several connected respects.

Piaget (Piaget and Inhelder 1969) stresses that the first state is one of 'adualism', in which 'there does not yet exist any consciousness of self; that is, any boundary between between the internal or experienced world and the world of external realities' (p. 22).

We can certainly understand the claim that the infant does not distinguish as we do between states of the self which are experiences of encountering objects, and the encountered objects themselves. Our distinction includes the idea that the objects, but not the episodic states of the self, are enduring, and this is just the conception the infant lacks.

Piaget's adualism has, however, a further and more difficult aspect. He tends to describe the early episodic phase as if it contained *no element of representation whatever* related to the later distinctions between internal and external, or self and other.

It is easy to see how these two aspects of adualism might be connected in Piaget's thinking. The idea would be that just as the infant's episodic objects are not properly regarded as objective until he represents them as enduring, so his experiences are not properly regarded as subjective until he represents them as in contrast to the objects themselves. So he cannot regard his own states as 'internal' or pertaining to himself, or his objects as 'external' or other. So – finally – he registers no distinction at all which bears on that between internal and external, or self and other.

The last step does not follow. It leaves out the obvious possibility that the infant's experience may contain distinctions between self and other, inner and outer, and so forth, which are not as full as ours, but which none the less shape his 'world'. Such distinctions might be precursors of ours, while still requiring to be developed or built up.[11]

Piaget's failure to consider this possibility entails both an implausibility and an incompleteness in his account. The implausibility comes out when he describes the behaviour of babies in terms of adualism.

> Insofar as the self remains undifferentiated, and thus unconscious of itself, all affectivity is centered on the child's own body and action, since only with the dissociation of the self from the other or non-self does decentration, whether affective or cognitive, become possible. The root notion in the term 'narcissism' is valid provided we make it clear that an unconscious centering due to undifferentiation is not at all like a conscious centering of one's emotional life upon the self which can occur in later life. (Piaget and Inhelder, 1969, p. 22)

This brings the reader up short. For the idea that the young infant's feelings are focused on himself and his activities sharply contradicts the sense we have, in observing babies or relating to them, that their attention, feeling, and activity is almost from the first focused also on what they in some way already take as outer and other. Here our natural impression of infant behaviour surely draws us away from Piaget's argument and towards the idea that the baby has something in the nature of forerunners of our conceptions.

This consideration holds for experimental observation too. Thus Campos et al. (1983) report that infants of three months 'express fearlike withdrawal to looming stimuli', or again that infants of four months 'specifically orient their anger expressions toward the immediate source of what is frustrating' (pp. 813–24). The natural impression of withdrawal from something, or of anger directed at it, does not fit with taking fear or anger as 'centered on the child's own body and action'. Nor, of course, does experimental or common-sense observation of the infant's complex and apparently communicative early relation with his mother fit with the idea that the infant represents nothing as in any way apart from its own body and action.

The theoretical incompleteness in Piaget's account is closely related to this. He has specified a change in how the child represents things, describing both the first and final stages in the development. But he has apparently assigned the early representations no features which might explicate why or how they yield the later ones. So he appears to render the development in representation he describes quite inexplicable in terms of representation itself.

We can begin to see how this gap might be filled by considering the distinctions between self and other, and inner and outer a little further. An important part of our distinction between self and other is that a self has its own perspective, from which it confronts and encounters things. This aspect of the distinction is not necessarily dependent upon representing objects as opposed to experiences as enduring, since it concerns, as it were, only the opposed location of subject and object in an episode of experience. Part of what seems to convince us that babies take things and people as objects seems to be that they do occupy such a perspective in relation to things. Their perspective, or their occupation of it, may be as episodic as their objects; but it seems already to constitute some distinction in experience itself, as between subject and object.

Of course we cannot assimilate infantile and adult experience. The latter is not only informed by the concept of an enduring object, as Piaget stresses, but also by conceptions as to its own nature. When we see, for example, we take ourselves to do so, and we take ourselves to use our eyes. To regard infantile experience as lacking these sophisticated overlays, however, is not to cease to regard it as an encounter with something. So experience remains a perspectival matter, and hence one which encodes the distinction we want to understand. What we need to see, it seems, is how this minimal conception of perspective can be, or become, that of a self.

In connection with this it seems useful to consider a distinction which Piaget himself makes, between what he calls 'external' and 'internal' experience. Paradigms of external experience would be sight and hearing, which are from the first co-ordinated and focused upon what comes to be taken as external objects, and guide what comes to be intentional action involving them. As Bower (1977) stresses, an infant will from the beginning look towards a source of sound, and will be surprised if there is nothing to be touched when his hands are where an object appears to be; and also, early on, will reach and grasp things he sees. Examples of internal experience, by contrast, would be sensations of pain, pleasure, and satisfaction; as well, presumably, as those derived from flexing the muscles, breathing, and the like.[12]

To state the distinction between external and internal experience is to notice far-reaching differences in their nature and role. External experience has a variety of elements, which are elaborately co-ordinated, both in the way they occur and in their structure,[13] so as to specify external objects of perception and action as having a range of properties. Internal experiences do not specify such objects, but rather guide action, by association with it and objects. These differences – and others which could be brought out if the topic were treated more systematically – seem correlatives of the way the distinction relates to the idea of the self.

It seems that in having external experience, we naturally direct attention outward, and take ourselves to be encountering something apart from ourselves; whereas in internal experience, we direct attention inward, and feel something to be happening to ourselves. To look seems to be to look at what is apart, even where what is looked at is oneself. When an infant looks at his feet, for example, it seems he may at first take them as things apart from himself, and that it is only gradually, and through learning how they are sources of internal experience, that he comes to assimilate them to his perspective. Again, the connection between experiences like pain and the self seems inbuilt, and to have no intelligible presupposition. An infant has to master reaching to reach towards an aching tooth, and to learn about teeth to regard the phenomenon as toothache. But it is not clear what an infant could be supposed to have to learn to feel pain as something happening to himself. We have no conception as to how else he could feel it, nor any notion of further primitives from which this feeling could be built up.

This suggests that we may take experience itself as involving kinds of information and ways of presenting them which already serve to distinguish self and other, and inner and outer, and which determine how these distinctions are woven into the frame of a perspective. It may simply be, for example, that in having external experience the infant is inclined to take himself as encountering something as existing apart, whereas in having internal experience he feels things to be happening to himself. And granted even the barest distinction of this kind in experience, we can see how it would be in the nature of experience itself to fill it out.

External experience is a natural source of information about events outside and impinging on the body, and internal experience about events inside it. So external experiences systematically focus attention on events, objects, and places in the space around the infant's body, and internal experiences on the space inside it. The space outside his body is thus (normally) presented to the infant in ways systematically different from places within it. Since presentations of things outside form one connected field, and those of events inside another, the things outside can come to be uniformly taken as those the infant encounters as distinct, and has a perspective on; while what happens inside is presented as happening to him, and so comes to be part of the locus of the perspective itself.

Internal experience is felt as located in, and directs attention to, an area which extends from the centre of the body out to the skin. External experience directs attention and action in space beyond this. Tactile experience has a double focus, which marks a boundary in these fields. The feeling of tactile contact is that it is with something outer, which is a potential object of further external experience; and also that it is of something happening to the self, and so connected with internal experience originating from the place of contact. So the intrinsic nature of these experiences themselves seem to go some way towards starting, and also filling out, the delineation of what is, and is not, the self.

So far as such a bounded image is something a baby has to construct, it seems he may do so in part just by lying or wriggling and feeling contact, touching and seeing his own body, and so on. In this he may well both use and build up an image in which he is already partly distinguished from, but related to, what is not himself. Similar observations would seem to apply to basic bodily activities. like breathing, taking nourishment, and so on, in which volition is connected with external, tactile and internal experience, in a variety of ways.[14]

Although they contradict his strictest statements about adualism, these ideas about the self do not seem really opposed to most of Piaget's thought. His sensory-motor schemas can be regarded as representations in which internal and external experience play the contrasting roles mentioned. And in his descriptions of the infant's world he often implies distinctions passed over in his summarizing comments. For example, speaking of the kind of coordination of external experience stressed above, Piaget (1955) says that 'if the object thus begins to be deployed in space, this space remains delimited by the child's zone of action; space, therefore, does not yet consist in a system of relations between objects, but is only an aggregation of relations centered on the subject' (p. 118).

Here the idea is that the child inhabits, and relates to things in, an egocentric space, which he will later locate within the objective one of adult thought. This seems correct, but also to involve precisely the sort of natural distinction between self and other that we have been considering. An egocentric perspective is one in which subject and object are distinguished, with the self at the centre. Piaget's phrase 'relations centered on the subject' suggests that he takes the things related to this centre as presented as apart (from the centre), and so, in effect, as distinct from the self.

Had Piaget considered internal experience in this context he would surely have had to regard it, not as centred on the self, but rather as further determining where the centre was and what it was like there. And this would, in fact, be an area potentially marked off and bounded by tactile experience, and so relatively fully demarcated as that of the infantile bodily self.

III

In light of the above it seems that an account of infantile experience should allow for an early, if rudimentary, distinction between self and other. So let us now consider how Piaget's views might be affected, if this were taken explicitly into account.

One of Piaget's findings is that young children systematically attribute to things they encounter psychological properties related to their own: the child who fears fire regards it as malevolent, and so on. Piaget (1929) stresses that this animism is 'a primitive property of mind' (p. 262), exercised in response to certain kinds of movement. Evidently it exists *ab initio*, and is only restricted to appropriate objects over time.

Piaget does not consider this in discussing episodic objects, presumably because he takes it that for them there is no distinction between self and other, and so no other to interpret this way. If we allow for the distinction, a natural extension of Piaget's thought would be to hold that this primitive tendency operates with respect to it. So the infant encountering the episodic as other will endow this other with feelings corresponding to its own. This, however, means in effect that it will have imagined object-relations, and with a very primitive sort of animate objects.

On this view the way we take the child to represent its episodic others will depend upon how we regard the psychology of the child itself. Both psychoanalysis and recent empirical work suggests that this should be taken as continuous with what shows later; and so as including the fundamentals of hatred, greed, envy, and so forth, as well as the more benign emotions we are used to associating with babies. In their recent survey of research on emotion, Campos et al. (1983) conclude that adult emotions are expressions of a set of differentiated core emotion states which are present throughout the lifespan and undergo development with time. So, following this view, we might assume that primitive core emotions are present in the episodic phase, and may change with it. Then it appears that early fantasized objects will be both experienced and animated in terms of very primitive feelings.

It seems that the most important objects of feeling and action for the baby include the mother's breast (or the bottle), and perhaps other parts of her body, such as her face and hands. Piaget (1955) describes the way the infant watches the breast or bottle intently, its ardour, greed, and passion in sucking it, rage when it is withheld, and so on. Observations of this kind gain further significance from the thought that the infant may endow episodic objects with feelings commensurate with its own, and also understand its relation to them in terms of its own bodily experience. Viewed this way, such ideas as that the infant may feel the breast as, say, something quite wonderful, and a source of soothing internal pleasure, or again terrible and a cause of frustration and pain, seem well within the realm of possibility.

Finally, it seems that experiences with such an object may naturally lead to its being construed in ways quite strange to adult common sense. Thus according to Piaget (1955), if a child feeds and experiences satisfaction, it should fuse 'into [the breast] the impression of effort, desire, and satisfaction which accompany the [feeding]' (pp. 42, 43). The infant will presumably also not distinguish the breast from the milk taken in, so there will be a continuous episode in which an object (or a series of related objects) is registered in external, then oral, then internal experience. In such a case it may be that the infant feels it takes in something which was external, animate, and satisfying, and that this has a fate within, or becomes assimilated to, itself. This, however, begins to approach Klein's account of the infant's internalizing the breast in fantasy, and imagining that it has good or bad things inside, which can sometimes be got rid of by defecation, and so on.

It thus appears that once we grant a distinction between self and other, and hence animism and emotion, in an episodic phase, natural extensions of Piaget's views approximate Klein's. The degree of approximation, indeed, will evidently depend in large part upon which of Piaget's views are emphasized. As we have seen, Piaget takes children to alter their psychological representations of others in accord with such Freudian mechanisms as projection, and there is no reason why these should not operate early, or be inbuilt. And the main constituents of Klein's account of the paranoid–schizoid position are the closely related mechanisms she described, together with very primitive emotions and relations to episodic objects.

These speculations gain point from the fact that experimental evidence suggests that there is indeed such an episodic phase of representation as Klein and Piaget describe, and that it begins to be resolved in early infancy. Thus Bower (1977) describes

> a simple optical arrangement that allows one to present infants with multiple images of a single object. . . . If one presents the infant with a multiple image of its mother – say three 'mothers' – the infant of less than 5 months of age is not disturbed at all but will in fact interact with all three 'mothers' in turn. If the setup provides one mother and two strangers, the infant will preferentially interact with its mother and still show no signs of disturbance. However, past the age of 5 months (after the coordination of place and movement), the sight of three 'mothers' becomes very disturbing to the infant. At this same age a setup of one mother and two strangers has no effect. I would contend that this in fact shows that the young infant (less than five months old) thinks that it has a multiplicity of mothers, whereas the older infant knows that it has only one. (p. 217)

This surely admits interpretation along the lines Bower indicates, as showing that although at 4 months the infant takes its mother as a psychological other, it does not regard her as a single object as opposed to a multiplicity of episodic ones. But by 5 months, apparently, it opposes uniqueness to episodic multiplicity, and takes mother as one.

Also, it seems that at 4 months the infant takes distinct bodily parts, rather than a person as a whole, as the object of experiential encounters. Thus consider an observation cited by Campos et al. (1983).

Stenberg and Campos did address the socialization of the target of a specific emotional frustration. They reported that by 4 months of age, infants specifically orient their anger expressions toward the immediate source of what is frustrating them (the experimenter's hands); by seven months of age, they direct their anger towards the social source of the frustration (the experimenter or the mother who is permitting the impediment to movement. (p. 824)

This suggests that the 4-month-old baby takes its mother's hands as things to be angry with, and so on, and hence as (part) objects. The same would presumably apply to other parts of her body, such as her face and eyes, and also and particularly her breasts. Later, apparently, the baby directs anger towards the person, a more unified representation of whom would thus seem to have been built up in the interval.

Together these experiments can be taken to indicate that in the fifth month the infant begins to move from representing its mother as a multiplicity of episodic and part objects to taking her as a single and physically unified person. If this is so then such a synthesis as Piaget assumed, and Klein described as the transition from the paranoid–schizoid to the depressive position, does indeed take place, and at the time in infancy Klein located.

Such a change must on any understanding be an important one. So it may now be of interest to consider it more abstractly. This may help us to see both how features of Klein's and Piaget's theories are related to the general notions of experience and identity involved in them, and also the sort of role these notions might be expected to play in other descriptions of this development.

Taking experiences as encounters with objects, as we naturally do, serves to integrate them and render them comprehensible, by connecting them via the concept of the object. Thus while encountering everyday things and persons we have a vast range of variety of sensory and emotional experience, and in using our everday concepts of objects, we connect these experiences in a picture of a stable and comprehensible world.

When we understand an experience as an encounter with an object of a certain kind, we assume that it is actually or potentially related to many other experiences, of the kind that would also be had in encountering such an object. This is part of the connection in question, and allows us to distinguish how things subjectively seem from how they objectively are. In the absence of appropriate further experiences we are bound to revise our original understanding, and account for it by some such means as deceptive appearance, illusion, and so on.

Now it seems natural that a phase of representing things egocentrically and episodically should precede that of representing them in a more objective way. This is because of the natural assumption that a creature trying to understand things on the basis of a flow of data will first gain some grip on what happens in important episodes, and then extend his spatial and temporal horizons from these. A conception of episodic objects would enable him to do this. As this suggests, however, such a conception should connect fewer data, and less stringently, than one of objects as enduring.

In an episodic world, data would first be integrated in the conception of an object during an episode. In agreement with this, infants very early seem to take objects as things which can be seen, heard, tasted, and the like. Such a representation can evidently be improved in various ways. Episodes can be lengthened to encompass more data, as they apparently are. Also, episodic objects can be compared and contrasted. The ways they accompany or follow one another, the ways they are affected by strivings of various kinds, and so on, can be registered and thought about. Still, this seems likely to be logically weaker than the connections effected by conceiving the same experiences as encounters with objects which last from episode to episode. For in this case data are still linked in episodes, and these registered and compared; but in addition each episode is itself connected with others, as it was not before, as an encounter with one object met on numerous occasions. This seems to be integration of another order, as well as that which we take to correspond to reality.

Thus it seems we should expect an episodic phase to begin with objects having, as it were, the minimum of objectivity, and to work up from there. Conversely, we should expect the early episodic world to be not only unintegrated, but also subjectively deformed. There would seem little way of distinguishing what an object was like from how it seemed in an episode. Early episodic feelings, and early projections or animations, should be relatively unconstrained and unmitigated by recognition of the possibility of error, bias, or complexity in the object. Again normal control of experience, or wilful distortion of it, would seem hard to distinguish episodically from the exercise of power over objects. For example, terminating an episode by breaking off sensory contact might be confused with anihilating an object, and fantastic egocentric imagining could be conflated with experience of reality generally.

Now the shift from episodic representation, as located by Bower's experiment, seems to have a number of observable concomitants. The fifth month is, as Bower notes the time at which at which infants co-ordinate place and movement, in tracking objects in space; and they also apparently start to use visual cues that specify the structure of the human body.[15] At the same time they seem to begin to scan reliably the interior details of the face which encode emotional information, and to respond to this, and to other indications, such as tone of voice, more appropriately. Also, it seems that by six months babies move about better, and hence are better able to direct the extension their own experience.

This apparently leads to a more realistic apprehension of the mother's relation to the baby. Stenberg et al. (1983) studied the results of making babies angry by taking a biscuit away. They used both the mother and a stranger, and found that the infant's response apparently depended upon roles which it assigned to both.

> the *elicitor* of the expression of anger seems to be important, even for the 7-month-old. Although the infants reacted angrily regardless of who took the biscuit away, the magnitude of the reaction was influenced by whether the mother or stranger initiated the trials ... when the mother tested the infant after the stranger had removed the biscuit a number of times, the infant showed particularly angry expressions toward the mother. On the other hand, when the frustration was initially produced by the mother, no similar increase in anger expression to the stranger was evident ... it appeared to us that that the infant may have expected the mother to comfort him or her and to end the frustrating task; when she did not, the infant expressed the anger more intensely. (p. 181)

Concentration on the role of identity may help explain why these and other developments go together. Taking the mother as one is taking her as the same entity, physically and psychologically, from episode to episode of experience. Apparently this requires working representations of encounters with various parts of her body, first felt as episodic presences, into a representation of a person who is depended on to act in certain ways. To represent its mother's body as unified the infant must take it as a spatial whole which it can to some extent keep track of, and so represent the parts as in co-ordination and as moving in space. To take the mother as the same person from episode to episode would seem to require a comparable psychological unification. The infant would have to form a psychological image of her which included and co-ordinated information from various encounters. This would mean, in effect, representing her as something like psychologically whole – as having a range of consistent and interrelated psychological characteristics, which were displayed episodically.

Consideration of these changes suggests, among other things, that in them the infant should come to think of itself as having experiences which are distinct from their objects, and liable to error.

First, the changes bring to the fore the distinction, both as regards the physical and the psychological, between episodes of experience – which are plural and temporary – and the object of experience – which is one and lasting. Secondly, the infant will presumably not go from ideas of a range of episodic objects, each of which has certain properties, simply to an idea of an enduring object which has all the properties previously manifested in episodes. These properties would not, so to speak, all just fit together in one object. Rather, representing a new sort of object will go with assigning it different, connected, properties, and hence with revising ascriptions from the previous phase. So after the episodic phase the infant should have reason to distinguish experience from its object, and to take it as admitting something like a distinction between appearance and reality.

The categories the infant uses for representing another should also be applicable to its own case, and vice versa. If so, it should also be able to think of itself as unified and lasting, both psychologically and physically. Thus as the infant distinguishes experiences from their object it should also be able to come to regard experiences as involving changes in itself, and to link these with its body. Also, if the infant can regard experience as potentially inveridical, it should be able to take itself as liable to respond to things and others inappropriately as well as appropriately.

It may be that something of this development can be seen in the behaviour of babies confronted with a 'virtual' object – an intangible visual appearance, as of an object in front of them. According to Bower (1982)

The young infants (from 4 days) showed some considerable degree of upset when their hands arrived at the location of the seen object but contacted nothing. This upset must reflect the violation of an expectancy that seen objects will be tangible. . . . If one studies the reaction of older infants to the virtual object, it is hard to see any change up to the age of approximately six months. . . . The infants are still startled by the virtual object; however, their grasping behaviour is quite different. Younger infants close their hands on the virtual object and, indeed, usually end up with their hands clenched at the object focus. Older infants stop the grasp action with their hands still open. One may also observe in older infants a variety of behaviours such as prolonged hand regard, rubbing the hands together, and banging the hand on a surface – all interspersed with further single attempts to grasp the virtual object. One could say that the infants were trying to verify that their hands were really working and had not suffered a loss of sensitivity. If one persists in observing the infant in this situation, one can usually then observe a range of exploratory *visual* behaviours. For example the infant may sway its head from side to side through an extreme arc, thereby picking up the maximum amount of motion parallax. The motion parallax thus generated is the opposite of normal . . . and is highly abnormal visually. The infant will usually then stop reaching for the virtual object. If presented with new objects in this situation, infants will not reach out until they have tested the parallax properties of the objects; then they will only reach for those objects that have normal parallax properties. (p. 124)

The progress charted here can be seen as a consequence of that from episodic to enduring representation. The 6-month-old baby seems to integrate a large range of experiential episodes, and to have a picture of the working of its own body in relation to various experiences taken as distinguished from, but related to, their objects. Hence, apparently, it can regard the experiences as veridical or misleading, and itself as judging rightly or wrongly. These differences suggest that it may be in the change from episodic to enduring representation that infantile experience acquires many of the features we associate with our own.

The behaviour shown in these observations exemplifies what Freud called 'reality testing', applied to everyday physical objects. Since a system of enduring objects and persons partly constitutes what we mean by reality, and the hypothesis of such a system allows us to integrate coherently the contents of virtually every episode of normal waking experience with every other, we can see that the change from episodic to enduring representation should coincide with what Freud calls the 'establishment of the reality principle'. Klein concentrated mainly on psychological reality, but similar points should apply to this. So perhaps something like testing the feelings of others, and willingness to assign responsibility to the self when interactions go wrong, can be seen to lead to the increased understanding apparently shown at 7 months, and the better communication evident by 8 or 9 months.

Since psychoanalysis traces pathology to infantile fantasy, the opposition of fantasy and reality is taken as particularly important. As we have seen, fantasy should be relatively unconstrained in an episodic phase; and the naturally egocentric quality of fantasy should be further heightened, since while the infant does not construe its mother as one and lasting it has no need to take her as existing apart from her contact with itself, and so less reason to take her as an independent object upon whom it depends. In these circumstances, it seems, the infant is relatively free to represent itself wishfully as the centre of a world over which it exercises great power. Hence for both Klein and Piaget, the achievement of enduring representation forces a 'decentering' which is comparable to a Copernican revolution. What Klein calls the manic defences against the depressive position are a sort of Ptolemaic counter-revolution, in which the infant again tries to represent itself as at the centre of things, and controlling them. Still, her account suggests that release from responsibility for the intemperate and egocentric exercise of unbridled power more than compensates for loss of it.

Now the processes which Klein describes in terms of splitting and projection seem familiar in everyday life, in the tendency people have to see themselves, their families, clans, races, or nations as at once unrealistically good and threatened by correspondingly bad others – the familiar and ubiquitous pattern of good us/bad them. Such mechanisms may therefore be supposed to have a role in organizing people into co-operating and competing groups which is complementary to their significance for the individual, and important in its own right. For this reason I should like to conclude by considering some further observations in this light, although the connections between theory and data in them are even weaker than those above.

One notable regularity in infant behaviour seems to be the emergence of what is called stranger anxiety. Many babies seem relatively unconcerned about strangers until about 8 months, and then become notably wary or even very frightened of them, watching them closely, looking away or screaming when they approach, and so on. At about the same time there also emerges a new kind of interaction between infant and mother, which Campos et al. (1983) describe as characterized

> by the communication between infant and another becoming extended to include a whole event in the environment. During this period the infant can appreciate what in the environment is the target of the other person's emotional reaction, much as the infant at this age begins to understand the referent of the mother's pointing or gaze behaviour.... Accordingly, during this period social referencing begins. Social referencing is the deliberate search for emotional information in another person's face, voice, and gesture, to help disambiguate uncertainties in the environment, and is an instance of a two-person communication about a third event. (p. 825)

These phenomena can be partly related, since it is plausible that the baby seeks such information partly to cope with the approach of strangers, who may be feared. Other research (Feinman and Lewis, 1983) seems to indicate that this is so. There still seems to be no explanation, however, as to why infants should come to see strangers as particularly threatening, and at this time in particular.

I do not know whether Klein addresses this matter explicitly, but her theory seems to have a fairly clear application to it. So far as the infant does not fully work through the depressive position, maintaining a relation with a good object can require the setting up of a bad object elsewhere, as, so to speak, a receptacle for the unmitigated and inadmissable badness. So on this account the consolidation of a representation of the mother as a good object in a good relation to the child should be accompanied by the appearance of a 'bad' figure or figures, outside the circle of familiars. This would be the first obvious instance of the pattern noted above, with the infant representing the couple engaged in referencing as the good us, alert, among other things, to the possibility of 'bad' others.

This explanation would also fit the way a form of stranger anxiety can be observed in connection with separation protest, which seems to acquire particular force and specificity just before this time. As Schaffer (1971) reports

> crying or some other form of protest on termination of contact with an adult was apparent from the early months on ... in the first half-year infants were found to cry for attention from anyone, familiar or strange, and though responsiveness to strangers tended to be somewhat less immediate and less intense than to the mother, both could quieten the infant and the departure of

both could evoke protest. At the age of approximately seven months, however, a change took place. The infants still protested in the same situations, but now their protests were directed at solely at certain *specific* individuals. The departure of these alone elicited crying and only their renewed attention terminated the infants' distress. Strangers, quite on the contrary, upset the infant by *approaching* him. (p. 117)

Now the increase in focus on familiars here cannot be explained on the supposition that before 7 months the infants did not discriminate or remember their mothers, since they seem to have done so. Rather it seems that the mother, and her absence, came to acquire a new significance. This would be so if the infants had now worked out that she was unique, and so irreplaceable as a good partner. Such a focused image of good enduring familiars, however, seems to have as its corrollary one of potentially bad strangers, as required on the hypothesis above.

This seems to provide a picture into which the marked emergence of separation protest and stranger anxiety would both fit, and together with their precursors in earlier months. The idea would simply be that the early behaviours were episodic precursors of the later ones. The more mature versions would be more salient, both because later the objects were taken as more singular and significant, and because behaviour towards them was displayed less episodically.

Something like early stranger anxiety, in fact, seems particularly noticeable where the mother herself is presented to the infant in a way that renders her partly alien. Carpenter (1975) described how babies in the first months behave, when their mother's face is presented in strange circumstances. 'Infants would tense as they averted their gaze appearing to keep the target in peripheral view. From this position they would frequently take furtive glances. Sometimes they would turn ninety degrees and cry (p. 134). She noted that looking right away, as if to try to end the episode, was particularly frequent when infants were shown their mother's face, but speaking with another's voice. A natural explanation of this would be that the infants were taking such strange presentations of the mother as bad episodic objects which had to be watched or avoided.

Again, Cohn and Tronick (1983) observed babies of just over 3 months, comparing the way they related to their mothers in normal circumstances with their responses when the mother deliberately behaved in a 'depressed' way. The mothers gazed at the infant while keeping an expressionless face, spoke in monotone, and minimized movement and touch. Normally the infants alternated among behaviours which were interpreted as monitoring the mother, showing positive feeling towards her, and playing with her. In the abnormal circumstances, by contrast, the infants showed wariness and negative feeling, and alternated among wary watching, protesting, and looking away.

The authors took this as a response to maternal depression. It may be, however, that what most affected the infants was not the simulation of depression in particular, but rather the fact that the mother had become strange, and in a way that prompted the idea she might be bad. The observations would then be comparable with those of same sort of behaviour by Carpenter, and another instance of the way the infant shows feelings towards a strange episodic mother comparable to those later displayed towards strangers.

In the early case, on this hypothesis, the infant would have images of its mother as mutually exclusive good and bad episodic presences, and would be consolidating an episodic image linking itself and the good mother. In consequence, it would be liable to be particularly wary of something recognizable as mother-type, but strange. Later it would have an image of mother (and other familiars) and itself as persons, and more or less good. So it would now have an image of bad persons, as located outside the circle of familiars, and would be liable to be particularly wary of something recognizable as a person, but strange. Both behaviours would be instances of the familiar pattern of good us/bad them. The difference would be that early on the mother played the bad as well as the good part.

On this supposition the emergence of separation protest and stranger anxiety at after 6 months would be different aspects of the same synthesis, and closely connected with social referencing. As the mother and other familiars were represented as one, the split between good and bad in their episodic images would be transformed into, and maintained as, the first such division in the social world. I do not know how much weight should be placed on such data, since they lack the fullness of content which enables psychological concepts to get a grip. But here, as well as elsewhere, Klein's theory seems to provide explanations of phenomena which seem important, and which deserve further consideration.[16]

NOTES

1 Some recent work related to experiment is surveyed in Mussen (1983). I take two articles from there as reference points: Harris, 'Infant Cognition'; and Campos, Barrett, Lamb, Goldsmith, and Stenberg, 'Socioemotional Development'.

   Two full, lucid, and authoritative introductions to Klein's work have been written by Hanna Segal (1978, 1981).

   Although Klein's theories remain controversial, particularly in the United States, the degree of acceptance acknowledged – as long ago, say, as in the critique in Kernberg (1969) – is in fact considerable, and apparently growing. Most of the views discussed below now seem, so far as I can determine, fairly common among Freudian (and also many Jungian) analysts.

   Further work directly related to both Piaget and psychoanalysis, and touching many issues not discussed below, is reviewed in Greenspan (1979).

2	Confirmation in common-sense psychology and the relation of this to psycho-analysis are discussed in Hopkins (1986).

3	Piaget (Piaget and Inhelder, 1969) agreed with this sort of interpretation of play, stating that 'Symbolic play frequently deals with unconscious conflicts: sexual interests, defense against anxiety, phobias, aggression or identification with aggressors, withdrawal from fear of risk or competition, etc.' He refers to Klein and Anna Freud in this context, and holds that the symbolism of play resembles that of dreams, although with a difference of emphasis. 'The vague boundaries between the conscious and the unconscious as evidenced in the symbolic play of children suggests rather that the symbolism of the dream is analogous to the symbolism of play (p. 62).

4	This can be seen, for example, in his case history of the Rat Man, so called because one of his main symptoms was a propensity to imagine that his father was being tortured by rats gnawing into his anus. Freud (1975, vol. X, pp. 155ff) describes his infantile neurosis, and the derivation of his symptoms from childhood Oedipal hostility towards his father. For the emergence in transference and memory of some persecuting images of the patient's father, plausibly constitutive of his super-ego, see the episode described in Freud's notes on pp. 283–5. The 'mouse or Butzen' or the faecal flea reported from Klein's patients below were plainly similar in role to the rats in this patient's imaginings, and Klein explained them in the same way as Freud had. Some other connections between this case and Klein's theories are noted in Hopkins (1982).

5	Freud had indicated something like this in the case of the Rat Man, noting how both his falling ill and his recovery seemed to turn on his finding 'a living like-ness' of himself in the rats which tortured his father (vol. X, p. 216).

6	Klein introduces the term 'projective identification' (vol. III, p. 8) for the mechanism instantiated when a person imagined part of himself entering and becoming identified with another in this sort of way. This concept became central to her later work, and has been developed in a number of important ways by her followers, particularly Bion. On this see the discussion in Segal (1978). Ogden (1982) relates this notion to some work in the United States.

7	The relation of Freudian and Kleinian accounts of introjection, fantasy, and identification to the the concept of the self as a whole is discussed philosophi-cally in Wollheim (1984).

8	Klein (1975, vol. IV, pp. 204–6). Richard could be seen to form such images regularly: cf. his fingering Klein's frock and speaking of the 'funny old woman' (p. 219), or the appearance of the 'monster' (p. 321), and the discussion in Klein's Note II, pp. 325–6.

9	In addition to children, Klein had analysed both depressive and manic patients, in which such anxieties and defences played a particularly significant role. Thus a person's imagining that he had irreparably damaged the good object might be a source of depression, or as against this he might manically imagine that everything was wonderful, or his feelings might swing between such alternatives.

A number of Klein's pupils were able to use her concepts in the analysis of schizophrenia. Segal (1978) contains a very clear account of the inter-pretation of splitting, projective identification, and other phenomena in the analysis of a schizophrenic patient (p. 62ff), and notes to other work in this field.

10 There have been a number of philosophical discussions of the connection between identity and objectivity. Hume sketched the way he thought we 'unite the broken appearances' so as to take distinct but resembling perceptual impressions of the same object, and thereby postulate bodies existing continuously, and independently of our minds. Kant put the matter in the explicitly wider framework taken up by Piaget, arguing that our representations of external reality and mind were interdependent. Mental items had to be unified to be taken as related to objects, but also to be taken as parts of the subject's mind. Through one activity, which Kant called 'synthesis in the imagination', we form a representation of ourselves at once as inhabiting a world of spatiotemporally and causally ordered objects, and as possessors of united, self-conscious minds. Piaget and Klein can be seen as continuing the Kantian tradition, but in science, and partly describing the relevant synthesis in complementary ways.

An outstanding recent discussion is that of Strawson (1954), especially chap. 2.

11 The sense that Piaget has left this out is strengthened by further reflection. His description of adualism assimilates three distinct ideas. Each is consistent with the possibility that the infant uses concepts or makes distinctions which are precursors of our later ones, but his discussion obscures this.

The first idea is that the infant is not self-conscious, that he does not at first think of himself as himself, as a self, or whatever. This is clearly consistent with the idea that he does make distinctions which pave the way for, or partly constitute, his later representation of himself in this way.

The second is that for the infant there is no boundary between what is internal and external. Presumably there would be such a boundary if the infant were fully self-conscious. But lack of self-consciousness does not entail absence of a boundary, for there might be one which was not yet thought of as such. Also, there is a difference between a distinction and a boundary if the latter implies knowledge of the things bounded. For clearly a baby might distinguish, for example, between episodes of vision which we should take as pertaining to the outer, and pain, which we should take as inner, but without yet knowing what is distinguished from what, and so without taking the distinction as a boundary.

The third is that the infant does not distinguish between experiences themselves (as opposed, for example, to spatial locations) as external or internal. This is yet another point, and again not inconsistent with the idea of related precursor distinctions. For the baby could distinguish different sorts of experience, in the sense of responding (feeling or judging) differently to or because of having them, but without yet representing experience as opposed to external reality explicitly at all. This point is touched on in recent psychological work, which describes the infant's early experience as *amodal*, that is, not yet represented by him as in one sensory mode as opposed to another, nor, again, related by him to one sense-organ or another (Harris, 1983, pp. 707ff).

12 Piaget makes this distinction only to stress that it is without significance in the context of adualism. For example he argues against 'a realism which is as

unpsychological when it deals with internal as when it deals with external experience' which would mean that 'all the impression of effort, expectation, satisfaction, etc., which intervenes in the course of the actions, should be attributed to an internal substantial subject located in the consciousness' (Piaget, 1955, p. 224). The idea of an internal substantial subject, however, is very far from that of infantile subjectivity which consists partly in having a perspective.

13   Bower (1977) illustrates the way the outer senses employ information with a common structure, and hence represent objects as in a connected field. Shape seems registered in oral (tactile) as well as visual experience, from the first (Meltzoff and Borton, 1979).

14   The idea of the self thus built up would be that of a bodily self engaged in basic physical activities, and hence, in effect, Freud's bodily ego. This seems to reflect facts about what we are. That external and internal experience should draw the boundary in this way seems a natural consequence of the information they give and the way they do so.

      In connection with the sense of self, Harris (pp. 745ff) mentions observations by Gibson and Butterworth, and also data about self-recognition in mirrors. This seems to be a more complex phenonemon, involving not only a conception of the self as a body but also the ability to recognize that body as externally displaced.

      Psychoanalytic work on the self and skin includes Bick (1968) and Symington (1985).

      Since this section was composed I have seen Stern (1983), which, although written from an empirical perspective and directed to further conclusions, seems to me to anticipate and complement the arguments above.

15   See Bertenthal et al. (1985) and Campos et al. (1983, pp. 824–5).

16   The author would like to thank James Russell and Sharon Numa for helpful comments on an earlier draft of this chapter.

REFERENCES

Abraham, K. 1973: *Selected Papers on Psycho-Analysis*. London: The Hogarth Press.

Bertenthal, B. I., Proffitt, D. R. Spretner, N. B. and Thomas, M. A. 1985: The development of infant sensitivity to biomechanical motion. *Child Development*, 56, 532–43.

Bick, E. 1968: The experience of the skin in early object relations. *International Journal of Psycho-Analysis*, 49, 484–6.

Bower, T. G. R. 1977: Blind babies see with their ears. *New Scientist*, 73, 255–7.
      1982: *Development in Infancy*. San Francisco, Calif.: W. H. Freeman.

Campos, J. J., Barrett, K. C., Lamb, M. E., Goldsmith, H. H. and Stenberg, C. 1983: Socioemotional development. In P. Mussen (ed.), *Handbook of Child Psychology*, vol. 3. New York: John Wiley.

Carpenter, G. (1975): Mother's face and the newborn. In R. Lewin (ed.), *Child Alive*. London: Maurice Temple-Smith.

Clark, S. and Wright, C. (eds) 1986: *Psychoanalysis, Mind, and Science*. Oxford: Basil Blackwell.

Cohn, J. F. and Tronick, E. Z. 1983: Three-month-old infants' reaction to simulated maternal depression. *Child Development*, 54, 185–93

Feinman, S. and Lewis, M. 1983: Social referencing at ten months: a second-order effect on infant's responses to strangers. *Child Development*, 54, 878–87.

Freud, S. 1975: *Standard Edition of the Complete Psychological Works of Sigmund Freud*. London: The Hogarth Press.

Greenspan, S. I. 1979: Intelligence and adaptation: an integration of psychoanalytic and Piagetian developmental psychology. *Psychological Issues*, 47/48, 34–49.

Harris, P. L. 1983: Infant cognition. In P. Mussen (ed.), *Handbook of Child Psychology*, vol. 2. New York: John Wiley.

Hopkins, J. 1982: Introduction: philosophy and psychoanalysis. In R. Wollheim and J. Hopkins (eds.), *Philosophical Essays on Freud*. Cambridge: Cambridge University Press.

1986: Epistemology and depth psychology: critical reflections on Grunbaum's *Foundations of Psychoanalysis*. In S. Clark and C. Wright (eds), *Psychoanalysis, Mind and Science*. Oxford: Basil Blackwell.

Kernberg, O. 1969: A contribution to the ego-psychological critique of the Kleinian school. *International Journal of Psycho-Analysis*, 50, 317–33.

Klein, M. 1975: *The Complete Works of Melanie Klein*. London: The Hogarth Press.

Lewin, R. 1975: *Child Alive*. London: Maurice Temple Smith.

Meltzoff, A. N. and Borton, W. 1979: Intermodal matching by human neonates. *Nature*, 282, 403–4.

Mussen, P. (ed.) 1983: *Handbook of Child Psychology*, vol. 3. New York: John Wiley.

Ogden, T. 1982: *Projective Identification and Psychotherapeutic Technique*. New York: Jason Aronsen.

Piaget, J. 1929: *The Child's Conception of the World*. London: Routledge and Kegan Paul.

1955: *The Child's Construction of Reality*. London: Routledge and Kegan Paul.

Piaget, J. and Inhelder, B. 1969: *The Psychology of the Child*. London: Routledge and Kegan Paul.

Schaffer, H. R. 1971: *The Growth of Sociability*. Harmondsworth, Middx.: Penguin Books.

Segal, H. 1978: *Introduction to the Work of Melanie Klein*. London: The Hogarth Press.

1981: *Klein*. Glasgow: Fontana.

Stenberg, C. R., Campos, J. J. and Emde, R. N. 1983: The facial expression of anger in seven-months-old infants. *Child Development*, 54, 178–84.

Stern, D. N. 1983: The early development of schemas of self, other, and 'self with other'. In J. D. Lichtenberg and S. Kaplan (eds), *Reflections on Self Psychology*. New York: The Analytic Press.

Strawson, P. F. 1954: *Individuals*. London: Methuen.

Symington, J. 1985: The survival function of primitive omnipotence. *International Journal of Psycho-Analysis*, 66, 214–31.

Wollheim, R. 1984: *The Thread of Life*. Cambridge: Cambridge University Press.

Wollheim, R. and Hopkins, J. (eds) 1982: *Philosophical Essays on Freud*. Cambridge: Cambridge University Press.

PART IV

Issues in Stage Theory

8

Concept formation and moral development

Gareth B. Matthews

Is it a good idea to conceive moral development as concept displacement? That is, is it a good idea to conceive moral development as getting a better concept than one used to have of honesty, courage, justice, obligation, or whatever, and then, perhaps, an even better one than that?

How would the story go? Consider the concept of obligation. One might say that a child starts out with a very external concept of obligation. An obligation would be, according to this primitive concept, something someone *else* holds one responsible for. Typically, that someone else would be an authority figure – Mother, Father, Teacher, Priest, Policeman. The embedded concept of being held responsible might also be external in that it had to do with physical punishment and material reward. Mother tells me not to raid the cookie jar. She goes off to the grocer's. I am obliged not to eat any cookies while she is away. If I am very small, perhaps my understanding of being held responsible for keeping my hands out of the cookie jar would be limited to the understanding that if I do take another cookie and Mother finds out, I shall be spanked.

Getting a more advanced concept of obligation might then consist in getting a more nearly internal concept of what it is to be held responsible, and then, later, as coming to think of oneself as a moral authority. At a certain point, then, physical punishment might no longer need to be the sanction; the look of disappointment on Mother's face would be enough. At this point, though, my concept of obligation would still be somewhat external in that there would have to be someone outside me, some external authority figure, to hold me responsible for whatever it is I am obligated to do. But now approval would itself be reward enough and disapproval a satisfactory punishment.

In the third stage of moral development I would sometimes be my own authority figure, my own lawgiver. I could then recognize an obligation to be brave or to tell the truth, even when there was no likelihood that Mother or Father, Teacher or Priest, would catch me out. To be sure, if I did fulfill my obligation, I might want the approval of some authority figure. I am only human. And if I lied or behaved in a cowardly fashion, I would doubtless prefer that no authority figure found out. But at the third stage I would find nothing odd or paradoxical in the suggestion that I have obligations to do this or that, or to behave in this way or that, that are not responsibilities specifically laid on me by Mother, Father, Teacher, Rabbi, or Policeman, and that are not backed by the promise of external reward or the threat of external punishment.

Is this a good way to think of moral development?

In a certain way it parallels the story of cognitive development Piaget tells in much of his early and middle writing. For a whole range of concepts (for example, concepts of life, causality, time, shadows, thinking, and so on) Piaget supposes there are sequences that satisfy this complex requirement:

(R)   There are at least two distinct and non-identical concepts, $C_1, (C_2) \ldots C_n$, such that
   (i)   each later concept in the series comes to displace its predecessor in the child's thought;
   (ii) only the last concept, C_n, can be recognized to be our adult concept of (an) F (for example, life, shadow, thinking, cause); nevertheless
   (iii) each of the earlier concepts, $C_1, (C_n) \ldots$ can be recognized to be a concept of (an) F; moreover
   (iv) this sequence of concept displacements recapitulates the history of science, or a development in the race or the culture.

Consider an example. In chapter VII of Piaget (1930), we are told that the concept of a shadow evolves through these stages (where each of the following definitions, or 'analytical hypotheses', expresses a concept specific to a single stage):

Stage 1: x is a shadow$_1$ = $_{df}$ x is stuff that emanates from objects and participates in the night.
Stage 2: x is a shadow$_2$ = $_{df}$ x is dark stuff that emanates from objects.
Stage 3: x is a shadow$_3$ = $_{df}$ x is dark stuff that emanates from objects in an effort to 'flee' the light.
Stage 4: x is a shadow$_4$ = $_{df}$ x is a region that some obstruction causes to be left unilluminated.

Piaget's idea seems to be that the body of data that speaks for this series of definitions supports the idea that there is a series of genuinely distinct shadow concepts, not just a series of stages of ever-increasing information about shadows, but a sequence of better and better concepts of what a shadow is.

It is indeed plausible to suppose that the concept captured by each of the later definitions above drives out its predecessor. After all, we adults have no place for a concept of stuff that 'emanates from objects' or tries to 'flee' the light. Thus (i) of requirement (R) would be satisfied for shadow concepts.

Presumably only the Stage 4 concept is our adult concept of a shadow; so (ii) of requirement (R) would be satisfied for these shadow concepts as well. Suppose, now, that we could somehow recognize each of these concepts captured by definitions 1–4 as *a* concept of a shadow (though not *our* concept). Then (iii) of requirement (R) would also be satisfied. Finally, if there were evidence from the history of science or of culture sufficient to make (iv) of (R) plausible, this succession of shadow concepts would seem to satisfy (R) as a whole.

This account from Piaget of the evolution of our concept of a shadow is, moderately plausible. But let us now turn to a much more celebrated application of (R), an application that is, in fact, rather unsuccessful. In *The Child's Conception of the World* Piaget (1929) claims to chart the development in the child of the concept of life (or, as I should prefer to say, of the concept of being alive):

> During the first stage everything is regarded as living which has activity or a function or a use of any sort. During the second stage, life is defined by movement, all movement being regarded as in a certain degree spontaneous. During the third stage, the child distinguishes spontaneous movement from movement imposed by an outside agent and life is identified with the former. Finally, in the fourth stage, life is restricted either to animals or to animals and plants. (pp. 194–5)

The analytical hypotheses or definitions that would express this succession of concepts seem to be these:

Stage 1: x is alive$_1$ $=_{df}$ x can do something.
Stage 2: x is alive$_2$ $=_{df}$ x can move.
Stage 3: x is alive$_3$ $=_{df}$ x can move itself.
Stage 4: x is alive$_4$ $=_{df}$ x is an animal or a plant and x can move itself.

This time it is quite implausible to suppose that requirement (R) is satisfied. Consider (i) of (R). Each of the concepts expressed in the definitions 1–3 is a concept that we adults still have! Thus we, too, have the concept of a thing's being able to do something, of a thing's being able to move, and of a thing's being able to move itself. Thus it is simply false that later concepts in the series drive out their predecessors.

It might be, of course, that young children make the mistake of using the world 'alive' to express these other concepts, for example, to express the concept of a thing's being able to move. It might even be that children misuse the word 'alive' and its cognates to express these other concepts in just the order and at just the ages Piaget says they have these, as he supposes, other concepts of life. But such misuse, even, let us suppose, such predictable misuse, would not mean that there are early concepts of life expressed by the misuse. In particular, it would not mean, as clause (iii) requires, that *we* could recognize these other concepts to be primitive concepts of life.

This point is far from trivial. Piaget contends that the thinking of young children is characterized by something he calls 'child animism' – see, for example, 1929, Part II. Animism, the attribution of life and consciousness to beings *we* know to be inanimate, is one of the major parallels Piaget thinks he finds between the thinking of (adult) 'primitive' peoples and the thinking of young children in our own culture. It supplies a significant part of the backing for Piaget's suggestion that children are like primitives. But what does 'child animism' come to? The idea seems to be that there is an age at which young children show that they subscribe, implicitly anyway, to this statement:

(a)   Everything that can do anything is alive.

A little later they reject (a), but subscribe, at least implicitly, to

(b)   Everything that can move is alive.

Later still, they reject (b), but accept, implicitly,

(c)   Everything that can move itself is alive.

What are we to suppose that a child who implicitly accepts (a) would mean by the world, 'alive'? If such a child's concept of life is just the concept of being able to do something, then, for such a child, (a) comes only to

(a*)   Everything that can do something is a thing that can do something.

Far from being the expression of a remote and primitive mentality, (a*) is the expression of a trivial truth. Of course *we* would say that the trivial truth (a*) is not properly expressed by the false sentence (a). But we would have to agree that a child who misuses 'alive' to mean 'can do something' would be mistakenly using (a) to express, not anything excitingly or outrageously false, but only the boring tautology (a*).

Similarly, the later stages of 'child animism' would come to nothing more than the acceptance of these trivial truths:

(b*)   Everything that can move is a thing that can move.
(c*)   Everthing that can move itself is a thing that can move itself.

What has gone wrong? And why is it that Piaget's story about the evolution of our concept of a shadow strikes a reader as plausible, whereas Piaget's account of the development of the concept of life seems so riddled with confusions?

I think the answer is this. In the shadow case we can suppose that children only 5 years old (the beginning of the first stage for shadow concepts) are quite good at *picking out shadows*. They may make the occasional mistake, but they are good enough at shadow identification that it is appropriate to think of them as entertaining successive *theories* about what shadows are, that is, theories about those very things that we all agree are shadows, even if we disagree about what it is to be a shadow. The successive theories are what Piaget calls 'successive shadow concepts'.

The case with the concept of life is entirely different. In that case Piaget wants us to suppose both that young children are impossibly poor at picking out living things (they suppose the sun, or a stone, or a bicycle, is alive!) and also that they develop various conceptions of what it is to be a living thing. But if young children are extremely poor at picking out living things, then they are not in a cognitive position to develop conceptions of what it is to be a living thing, even very poor and inadequate ones. They may succeed in misusing the word 'alive' and its cognates, they may even misuse them in predictable ways; but in and of itself such misuse reveals nothing about whether they even have a concept of life at all.

This conclusion squares well with recent efforts to outline a semantics that will make sense of the history of natural science. I have in mind especially the problem of understanding how it can be that, for example, in developing the science of chemistry our ancestors came to a better understanding of what water is.

Here is the puzzle. Suppose that immediately before the development of chemistry people thought of water as that one of the four elements (the others being earth, air, and fire) that is both cold and wet. In learning that water is H_2O nobody learned that the single element that is both cold and wet is H_2O. As we now know, there is no such thing as the single element that is both cold and wet. In learning that water is H_2O people actually learned to reject the Aristotelian theory of the four elements and to substitute for it a new theory. But then if, before the development of modern chemistry, people did not really know what water is, they did not have any beliefs about it at all, not even mistaken beliefs. Thus modern chemistry, it seems, could have given them a *better* understanding of what water is.

Saul Kripke (1980) has advised us to deal with such puzzles by recognizing that the expression 'water' is, in his terminology, a 'rigid designator' that picks out the natural kind, water. To be sure, we might use an accidental description to help us identify the natural kind. This description could be something quite informal, such as 'the stuff that makes up rivers and lakes, or that comes from the clouds when it rains'; it could even be the now defunct Aristotelian description, 'the elemental stuff that is both wet and cold'. The job of the description is to 'get us to' good samples of the natural kind. It can do this successfully even though it is not really a correct description of the samples it 'gets us to', let alone the expression of an adequate conception of what water is.

Now, how is it that modern chemistry brought with it a better understanding of what water is? It was by our ancestors being able to pick out water pretty successsfully long before anybody had a good theory of what *that stuff*, the natural kind, water, is. Then chemical theory came along and gave them a better understanding of what that very stuff is.

Shadows constitute a natural kind. If we suppose young children to be reasonably good at picking out shadows, we thereby suppose them to be in a cognitive position to form successively better theories as to what a shadow is. For all I know, their successive theories parallel theories in the history of science, or of culture, as to what *those very things* (shadows) are.

Living things also constitute a natural kind. But it is part of Piaget's contention that children start out with miserably poor abilities to pick out living things. According to Piaget, they start out supposing that stones, the sun, and bicycles are living things. If Piaget is right, children start out completely unable to pick out the natural kind, living thing. Having no cognitive anchor in the natural kind, they are not in position to develop better and better theories (or concepts) of what a living thing is. Piaget's account is thus incoherent.

All this has interesting parallels in moral development. It is significant that Piaget, though he wrote a very important book on moral development (Piaget, 1948), tended to shy away from conceiving moral development as concept displacement. In his book he gives us evidence that could be used to try to tell a concept-displacement story; but he does not himself tell that story.

Consider, for example, the evidence Piaget gives us of the stages in which children come to understand what lying is. First, there is the stage at which the child can say no more in answer to the question, 'What is lying?' than 'It's naughty words' (Piaget, 1948, p. 141). Second, there is the stage at which the child will respond by explaining that to lie is to say something false. Third, there is the stage at which the child can first explain that lying is saying something that is false with the intention of deceiving someone.

So we could have these three analytical hypotheses:

x is a lie$_1$ $=$ $_{df}$ x is something naughty to say.
x is a lie$_2$ $=$ $_{df}$ x is a false statement.
x is a lie$_3$ $=$ $_{df}$ x is a false statement made with the intention of deceiving someone.

It is highly significant that Piaget makes, at most, half this move. It is also significant that he never makes entirely clear what reason he has for not making the whole move. Thus, after giving us the evidence that would seem to support saying that children at the first stage have the concept of lying given in the first analytic hypothesis above, he says this:

> It should be noted in the first place that no mere verbal confusion is here at work. The child who defines a lie as being a 'naughty word' knows perfectly well that lying consists in not speaking the truth. He is not, therefore, mistaking one thing for another, he is simply identifying them one with another by what seems to us a quaint extension of the world 'lie'. (1948, pp. 141–2)

Piaget never tells us how he knows, or how we could know, that 'the child who defines a lie as being a "naughty word" knows perfectly well that lying consists in not speaking the truth'.

Piaget does suggest that, at the second stage the child may have difficulty distinguishing between 'an involuntary error' and 'an intentional lie', that is, a lie more properly so called. He speaks of a tendency in children at this stage 'to consider lies in a purely realistic manner and independently of the intentions involved' (p. 145). So, in effect, he does distinguish two alleged concepts of a lie, the one given in the second definition above, the other given in the third.

Why then does he not accept the concept of 'naughty words' as a primitive concept of a lie? The answer may be that it is too implausible *for us* to consider 'naughty words' as a concept of a lie, even a very primitive concept of a lie. (But notice, it is also too implausible for us to consider 'can do something' as a concept of life, even a very primitive concept of life.)

The second putative concept obviously fares much better. We, in our dealings with children, move effortlessly from talk of 'telling lies' to talk of 'telling falsehoods', where the requirement of deceptive intent is left out, or at least left unstated. When we are fighting deception we tend to concentrate on the goal of truth-telling and ignore the difference between honest mistakes and falsehoods that are meant to deceive.

The fact remains that a child who has not mastered the idea of intentional deception does not yet have the concept of a lie. Why not simply say that? Of course one consequence of saying that might be that, strictly speaking, there would be no such thing as moral development with respect to understanding what lying is. Perhaps the only development relevant to an appreciation of what lying is would be the change from pre-moral thinking about telling the truth to moral thinking about telling the truth. Piaget seems not to want to limit himself to that. Nor do I. So we should cast about for another way to approach the data.

The child's developing sophistication about shadows, we should recall, can be certified as better and better thinking *about shadows* (rather than merely a transition from pre-shadow thinking to genuine shadow thinking) if, even at the early stages, the child is reasonably good at picking out shadows. By contrast, Piaget's data on concepts of living things in young children seem not to allow for a similarly coherent account of increasing sophistication in thinking about living things. The data suggest that young children are hopelessly bad at distinguishing living things from non-living ones. If that is so, young children could hardly be said to have latched onto the natural kind, living thing.

Is there a way of providing for the child's increasing understanding of what lying is that parallels, or parallels somewhat, the suggested story about shadows, rather than the unsuccessful one about living things?

There is; but to exhibit the parallel a concession must first be made and then things complicated a bit. The concession is that moral kinds – deeds such as lying and acting bravely, virtues such as courage and fairness, and vices such as dishonesty and cowardice – are not natural kinds. (I cannot defend that claim here. A helpful defence would require another chapter.)

Still, although moral kinds are not natural kinds, they do have a cognitive structure based on shared paradigms that enables each of us in our culture to latch onto several moral kinds at a very tender age. As we grow up our understanding of each moral kind tends to get deepened along four different dimensions: one enlarges one's stock of paradigms; one undertakes to isolate the relevant features that the paradigms share and so to analyse the nature of the kind; one comes to appreciate the range of non-paradigmatic instances that are close relatives of the kind; and one learns to adjudicate conflicting moral claims that arise from different moral kinds.

For the moral kind, lying, a central paradigm in our culture is the case of falsely denying one has disobeyed an authority figure so as to escape blame or punishment. For example, one denies having taken the cookie from the cookie jar, or having played with and dropped Father's cherished meerschaum pipe. Taking the cookie, or playing with the pipe, was a naughty thing to do. Denying that one did it is an additional naughtiness.

This kind of case remains central to our understanding of what lying is, even after Father and Mother cease to be the central authority figures and even when denying misdeeds is only one kind of case that is important. A child who can recognize the relevant naughtiness as lying has already latched onto the moral kind, lying.

It will be objected that I am making a naïve mistake here of the kind that Socrates's hapless interlocutors are always making in the early Platonic dialogues. An example of lying, even a paradigm example, is not *what lying is*. Surely, the objection continues, only someone who can define 'lying' satisfactorily really knows what lying is and only such a person has succeeded in latching onto the moral kind, lying.

The reply to this is twofold. First, it is an open question whether any of us can give an entirely satisfactory definition of 'lying'. (We should not be surprised that the early Platonic dialogues end in perplexity!) Yet most of us have a working grasp of what lying is. Therefore, having a working grasp of what lying is, is something other than being able to give an entirely satisfactory definition of 'lying'. In fact, it can consist in having a basic understanding of central paradigms of lying.

Second, Socrates's technique in the early Platonic dialogues requires his interlocutors (and his readers!) to test out suggested definitions with their own intuitions. Thus Socrates in Book I of the *Republic* rejects Cephalus' definition of 'justice' ('telling the truth and paying your debts') by asking, rhetorically, whether one should return a weapon to its owner if, in the meantime, the owner has gone mad. As readers we are expected to answer, confidently, 'No'. But on what basis can we give that answer if we have, as yet, no definition of 'justice'? Clearly such testing of suggested definitions by counterexample is a futile exercise unless we already have a working grasp of the relevant moral kind. Having such a grasp may consist simply in having a basic understanding of central paradigms.

Piaget, we recall, claims that, quite early on, children can recognize lying pretty well, though the best they can do at explaining what a lie is, is to say something like 'Lies are naughty words'. My suggestion is that a somewhat fuller description, such as, 'Saying something naughty the way I did this afternoon', may indeed be sufficient to latch onto a core paradigm for lying.

Moral development takes place, then, across four dimensions. First, there is the dimension of paradigms. A fabrication to escape punishment is a good first paradigm for lying. A misrepresentation to gain advantage may be a second paradigm. (Susan says she doesn't know what time it is – though she does, really – so as to be able to watch the rest of the TV programme.) A group conspiracy to flout authority may be a third. (Albert tells the teacher he did not see who shot the spitwad even though he saw Leonard to it; perhaps Leonard is Albert's friend, perhaps Albert is afraid of Leonard; perhaps Albert succumbs to group pressure.)

A second dimension of moral development is relative success in offering defining characteristics. 'Saying something naughty like that' is a beginning, 'Uttering a falsehood' is an improvement. 'Uttering a falsehood when you know better' is a further improvement. 'Saying something false to deceive someone else' is even better than that.

It is important to recognize, however, that none of these definitions is entirely satisfactory. Consider the last one ('Saying something false to deceive someone else'). Now suppose you want to get my friend, Ben, in trouble. You want me to verify your story that Ben called the boss 'a bastard'. Protecting Ben, I deny your story. To lie I need not be trying to deceive anyone. I may simply reason that you cannot get Ben into trouble unless I corroborate your story. You may realize that I am denying your story to protect Ben. The boss may even realize this, but be unable to do anything unless someone will corroborate your story. So I can lie to protect Ben without having any intention of deceiving anyone.

Perhaps someone can offer a definition of 'lying' that fits all our cherished intuititions and is also informative. But the important point is that no one needs to be able to do this to have a working grasp of what lying is. And to begin with one need only have a basic understanding of one central paradigm.

A third dimension of development concerns the range of cases that fall under the kind, or are closely related to it. Is writing a bad cheque lying? Is it, anyway, closely enough related to genuine lying to share much of the wrongness of lying? What about painting or drawing a misleading picture? Can a photograph lie? Is it lying for a college dropout to wear the college tie?

A fourth dimension of moral development concerns the adjudication of conflicting moral claims. Sometimes lying is not really naughty; sometimes it is one's duty. How can this be? Though it is *prima facie* wrong to tell a lie, other moral claims may override the demand to tell the truth.

All this suggests a very traditional picture of moral development – although it is one that had gone out of favour until a decade or so ago. It is a picture that derives from Aristotle and invites us to identify virtues and vices such as honesty and dishonesty, courage and cowardice, justice and injustice. According to this picture, the child develops moral virtues by modelling adult moral behaviour and by following explicit adult instructions ('Tell the truth!', 'Don't cry in the surgery when you get a needle stuck into your arm!', 'Divide the cake into four equal pieces, one for each of you!').

According to this picture, a child's first efforts to model adult moral behaviour will not qualify fully as moral behaviour. The child's first truth-telling behaviour is not really an expression of honesty. Nor is the first cry-suppressing behaviour the expression of courage, or the first equal-distribution behaviour the expression of fairness. Only when one acts from a 'firm and settled disposition' (as one might translate Aristotle's observation) can one lay serious claim to acting in expression of those virtues. By repeatedly doing what an honest or brave person does one comes to act honestly, or bravely, from a firm and settled disposition; then one is honest (brave).

Still, telling the truth in challenging circumstances is being honest, whether or not the action is an expression of honesty in the agent. Even basically dishonest people are sometimes honest, that is, they say what the honest person would say. And even a child who has not yet developed a firm and settled disposition to tell the truth may do the honest thing on a given occasion. There is thus an important continuity between the child's very first efforts to model moral behaviour and the actions of a fully mature moral agent.

Let us pause here to take stock of the discussion so far. It began by asking whether it is a good idea to try to understand moral development as concept displacement, getting a better and better concept of obligation, bravery, lying, or whatever. It was then pointed out that the development story Piaget tells about the concept of life is unsatisfactory because the concepts of life Piaget attributes to very young children are not concepts we adults can understand to be concepts of life at all, not even primitive ones. (This fact it was said, vitiates Piaget's claim that young children are animists, for the putatively objectionable beliefs – for example, the belief that everything that can do anything whatsoever is 'alive' – turn out to be truisms – for example, the truism that everything that can do something can do something.)

Piaget's account of the development of the shadow concept in children is more promising, it was suggested, because Piaget does nothing to cast doubt on the reasonable assumption that even children at Stage 1 are reasonably good at picking out shadows. (By contrast, he suggests that children at Stage 1 are hopeless at picking out living things.) What Piaget considers increasingly satisfactory shadow concepts can then be understood as increasingly satisfactory theories about something children are able to latch onto from a very early age, namely, the natural kind, shadow.

Somewhat parallel to natural kinds, such as water and shadows, I went on to suggest, are moral kinds. A young child is able to latch onto the moral kind, bravery, or lying, by grasping central paradigms of that kind, paradigms that even the most mature and sophisticated moral agents still count as paradigmatic. Moral development is then something much more complicated than simple concept displacement. It is: enlarging the stock of paradigms for each moral kind; developing better and better definitions of whatever it is these paradigms exemplify; appreciating better the relation between straightforward instances of the kind and close relatives; and learning to adjudicate competing claims from different moral kinds (classically the sometimes competing claims of justice and compassion, but many other conflicts are possible).

The simple concept-displacement story of moral development is inadequate for two different sorts of reason. First, it leaves us unclear about why the early concepts count as concepts of lying, bravery, obligation (or whatever) at all. (Answer: they count, even though they are woefully inadequate, because they are attempts to model what genuine paradigms exemplify, paradigms that even an apprentice moralist who does not understand them well can use as examples.) Second, it ignores

other dimensions of moral development besides the definitional dimension.

In the remainder of this chapter I want to apply what has been said so far
by taking a few steps towards assessing the work of Lawrence Kohlberg on
moral development.

Kohlberg presents subjects with moral dilemmas and then grades their
responses, in particular, the *justifications* they offer for their solutions to
the dilemmas, so as to locate each subject at one of six stages (stages 1–6)
of moral development.[1] The most famous of these dilemmas is the
following 'Heinz' dilemma:

> In Europe, a woman was near death from a special kind of cancer. There was
> one drug that the doctors thought might save her. It was a form of radium that a
> druggist in the same town had recently discovered. The drug was expensive to
> make, but the druggist was charging ten times what the drug cost him to make.
> He paid $400 for the radium and charged $4,000 for a small dose of the drug.
> The sick woman's husband, Heinz, went to everyone he knew to borrow the
> money, but he could only get together about $2,000, which is half what it cost.
> He told the druggist that his wife was dying, and asked him to sell it cheaper or
> let him pay later. But the druggist said, 'No, I discovered the drug and I'm going
> to make money from it.' So Heinz got desperate and considered breaking into
> the man's store to steal the drug for his wife. (Kohlberg, 1984, p. 640)

At Stage 1 a subject will exhibit what Kohlberg calls 'the punishment
and obedience orientation'. At Stage 2 an elementary reciprocity emerges,
but it amounts only to 'You scratch my back and I'll scratch yours'.
Stages 1 and 2 constitute what Kohlberg calls the 'Preconventional Level'.

Stages 3 and 4 make up the 'Conventional Level'. At Stage 3 one has
achieved the 'good-boy-nice-girl orientation'; Stage 4 is the 'law and
order' orientation.

Stages 5 and 6 constitute what Kohlberg calls the 'Postconventional',
'Autonomous', or 'Principles' Level. Stage 5 is a social-contract orientation. And, finally, at Stage 6 'right is defined by the decision of conscience
in accord with self-chosen *ethical principles* appealing to logical com-
prehensiveness, universality and consistency' (Kohlberg, 1971, p. 165).

After some 30 years of investigation, Kohlberg and his collaborators
have amassed a staggering amount of evidence to show that the order of
this development is fixed in that none of us can reach stage $n + 1$ without
first going through stage n and there is no regression to an earlier stage.[2]
Moreover, despite various claims to the contrary, the best recent evidence
suggests that there are few, if any significant gender-related differences in
distribution across stages (Walker, 1984).[3]

It also seems that Kohlberg's scheme shows little interesting cultural
bias. (By 'interesting cultural bias' I mean bias that cannot be eliminated by

the sensitive redescription of Kohlberg's dilemmas to fit other cultures.) As one recent investigator has put the matter,

> The evidence suggests that Kohlberg's interview is reasonably culture fair when the content is creatively adapted and the subject is interviewed in his or her native language. The invariant sequence proposition was also found to be well supported, because stage skipping and stage regressions were rare and always below the level that could be attributed to measurement error. (Snarey, 1985, p. 226)

All this means that Kohlberg's theory is one of the best articulated and most thoroughly supported theories we have in all developmental psychology. Nevertheless, many people are profoundly dissatisfied with it. Perhaps one of the points that has already been made here can be used to illuminate important sources of that dissatisfaction.

Recalling Piaget's unsuccessful attempt to outline stages in the (alleged) development of the concept of life, we might ask whether Kohlberg's theory gives us any understanding of why a person at Stage 1 or Stage 2 might be said to have any grasp of morality at all. Does Kohlberg's theory make clear why the concept of obligation one has at Stage 1 (the 'punishment and obedience orientation') or Stage 2 ('You scratch my back and I'll scratch yours') is a moral concept at all, even if only a primitive moral concept? The answer seems to be 'No'.

Of course Kohlberg might reply that the first two stages are characterized as the 'Premoral Level'. He might add that the concepts of obligation one has at these stages are moral only in the sense that one has to develop each of them and move on to something else in order to arrive at a genuinely moral concept.

Such a reply seems unsatisfactory for two reasons. First, it is surely implausible to suppose that one of those subjects at Stages 1 and 2 has any understanding at all of what morality consists in. Second, a similar difficulty recurs at Stage 3, and perhaps even at Stage 4. One who conforms to expectations simply to avoid disapproval (Stage 3) or even one who acts to maintain the 'given social order for its own sake' (Stage 4; cf. Kohlberg, 1971, p. 164) has not, it seems, *not for those reasons anyway*, attained a specifically moral understanding of obligation. It begins to look as though all stages before Stage 5, or even Stage 6, are really pre-moral stages. Since, according to Kohlberg, hardly anyone, perhaps no one, reaches Stage 6, and only a small minority reach even Stage 5, we are driven to the unwelcome conclusion that the vast majority of people do not have a specifically moral concept of obligation. It is not just that most people do not act morally most of the time; that would hardly be a surprising or objectionable conclusion. What is both surprising and objectionable is the conclusion that the vast majority of people really do not have any grasp at all of what morality is.

This worry is underlined by the fact that Kohlberg himself defines morality in terms of impartiality, universalizability, reversibility and prescriptivity. If Kohlberg is right and a judgement is moral if, and only if, it exhibits those formal features, then the concepts of obligation one has at lower stages of development are not even primitive moral concepts; they are not moral concepts at all.

This worry can be made concrete by appeal to a hypothetical example. Suppose Susan, age 6 years, is given a Kohlberg interview and is found to be at Stage 1. What this means is that her ability to reason her way through a moral *dilemma* to resolve a moral *conflict*, and her ability to articulate such a resolution are very primitive. Now suppose that when cookies and orange juice are distributed to Susan's class in school, Susan herself happens to get two cookies, whereas James, through an oversight, gets none, and everyone else gets one. We can imagine that Susan first rejoices in her good fortune, but then, noting that James has no cookies, gives one of hers to him. She has done the fair thing; she has done what the just person would do.

Of course she might give James a cookie out of fear that she would be reprimanded for having two when James had none. Or she might give him a cookie in the hope of praise from her teacher, or of favour from James. But there is no reason to suppose she *has* to act out of fear of punishment or hope of reward. In particular, and this is the crucial point, the fact that she scores at Stage 1 in a Kohlberg interview does not mean that she cannot act out of a sense of fairness when she is not confronted with a moral dilemma, let alone with the need to justify her resolution of a moral dilemma.

A Kohlbergian might reply that Susan does not really have a sense of fairness if her moral reasoning is at Stage 1. She may be modelling behaviour that she observes in others, or conforming to pressures from adults or peers, but she is not really acting from a sense of fairness unless she can give Stage 5 or Stage 6 reasoning to resolve a moral dilemma.

Here is where the analogy to the development of the shadow concept is helpful. Just as a young child with a very primitive theory of what shadows are may nevertheless be reasonably good at picking out shadows, so Susan, who, we may assume, will be very bad at telling us in a general way what justice or fairness requires, may have accepted some perfectly good paradigms of distributive justice and, using these paradigms, may be quite good at doing what fairness requires.

As Susan grows and develops we hope she will enlarge her stock of paradigms from cutting up pies and handing out cookies fairly to distributing work assignments fairly among workers of varied abilities, to, perhaps, refusing to change the rules in the middle of a game. And we hope Susan will grow along the other dimensions of moral development as well. But the simple paradigms of distributive justice will stay with her permanently. And no contrast between the virtuosity of her later reasoning and the naïvety of her early appeal to simple paradigms can establish that those early actions were not really performed from a sense of justice.

Theories of cognitive and moral development encourage us adults to distance ourselves from children – both from the children around us and from our own childhood selves. Such distancing can produce a new respect for children. After all, it warns us against faulting children for shortcomings that express, according to the theories, immature cognitive and moral structures entirely normal for children of the given age range. But such distancing can also encourage condescension. If we suppose that children live in conceptual worlds that are structurally different from ours, but that will naturally evolve into ours, how can we fail to be condescending towards children as thinkers and moral agents?

The condescension, though understandable, is unwarranted. One reason it is unwarranted is that later structures are not entirely solid accomplishments of the maturation process; characteristically, they are problematic in ways that philosophers never tire of exposing. Thus it is an open question whether anyone at all can provide an entirely satisfactory theory of justice or, as remarked earlier, even an entirely satisfactory definition of 'lying'.

Another reason the condescension is unwarranted is that children, in their simple directness, can bring us adults back to basics. 'A little child shall lead them' (Isaiah 11:6) can be taken sentimentally; it often is. But it can also be taken to express something profoundly realistic. Any developmental theory that rules out, on theoretical grounds, the possibility of being led intellectually and morally by a child is, for that reason, defective; it is also morally offensive.

NOTES

1   There are complications, Kohlberg and his associates now speak of heteronomous and autonomous substages for each of the regular stages and also of the possibility of a 'soft' Stage 7. At the same time they seem less confident of Stage 6. See Kohlberg, 1984, chap. 3 and Appendix C).
2   For a time it seemed that there was indeed regression; but refinement of the theory now seems to have dealt with the problem. See Kohlberg (1984, pp. 437–8).
3   I am ignoring here the intriguing suggestion Carol Gilligan makes in her book, *In Another Voice* (1982), that women in our culture tend to have a different 'vision of moral maturity' from men, and that they are more likely to live by an 'ethic of care and responsibility' than by the 'ethic of justice' Kohlberg emphasizes. I am also ignoring Kohlberg's recent efforts, in response to Gilligan, to supplement his own account of the development of a sense of justice with some attention to love, care and responsibility (Kohlberg, 1984, see especially pp. 227–33).

190   *Issues in Stage Theory*

The account of moral development I have offered – concerned as it is with all the virtues, including charity, care and responsibility, as well as justice – provides, I think, a rich enough context in which to discuss these issues. But the issues are simply too complex for a brief treatment. I defer discussion of them to another occasion.

4 'Stage 6 has disappeared as a commonly identifiable form of moral reasoning as our stage-scoring concepts and criteria have developed from the continuing analyis of our longitudinal data' (Kohlberg, 1984, p. 270). 'We no longer claim that our empirical work has succeeded in defining the nature of a sixth and highest stage of moral judgement' (Kohlberg, 1984, p. 215).

REFERENCES

Gilligan, C. 1982: *In Another Voice*. Cambridge, Mass.: Harvard University Press.
Kohlberg, L. 1971: From is to ought: how to commit the naturalistic fallacy and get away with it in the study of moral development. In T. Mischel (ed.), *Cognitive Development and Epistemology*. New York: Academic press, pp. 151–235.
    1984: *Essays on Moral Development*, Volume II, *The Psychology of Moral Development: The Nature and Validity of Moral Stages*. New York: Harper and Row.
Kripke, S. 1980: *Naming and Necessity*. Cambridge, Mass.: Harvard University Press.
Piaget, J. 1929: *The Child's Conception of the World*. London: Routledge and Kegan Paul.
    1930: *The Child's Conception of Physical Causality*. London: Routledge and Kegan Paul.
    1948: *The Moral Judgment of the Child*. London: Routledge and Kegan Paul.
Snarey, J. R. 1985: Cross-cultural universality of moral development. *Psychological Bulletin*, 82, 202–32.
Walker, L. J. 1984: Sex differences in the development of moral reasoning. *Child Development*, 55, 677–91.

9

On Piaget on necessity

Leslie Smith

1 INTRODUCTION

One philosophical objection to Jean Piaget's account of the development of knowledge is its conflation of necessary with empirical issues. This objection, which is variously supported in philosophical (Hamlyn, 1971, 1978), psychological (Brown and Desforges, 1979) and educational (Egan, 1983) commentary, is concisely expressed in the key question:

> what precisely can it mean to describe the *empirical* relationships between the elements of the corresponding mental structures as being *necessary* relationships? (Feldman and Toulmin, 1976, p. 418; my italics)

In Piaget's account, a cognitive structure is formally characterized in terms of its constitutive principles; yet any such structure is also empirically tested by reference to children's performances. Philosophers who distinguish issues which are necessary (logical, normative, formal) – and so not empirical – and issues which are empirical (factual, psychological) – and so not necessary – contend that Piaget's account is objectionable because of the neglect shown to this distinction. Indeed, one appeal of this objection is due to the fact that it is easy to find passages which seem to show that the distinction is lost in the writings of Piaget:

> the psychological explanation of intelligence consists in retracing its development by showing how the latter terminates *necessarily* in the equilibrium described here. (Piaget, 1947, p. 55/1950a, pp. 48–9; my italics[1])

> a structure may impose itself with *necessity*, and by essentially endogenous means, as an outcome of progressive equilibrations. (Piaget, 1967a, p. 438/ 1971, pp. 316–17; my italics)

In such passages, Piaget is not claiming that the formal characteristics of one structure are necessarily related to those of some other but rather that the process of structural change is itself a necessary process.

Interestingly, this objection can be restated in a stronger form in that Piaget's own account is inconsistent. Such inconsistency can be illustrated in several ways. Thus Piaget (1966, pp. 132–43) denies that his account is open to a charge of psychologism – the account does not set out to validate a normative principle on the basis of empirical evidence; he also denies that his account is vulnerable to a charge of logicism – the account does not set out to provide a logical rationale for a psychological relationship. The fact of this denial – as opposed to its validity – indicates that Piaget is aware of the distinction between empirical and necessary issues. Again, Piaget's empirical study (Apostel et al., 1957a; Quine, 1960) into adults' understanding of the distinction between analytic and synthetic propositions shows that he has some understanding of this distinction. Again, a crucial difference is drawn by Piaget (1975, p. 50/1978, pp. 43*)between an observationally based judgement and one which is deductively necessary. To repeat: what is important here is not the use which Piaget's makes of this distinction but the fact that he makes it at all. Moreover, this distinction is not one which is confined to his recent writings. The distinction between observation and deductive inference is explicitly asserted in early papers (Piaget, 1922) as well as in his classic studies: what distinguishes a stage II from a stage III performance on conservation, inclusion or transitivity tasks is the use of an empirical or a deductive strategy respectively (Piaget, 1941/1952). Central to all of these cases is the distinction – or some analogue of it – which is presupposed in the main objection. It follows that the charge made against Piaget's account is not that there is neglect of a distinction which is accepted by others but rather that there is a failure to maintain a distinction which is accepted in the same account.

My strategy in this discussion is not to deny the distinction which is presupposed in the objection but rather to deny that it has an application to Piaget's account of structural change. There are two features of this discussion which can usefully be noticed at the outset. Firstly, an attempt will be made to distinguish three distinct ways in which Piaget uses the concept of necessity in his account. The three uses, which will be referred to as necessary conditionship, deductive necessity and constructive necessity, are discussed in more detail in the three central sections respectively. I shall try to show that the account offers empirically necessary conditions of the understanding of deductive necessity as an outcome of a necessary process of structural change. Secondly, within each section a variety will be used of material, including Piaget's own writings as well as both philosophical and psychological evaluations of his position. Such juxtaposition of material is deliberate and is intended to illustrate the central claim that an account whose presuppositions are necessary may have consequences which are empirical in character. Acceptance of this practice provides, in fact, some additional support for the rejection of the main objection to Piaget's account of structural change.

2 NECESSARY CONDITIONSHIP

The argument of this section is that Piaget's account of the growth of knowledge offers conditions which are (1) necessary rather than sufficient and (2) empirical rather than logical, but that (3) not all philosophers and psychologists accept that this is so.

2.1 *Necessary–sufficient*

To claim that an element X_1 is a sufficient condition of an element Y is to claim that whenever X_1 is present Y is also present. Such a relationship may occur in either of two forms. Either X_1 is sufficient for Y quite independently of the presence of some other element, say X_2, which is also independently sufficient for Y; that is, Y is present if X_1 is present but X_2 is absent or if X_2 is present but X_1 is absent. Alternatively, X_1 is sufficient for Y but only in conjunction with all those elements whose co-presence results in the presence of Y; that is, the presence of X_1 alone does not result in the presence of Y, even though the presence of Y does follow if X_1 is present jointly with those other elements whose co-presence is required for the presence of Y. In both cases, a claim that X_1 is sufficient for Y is invalidated by the production of a case where X_1 is present but Y is absent. Notice that the claim that X_1 is sufficient for Y is not invalidated by the production of a case where X_1 is absent but Y is present, for the presence of Y could be due to the presence of some other element which is sufficient for Y. To claim that X_1 is sufficient for Y is to claim that when X_1 is present, Y is also present; it is not to claim that when Y is present, X_1 is also present.

To claim that an element Z_1 is a necessary condition of Y is to claim that the absence of Z_1 is coupled with the absence of Y: whenever Z_1 is absent, Y is also absent. Such a claim is invalidated by the production of a case where Z_1 is absent but Y is present, for in such a case Z_1 is not a necessary condition of Y. Notice that the claim that Z_1 is a necessary condition of Y is not invalidated by the production of a case where Z_1 is present but Y is absent: the claim that when Z_1 is absent Y is absent is not the claim that when Y is absent Z_1 is also absent. Finally, whether Z_1 is the sole necessary condition of Y or whether Z_1 is one necessary condition in conjunction with Z_2 of Y, the absence of either Z_1 or Z_2 results in the absence of Y.

Piaget's account presents necessary conditions of the growth of knowledge and does not present sufficient conditions. His position is made explicit in his oration on receiving the Erasmus Prize. Defining assimilation as the integration of experiential data to a cognitive structure, Piaget states that:

> assimilation is a necessary condition, not sufficient, but necessary for all – even experiential – knowledge. Every reading from experience thus presupposes assimilatory frameworks and this is true of all the most refined scientific physics as well as the young child. (Piaget, 1972a, p. 30; my translation)

This position is in fact maintained by Piaget in earlier writings:

> all knowledge . . . presupposes an explicit or implicit system of principles of conservation. We simply assert that conservation constitutes a necessary condition of all rational activity, without being concerned to ascertain if that condition is sufficient. (Piaget and Szeminska, 1941, p. 16/1952, p. 3*)

Since conservation is here taken to be a necessary condition of all knowledge and since Piaget's task is to identify a cognitive structure whose use results in conservation, it follows that the use of such a structure is a necessary but not sufficient, condition of all knowledge. Further, Piaget's associates confirm this position: 'Piaget was often reproached for having seen structures as the sufficient source of all objective knowledge, whereas they are only one necessary aspect' (Inhelder, 1982, p. 414). In short, there is clear evidence, arising from a general statement of position, that Piaget's account does offer necessary conditions alone for the growth of knowledge.

2.2 *Empirical–logical*

To claim that a conditionship relation is empirical is to claim that the relation could in logic, but not in fact, be other than it is. By contrast, to claim that a conditionship relation is logical is to claim that the relation could, neither in fact nor in logic, be other than it is. The denial of a conditionship relation which is empirical results in an assertion which is, as a matter of fact, false. The denial of a conditionship relation which is logical results in a contradiction.

Piaget's account presents necessary conditions of knowledge growth which are empirical and not logical in character. One expression of this position occurs in Piaget's discussion of genetic epistemology. Genetic epistemology shares with philosophical epistemology the investigation of the *ipse intellectus*: this allusion to the work of Leibniz (1949, p. 111) is evident in Piaget's (1953, pp. 2–3) discussion. Yet this reference is coupled with criticism. 'As for Platonic, rationalist or apriorist epistemologies, each took itself to have found some fundamental instrument of knowledge which was extraneous, higher or prior to experience. . . . These doctrines have neglected to *verify* that that instrument was actually available to the subject. Now that, whether one likes it or not, is a factual matter' (Piaget, 1970, p. 12/1970, p. 5*). Piaget takes it to be one virtue of his genetic epistemology that his approach is empirical, i.e. directed upon the verification that a specified instrument of knowledge – Platonic form, Cartesian innate idea, Kantian category – actually is available to a knowing subject. Piaget's objection to philosophical epistemologies is not that each is contradictory but rather that each is empirically false: each represents a logically possible but not the actual way in which knowledge arises. In short, Piaget supposes his own account to be both non-contradictory and empirically verified. It is for this reason that the instrument of knowledge identified in his account, namely a cognitive structure, is an empirically necessary condition of knowledge growth.

This same conclusion is supported by reference to Piaget's discussion of two central postulates. One postulate is that any assimilatory structure has a tendency to be used. The second postulate is that any assimilatory use requires structural accommodation. Piaget (1975, p. 13/1978, p. 7*) then asserts that both postulates have an empirical basis since each is derived from factual investigation. It would be logically possible to maintain that no structural change occurs in that the same structure is used throughout experience. Such a view is denied by Piaget, both in the present claim and by his use of the distinction between functioning and structure (cf. Piaget, 1931, p. 151). As a structuralist, Piaget accepts that all experience is structured; yet this assertion is compatible with the use of different structures throughout experience. What is invariant to experience is the functioning of some structure, even though any specific structure is a variable feature of functioning. The use of some structure in experience does not require the use of some *specific* structure in experience, still less the numerically same structure throughout experience. In short, it is an empirical question as to which assimilatory structure is used by individuals at different developmental points.

2.3 *Comment*

It is evident that the interpretation of Piaget's position presented here is not always accepted. Specifically, developmental psychologists tend to attribute to Piaget the view that his account offers sufficient conditions of knowledge growth, whilst philosophers tend to stress the necessity of Piaget's conditions.

Consider first the position taken by psychologists. Certainly, some commentators (Gallagher and Reid, 1981, p. 40) attribute to Piaget the view that the conditions outlined in his account are necessary conditions, though this is not accepted by all. Some commentators (Flavell, 1963) do not specify the type of conditionship relation at all; others state that it is Piaget's view that genetic, environmental, and social conditions are all necessary conditions in that account without specifying the nature of Piaget's own conditions (Furth, 1981, p. 207); others contend that Piaget's account offers conditions which are both necessary and sufficient (Vuyk, 1981, p. 36), in the absence of any justification of this assertion. And one philosophical commentary on Piaget's psychology offers the criticism that Piaget's own conditions are not sufficient, even though they are (merely) necessary conditions (Hamlyn, 1978, p. 55). What is common to all of these commentaries is an omission of a detailed specification of Piaget's position, an omission which sections 2.1 and 2.2 above partially rectify.

Typically, however, psychologists do not discuss the nature of Piaget's conditions at all, following the example initially set by Flavell (1963). What is implicit in their investigation is the view that Piaget's account offers sufficient conditions. Certainly, this attribution is rarely made explicit. It is, however, presupposed in their practice. There is a threefold basis for this conclusion. Firstly, success on certain tasks is taken to be criterial (Winer, 1980, p. 309) in the attribution of ability to a child. Thus children's logical abilities are to be attributed on the basis of successful performance on conservation, inclusion, or transitivity tasks. (For a recent review, see Gelman and Baillargeon, 1983.) Secondly, it is contended that Piaget's account presents a 'bleak and negative' construal of children's abilities (Donaldson et al., 1983; see also Bryant, 1984) and that such a construal is a consequence of his failure to investigate the role of other variables whose manipulation differentially affects performance (Brainerd, 1978). Thirdly, a positive and optimistic construal of children's abilities is available on the basis of the actual control of such variables, whether perceptual, linguistic, contextual, or cognitive, on inclusion (Winer, 1980), conservation (McGarrigle and Donaldson, 1974; Samuel and Bryant, 1984), or transitivity (Bryant and Trabasso, 1971) tasks. Now the acceptance of such a research strategy focuses attention upon Piagetian tasks where the critical question is: what are the population norms for success or failure on such-and-such a task? If the experimental manipulation of some variable leads to successful performance on that task, in contrast to the lack of success shown by children who perform under Piagetian conditions, the conclusion drawn is that Piaget's account may be set aside. It may be set aside since it runs counter to the available evidence. Yet this conclusion only follows if Piaget's account is taken to present *sufficient* conditions and it does not follow if the account is taken to offer necessary conditions. If the conditions stated in Piaget's account are necessary conditions, they cannot be bypassed in this way.

It will be replied: the substantive question is not whether the conditions stated in Piaget's account *are taken* to be necessary but rather whether those conditions *are* necessary. The previous argument begs this question by assuming that the latter is the case. Yet this reply is open to objection since the research strategy at issue is, in principle, flexible enough for the investigation of Piaget's own conditions to occur but that, in fact, this has not happened. Attention is focused upon Piagetian tasks and the antecedent variables whose control differentially influences performance on them. Attention ought, for the reply to be sustained, to be focused upon Piaget's conditions as well as Piagetian tasks. In fact, the latter is conspicuous by its absence. It is a reasonable explanation of this practice to claim that it rests upon the implicit attribution to Piaget of the view that his account offers sufficient conditions of performance on his tasks. Such an attribution is incompatible with the attribution outlined in section 21. above.

Incompatible with the attribution outlined in section 2.2 is the view that since Piaget's account specifies relationships which are logically necessary, his conditions do not require empirical testing. The basis of this conclusion is twofold. Firstly, it is argued that Piaget's account does specify relationships which are logically necessary since, for example, stage transition is a progression from particular to general (Atkinson, 1983; Hamlyn, 1971) or since stage characteristics are linked by the relation of logical inclusion through their own definition (Feldman and Toulmin, 1976). Secondly, it is concluded that a logically necessary relationship does not require empirical testing, presumably because the relationship holds *tout court*. Certainly such philosophers (Atkinson, 1983, p. 163; Feldman and Toulmin, 1976, p. 466; Hamlyn, 1978, p. 46) are careful to notice that logical and temporal priorities do not have to coincide. Equally clear is the failure to maintain this position. This failure amounts to the claim that if a relationship is necessary, it is 'a waste of time' (Brown and Desforges, 1979, p. 90) to submit that relationship to empirical testing, for example: 'the relations between many of Piaget's so-called "stages" are logical relations. ... [In consequence] many of Piaget's so-called empirical discoveries are in fact disguised analytic truths' (Atkinson, 1983, pp. 94–5). Now such a contention is open to objection (Smith, 1987). Suppose, for example, three stages in development are identified as A, B and C and suppose also that stage A is *defined* in terms of the propositional calculus, stage B in terms of the predicate calculus and stage C in terms of a (weak) system of modal logic. Following Hughes and Cresswell (1972), stage A, so defined, is a logically necessary condition of stage B and stage B is, so defined, a logically necessary condition of stage C. What is also apparent is

tinction at issue is not one which arises from the question of whether acceptance of a belief commits an individual to all of its logical pre-suppositions and consequences (Stroud, 1979). Rather, the distinction concerns whether an individual, the content of whose belief is a necessarily true, accepts the necessity of that belief. The discussion is in three parts, including (1) a review of Piaget's account of children's understanding of deductive necessity, (2) a critique of psychological research which derogates issues of modality in favour of issues concerning truth-value and (3) an evaluation of the genetic fallacy in relation to philosophical analyses of the concept of knowledge.

3.1 *Understanding deductive necessity*

Piaget's interest in children's understanding of deductive necessity is evident in his first psychological papers. At issue is not merely whether children give a correct response on a task but whether the response is based on inference. 'Reasoning is here called formal which draws a conclusion, from one or several propositions, to which the mind adheres with certainty, without recourse to observation. What is incontestable is that such reasoning exists' (Piaget, 1922, p. 222; my translation). Piaget's position here reflects the distinction – illustrated by reference to his account in the introduction to this chapter – between the empirical and the normative. His argument is that a belief which arises on the basis of observation is not a belief which is inferential and so necessary. This position was, however, modified by Piaget in his structuralist (cf. Smith, 1986) writings. In the latter, Piaget is committed to there being a cognitive structure whose use underpins the acquisition of all, including observational, knowledge at any developmental point.

'Neat' experience in the sense of simple registration of external data – in the absence of a contribution from a subject – does not in fact exist . . . physical experience is always indissociable from a logico-mathematical framework. (Piaget, 1969, p. 127; my translation)

let us recall that, even from the beginning and already with the youngest subjects, a physical fact is registered only by means of a logico-mathematical framework, however elementary. (Piaget, 1977b, p. 321; my translation)

A structure which is logico-mathematical in character is used from infancy onwards in the acquisition of knowledge. In consequence, the distinction between inference and observation is, for Piaget, a distinction which is to be drawn by reference to the specific character of the cognitive structures used by individuals at different developmental points. There is an inferential aspect to the acquisition of even observational knowledge and so the distinction between inference and observation is essentially one which depends upon the specific type of inference at issue.

The specific type of inference at issue is clarified in many places: the account is concerned with deductive inferences appropriate to the understanding of inclusion or transitivity (Piaget, 1950b, p. 146), inferences which are necessary, rather than probable, in the deductive sense (Piaget, 1967, p. 14). Whereas Piaget's pre-structuralist work was directed upon the question of when children can make such inferences, his structuralist work is directed upon the question of whether children can make such inferences. In the latter, Piaget rejects the assumption of the Miniature Adult, namely that what is logically necessary to an adult is similarly necessary to a child (Inhelder and Piaget, 1964, p. 282). In rejecting this assumption, Piaget is disinclined to use an *a priori* approach; indeed, his account offers conditions which are empirical, rather than logical, for precisely this reason. Thus Piaget requires some empirical criterion by the use of which an attribution of logical ability to a child may be justified.

Two objections might be raised here. The first objection is theoretical, consisting in the reminder that an attribution of inability to a child on the basis of the child's unsuccessful performance on some task is invalid. A child's successful performance renders valid an attribution of corresponding ability to a child: *ab esse ad posse valet consequentia*. Notoriously, the absence of the former does not render valid an attribution of the lack of the corresponding ability. There is, however, an adequate reply to this objection (Smith, 1987). An empirical approach is directed upon the production of empirical evidence on the basis of which an attribution of ability is to be made. It is legitimate, with respect to a given task, to check whether a child's performance on that task is successful or not. If the child's performance is not successful, the conclusion to draw is that there is no evidence from this task on which to base an attribution of some corresponding ability to the child. Of course, the child might perform differently on some other task or on the same task on some other occasion; which is an empirical question. The child's unsuccessful performance does, however, warrant the conclusion that there is no evidence on which to base an attribution of some ability.

The second problem is methodological in that an attribution of ability may be incorrect in one of two ways (Flavell, 1977). A 'false-positive' attribution is one in which an ability, which is in fact absent, is attributed to the child; a 'false-negative' attribution is one in which an ability, which is in fact present, is not attributed to a child. Certain psychological critics contend that Piaget's account is objectionable because of the occurrence of attributions of the latter sort (Brainerd, 1973; Wheldall and Poborca, 1980). In essence, such critics recommend that adequate task-design legitimizes a reliance upon a child's judgements alone – on which an attribution of logical ability will be based – in contrast to a reliance upon a child's judgements and explanations. It is Piaget's preference for the latter which generates the methodological objection.

One reply to this objection is to point out that Piaget's preference for a criterion of successful performance which requires a child to justify a judgement is deliberately adopted so as to avoid the making of 'false-negative' attribution. That is, he would accept the general need to avoid making such attributions but deny that the use of his empirical criterion actually results in the making of 'false-negative' attributions.

> The first point to notice is the onset of awareness of necessity: 'it has to be', etc. But the use of such a criterion is dangerous, if there is a pre-occupation with verbal statements and with states of consciousness, even though their onset generates an interesting problem. What has greater firmness is the fact that this necessity is used in behaviour and that it seems to correspond to the 'closure' of a previously incomplete structure. (Piaget, 1967b, p. 271; my translation)

The same logical principle, for example transitivity, may be utilized in the design of two tasks whose task demands are different: Burt's problem and Piaget's seriation task are illustrative (Piaget, 1947a/1950, p. 146). A 'false-negative' attribution of the ability to understand transitivity would arise if the former task, requiring an advanced linguistic ability, was used in preference to the latter task which is taken by Piaget not to demand the use of such an ability. Again, Piaget's decision not to use an introspective criterion, consisting in an individual's experience of necessity (Piaget, 1967/1971, p. 316), is rejected for the same reason. It is impossible to verify the presence of such experience, resulting in the making of 'false-negative' attributions of ability. That is, by deciding not to use an empirical criterion which is linguistic or introspective Piaget would contend that he does avoid the making of 'false-negative' attributions.

A second reply is to assert that the preferred criterion does require the individual to display an understanding of necessity in behaviour. Necessity is used in the child's behaviour when the responses made by that individual are co-ordinated in a system – a system whose formal description is isomorphic with that of a logical structure. From this perspective, an individual's responses are elements in an open system. An individual has access (*ouverture*) to new possibilities; yet an open system does not exclude closure (*fermeture*): the possibilities are integrated by the use of an inferential framework (Piaget, 1967, p. 220/1971, p. 155). Only by investigating both a child's judgements and explanations for those judgements can an observer establish, empirically, that the system of thinking used by a child is an open-but-closed system of thought. Thus when Piaget (1966, p. 174) contends that reversibility is an essential feature of deductive thinking, reversible thinking is open and closed in this way. The individual who can subtract from a superordinate class one of its subordinate classes, characterized negatively and inferentially, to yield some other subordinate class uses an open system. A new relationship is understood, namely linking complementary classes. The system is closed since such a relationship is necessitated by the positive characterization of the classes. Here is an example. In an array consisting of 10 flowers (class B) such that seven flowers are daisies (class A) and three flowers are roses (class A'), the addition of the two subordinate classes yields the superordinate class $(A + A' = B)$. The child who understands that the subtraction of one of the subordinate classes from the superordinate class *necessitates* the remaining subordinate class has an understanding of necessity by way of (partial) complementation. In this array, a flower which is not a rose is a daisy $(A = B - A')$ and a rose is a flower which is not a daisy $(A' = B - A)$. It is a valid inference to deduce that class A remains if its restricted complement, relative to a superordinate class, is substracted from the latter (Smith, 1982a). (A similar argument can be used with respect to the type of reversibility taken by Piaget to be applicable to relational thinking – see Piaget, 1966, p. 177.) In short, Piaget investigates both a child's judgements and explanations to ascertain whether the possible responses which a child may give when presented with a task are coordinated in a deductive system of thought.

No argument has been offered to suggest that Piaget is correct to distinguish concrete from formal operational thinking; nor that either type of thinking is to be characterized in the way that he suggests; nor that the formal descriptions of such cognitive structures are the ones outlined in his account (Piaget, 1966). Rather, the argument has been that if access to new possibilities and closure through their binding in a deductive framework is an essential feature of inferential thinking in childhood, their attribution requires a range of an individual's responses to be exposed to third-party scrutiny. No doubt 'false-negative' attributions of competence do arise from the adoption of such an approach but this is not to say that such attributions are a logical consequence of its adoption.

3.2 *Psychological research on children's inferences*

Not all psychologists with an interest in inferential ability consider Piaget's account to be a serious alternative. Typically, cognitive psychologists are uninterested in the development of ability because of a commitment to the psychological investigation of the end-point of such development. If the memory system is taken to be suitable for psychological analysis – by reference to its component system, schematic basis or semantic networks (Bransford, 1979; Norman, 1978; Tulving, 1985) – the system used by the adult subject is at issue (Murray, 1984). Such a commitment is, of course, open to Piaget's objection, noticed in section 2.2, that there is a failure to check that some selected cognitive instrument is actually at a subject's disposal.

Developmental psychologists have, however, taken seriously Piaget's account – for example, by exposing it to psychological testing. But it is evident that even developmental psychologists have tended to investigate the correctness of children's judgements rather than the child's under-standing of necessity. In support of this contention, consider psycho-logical research on three types of operational task: conservation, classification, and seriation. (For a general review of this research, see Gelman and Baillargeon, 1983.)

The essential nature of a conservation task is well described by Murray (1981). In essence, a child is (1) presented with two objects which are accepted to be observationally identical; (2) one of these objects, though not the other, is transformed by the experimenter; (3) so that the child may be re-presented with one original and one transformed object with a view to accepting, or rejecting, their equivalence. All agree that a conservation task requires these three steps. A further step (4) is required in Piaget's account since the basis of the child's answer must be checked – as well as (5) a check on the child's deductive ability. Yet, as Murray (1981, p. 164) points out, 'rarely is a direct assessment of necessity made'. In fact, in their comprehensive review, Gelman and Baillargeon (1983) fail to discuss this aspect at all since their concern is with the characterization of young in relation to older children's thinking rather than with children's under-standing of necessity. Some critics (Shultz et al., 1979) observe that there are certain conservation tasks – which were actually studied initially by Lunzer (1968) – which do not admit of a logical solution since empirical beliefs are also required. This observation would not be denied by Piaget whose position (see section 2.1) is that conservation is a necessary, not sufficient, condition of rational activity. In short, the paradigm example of a Piagetian task has been – *in practice* – investigated without reference to one of its defining features, namely its logical necessity. Whilst it is interesting to notice that external variables influence performance on a conservation task (McGarrigle and Donaldson, 1974; Miller, 1982; Samuel and Bryant, 1984), the crucial question of the modality of a child's (correct) understanding is left untouched.

A similar finding is applicable to the investigation of the child's classificatory thinking. Research on inclusion has typically been con-cerned with the role of different variables and their differential effects on children's understanding. Winer's (1980) comprehensive review is valu-able both since it is comprehensive and since it signals the lack of interest in the child's understanding of the necessity relevant to this relationship. Indeed, the previous subsection contains an indication of why Piaget's inclusion task is distinctive just because of its focus upon the necessity of the relationship. The explicit goal of some psychologists is to chart the developmental route, consisting in the understanding of collection terms, such as *family* (Markman, 1979), or mass-nouns, such as *money* (Markman, 1985). Yet it is clear that such research is directed upon more primitive types of classificatory thinking and that the necessity of the child's understanding is not a central issue. The conclusion is, once again, clear: questions about the correctness of a child's understanding have taken precedence over questions about the child's understanding of necessity to the extent that the latter is conspicuously absent from psychological research.

Piaget's work on seriation has primarily been evaluated by reference to children's abilities to make transitive inferences. The classic psychological study (Bryant and Trabasso, 1971) centres upon the age at which children have this understanding and upon the facilitating role of memory of the premises on which the inference is based. This study has been recently criticized because children who do remember the premises may still fail to make the inference (Russell, 1981) and because the degree of training required to ensure that children do remember the premises is such that monkeys given similar training outperform children (Chalmers and McGonigle, 1984). The two studies indicate that inference requires more than accurate recall of premises and that individuals who are exposed to sufficient training may perform successfully by using a non-logical strategy. In short, what is at issue is the correctness of the inferences made by individuals and what is left untouched is the modality of the child's (correct) understanding. The relevant conclusion is that the evaluation of Piaget's account should include the evaluation of its crucial component, namely the child's understanding of necessity. Such a conclusion is not new (cf. Breslow, 1981, p. 325). It is, however, a conclusion which is bypassed in the practice of developmental psychologists, whatever their declared intentions.

An inappropriate conclusion to draw from this review is that research in developmental psychology has been sterile and pointless. On the contrary: that research has been important in showing a systematic concern for issues which were not addressed in Piaget's account. The neglect was, however, quite deliberate (Smith, 1987). For the appropriate conclusion to draw is that Piaget's account was directed upon a restricted range of issues one of which was the child's understanding of necessity. The conclusion of the present section is that in practice psychologists have tended to ignore this issue because of a preferred concern with other issues – for example, issues where the correctness of the child's under-standing has priority.

3.3 Genetic fallacy

The genetic fallacy is committed if the truth or falsity of a conclusion is dependent upon the truth or falsity of an account as to how that conclusion is in fact accepted: what led someone to a view is irrelevant to determining whether the view is true (Carney and Scheer, 1964, p. 32). A special case of the genetic fallacy is the claim that 'if this evolved from that, then this must always be that; or at least, it must always be really or essentially that' (Flew, 1975, p. 102). Transposed to Piaget's account, a philosopher might say that the genetic fallacy is committed if it is thought that a question in philosophical epistemology can be answered by reference to Piaget's genetic epistemology. To make the same point: there is nothing in Piaget's genetic epistemology, *qua* account of how individuals actually do understand deductive necessity, which has any implications for philosophical epistemology, *qua* account of what understanding deductive necessity is.

This conclusion would be resisted by Piaget who takes his genetic epistemology to be a contribution to the solution of problems which have previously been the exclusive concern of philosophers. This stance is clear in the citation of the award of Distinguished Scientist conferred on him by the American Psychological Association (cf. Piaget, 1972b, p. 15). It is also asserted in his definition of genetic epistemology: 'the genetic method amounts to the study of the formation of knowledge (*connaissances*) by virtue of its real, or psychological, construction and to the construal of *all* knowledge as relative to a certain level of the mechanism of that construction' (Piaget, 1950b, p. 19; my translation and italics). Genetic epistemology is a method and, as such, does not prejudge which viewpoint – whether in philosophical epistemology or not – is acceptable. The method does not, for example, prejudge whether Piaget's epistemology is preferable to that of Plato. This is because no *a priori* stance is adopted as to whether a problem is a philosophical problem, and so amenable only to an *a priori* approach, or not philosophical, and so amenable to an empirical approach (Piaget, 1950b, pp. 14, 52). Crucially for the present argument, this method is taken to be applicable to knowledge at any developmental level – including that adopted in philosophical epistemology.

Here is one application of Piaget's position. The question 'What is knowledge?' has invited a traditional answer (Chisholm, 1977) in which a subject is classified as knowing a proposition p only if p is true; the subject believes p; and the subject is justified in believing p. One objection (Gettier, 1963) to this definition is that even if it is acceptable as stating necessary conditions of *knowledge*, it fails to state sufficient conditions since the three conditions listed may be satisfied and yet the individual in question would not normally be classified as knowing the proposition p.

Some philosophers take the 'Gettier objection' to be a refutation of the traditional analysis and so offer a causal theory of knowing (Goldman, 1978). Some philosophers accept that the 'Gettier objection' is an objection to the traditional analysis but argue that that analysis can be improved. For example, in one recent improvement, it is argued that scepticism is a strict consequence of the revitalized definition of *knowledge*: 'most of the knowledge claims we make in ordinary life are simply incorrect' (Kirkham, 1984, p. 512). What is common to both responses is the assumption that 'we' have an objective way of classifying when a true belief is, and is not, knowledge. But the question which arises now is: who are the 'we'? Whatever answer is given to this question, it is clear that human decision is involved since certain individuals are in fact using a normative principle in their classification of epistemic states of all individuals. The genetic method is an invitation to take seriously the *possibility* that any such normative principle may be studied as a psychological fact, i.e. studied by virtue of its own development in the minds of those who eventually use it. Acceptance of the genetic method does not exclude the possibility that the traditional analysis of *knowledge* is correct – but neither does it exclude the possibility that the classification of what is, and is not, knowledge is itself a developmental matter, 'relative to a certain level of the mechanism of that construction'.

Notice that the genetic method requires there to be a distinction between normative principles and empirical facts. There is an invitation to study any norm as a psychological fact. Genetic epistemology is the study of normative facts, i.e. the use of a norm in a cognitive system. The point of such a study is to investigate the formation of the norm in that cognitive system, that is, to show how the epistemic states of the system develop through time and result in atemporal norms (Piaget, 1966, pp. 143–5).

Someone will say: this reply begs the question in that the use of the genetic method must result in the a committal of the genetic fallacy if a philosophical position is rejected on the basis of the facts of development. In order to evaluate this reply, recall the problem set by Socrates in the *Meno* (Plato, 1956) in which a slave is asked to state the length of the side of a square double in area that of a square with sides 2 ft. long. During the dialogue, Socrates encourages the slave to accept that the length of the side will be equal to the diagonal on the original square. What is of some interest about Socrates' proof is not the question of whether the slave actually does understand it but rather the question of the logical competence required for its comprehension. The proof requires hypothetical thinking (Plato, 1956, p. 87A) as well as an understanding that things equal to the same are equal to each other, i.e. transitivity (p. 84D). Thus an individual who accepts this proof is one who can engage in hypothetical thinking and who can understand transitivity. Hence the individual who can do neither is not in a position to accept this proof and so is not in a position to justify the belief that the side of the square will be equal to the diagonal of the original square. Now if the traditional analysis of *knowledge*, or any similar philosophical analysis, is retained, any such individual will be debarred from understanding this proof. Acceptance of such an analysis leads to a construal of epistemic change as a transformation from one state, say belief, to some other, say knowledge. From this perspective, there is no epistemological difference between the slave, who has the requisite logical competence but fails to use it, and a child who does not have that logical competence in the same form. Yet there is an point of epistemological importance here since the child will not simply lack knowledge in this case but in an indefinitely large range of similar cases where these principles are instantiated. Whereas the slave could, in principle, gain knowledge in such cases, the child could not. This is a difference and is epistemologically important, important because of the consequences for an account of what knowledge is.

What is important is the distinction between idealized and minimal rationality (Cherniak, 1981). The traditional analysis of *knowledge* presupposes that a knowing subject is in principle capable of accepting all of the logical assumptions and consequences of any proposition. In general, any *a priori* account is committed to this same presupposition, unless some restriction is placed upon the extent of the individual's rationality. It is possible, in philosophical epistemology, to demarcate the bounds which are to be placed upon rationality and, in fact, Cherniak (1981, pp. 178–9) distinguishes the normative thesis (a person must make all and only sound inferences from accepted beliefs) from a descriptive thesis (a person must make some of the inferences from accepted beliefs). Yet the latter thesis is content free, if it is put forward on *a priori* grounds. Once it is agreed that the normative thesis is too strong – no knowing subject can have idealized rationality – a reliance upon the descriptive thesis requires the exact specification of what the logical competence of an individual actually is. Piaget's genetic method is ideally suited to the task of adding to the specificity of the descriptive thesis since it provides one empirically based construal of the 'cognitive universals' which are used by knowing subjects on the basis of their past development.

4 CONSTRUCTIVE NECESSITY

The discussion may now turn directly to the problem posed in section 1: in what sense, if any, is a process of structural change a necessary process? The short answer is that this process can be both empirical and necessary but that to see why this is so requires reference to Piaget's construal of the construction of structures, his account of equilibrium. The discussion is in two parts: (1) a review of four respects in which the process of equilibration can be both empirical and necessary and (2) a critique of Piaget's account of equilibration.

4.1 *Equilibration: empirical and necessary*

Piaget first made use of the notion of equilibration in his novel *Recherche* (Piaget, 1918) and his considered account (Apostel et al., 1957b) has not been translated into English. This latter is taken to be preliminary and tentative (Flavell, 1963, p. 244) and is even regarded as so much 'surplus baggage' (Bruner, 1959, p. 365). His revised attempt to articulate this notion preoccupied the last decade of his life; this account (Piaget, 1975/ 1978) is taken to be 'the definitive version of his theses' (Inhelder et al., 1977, p. 10), though Piaget's (1983; Piaget and Garcia, 1983) later work requires the reconsideration of that revised account. It is safe to say that the English translation (Piaget, 1978) is radically defective (Furth, 1981, p. 254; Smith, 1981). Some commentators (Furth, 1981; Vuyk, 1981) offer detailed reviews of the equilibratory model proposed by Piaget.

Leaving the details of that account to one side, there are at least four reasons why the account of equilibration is of relevance to the main problem, namely: a temporal process requires the use of atemporal norms; the genetic method requires the empirical instantiation of normative principles; philosophical theses and empirical testing; and equilibration as the elimination of modal error. Each of these now requires some attention.

Temporal–atemporal. The argument in section 3 was that Piaget's account concerns the individual's understanding of deductive necessity. In that account, it is contended that the use of a cognitive structure, which may have a formal (logical) description, is used as a condition of the individual's understanding of necessity.

If this argument is accepted, it is clear that the outcome of development is a form of understanding which is not open to further revision. Consider any of the tasks reviewed in section 2. A criterial performance on a conservation task requires the understanding of identity; that on an inclusion task requires an understanding of inclusion; that on a seriation task requires the understanding of transitivity. Piaget simply assumes that these logical principles are correct, simply assumes that such normative principles have an acceptable use in formal contexts. What he investigates is whether or not a child performs on a task in a way that indicates an understanding of the logic corresponding to such principles. It is logic- ally possible that any individual should have the cognitive competence to understand the logic implicit in the tasks – indeed, Piaget's rejec- tion of philosophical epistemology (see section 2.2) is based on the presumed empirical inadequacy of any such view and not upon its philosophical adequacy. Thus when Piaget (1980, p. 150) says that there are Kantian elements in his account, what he has in mind is his claim that there is structural, but not a functioning, *a priori*. The individual does not, as Kant would suggest, make use of the *a priori* at the outset of development as a condition of having knowledge at all but rather at the terminal stages in development (Piaget, 1971, pp. 313–17). Once attained, however, such understanding is not open to further change. Children who return incorrect performances upon Piaget's tasks may certainly be expected to undergo further development, including structural change. On the assumption that certain logical principles such as inclusion and transitivity are acceptable to logicians, the understanding of children who do perform correctly on those tasks – that is, the children do understand deductive necessity – is a necessary understanding. On the assumption that such logical principles are acceptable, such understanding *could not be other than it is*.

In short, the criterion of performance on Piaget's tasks makes essential use of normative principles of logic. Such principles partially define the task. In consequence, any performance which meets the criterion is not open to further change. Thus the normative principle is necessary in a formal sense; the child who performs to criterion has an understanding of deductive necessity; and that understanding is itself necessary: it has to be the understanding that it is. There is a way in which an individual's understanding which meets a criterion which is not specified through some normative principle may undergo change, namely through change in the criterion. But if a criterion is specified through a normative principle – that is, any principle which has a necessary modal status – then even if that principle is changed through its subsumption by some other normative principle it follows that any understanding which meets the criterion must be the understanding that it is.

It is not denied that a normative principle, used to specify the criterion, may itself be changed, for example by its incorporation in some richer system. Obvious examples of such subsumption, such as the incorporation of propositional in modal logic (Hughes and Cresswell, 1972), show the truth-preserving nature of the subsumption. Piaget (1971, p. 184; 1986) no doubt has such examples in mind when he recognizes that one formal system may take in another as a special case. Thus the 'passage from the temporal construction to atemporal necessity' (Piaget and Garcia, 1983, p. 27; my translation) is both an empirical, since temporal, and a necessary, since atemporal, process.

Instantiation of normative principles. There is a well-known distinction between a normative principle and its instantiation. The inference principle *modus ponens* is a logical principle which happens to be instantiated in the question (Piaget, 1967b, p. 277) posed to young children: 'If John is in school, then Mary is in school, John is in school. What can you say about Mary?' It is a main contention that the cognitive structure used by individuals is an instantiation of some normative system. A major psychological problem is how to characterize such a structure since there is some difference (Case, 1985; Halford, 1982) of opinion as to how a cognitive structure is to be described. *Pace* Seltman and Seltman (1985, p. 50), it is widely accepted that it is possible for a cognitive structure to have a formal representation in some logical system, even if it is unclear which system actually provides an adequate representation.

Using the argument of section 2, it is apparent that it is at least intelligible – without prejudging the question of whether this is also the case in fact – to suppose that a series of normative systems may be identified such that each simpler system is included in a complex system. For example, if the three systems are propositional, predicate, and modal systems respectively, there is strict inclusion of the simpler systems in the more complex systems. Such logical priority must be respected in any instantiation of these systems – for example, an instantiation of a predicate system must be an instantiation of the propositional system though not the modal system. But it does not follow (see section 3) that any specific temporal ordering is implicated by the logical priority in question. Indeed, it is Piaget's contention that if an empirical check is made, cognitive structures whose formal representation enjoy logical relationships are serially ordered in their psychological realization.

In short, quite independently of whether an individual has an understanding of deductive necessity, it is intelligible to suppose that the use of some cognitive structure underpins the acquisition of any knowledge: 'any knowledge whatsoever always and necessarily involves a fundamental factor of assimilation, which alone confers meaning on what is perceived or conceived' (Piaget, 1967, p. 21/1971, p. 5). It is also intelligible to suppose that the contention that all experience is structured does not entail that the same structure is at issue, since different structures may be used at different developmental points. Piaget (1931) draws a distinction between functioning and structure to make this point. In consequence, cognitive growth, if it occurs, must be growth of a certain sort, namely corresponding to the formal descriptions of the systems which happen to be temporally ordered in the growth of knowledge, whether in children or in the history of science (Piaget and Garcia, 1983, p. 18).

Philosophical theses and empirical testing. There is a sense in which it is intelligible to expose a viewpoint which is necessarily true to empirical evidence with a view to establishing their relation. If a philosophical thesis, which is taken to be necessarily true, is confronted with the available empirical evidence, the expectation would be that all of the evidence would be compatible with that thesis. Thus if there is empirical evidence which is incompatible with such a thesis, that thesis could be rejected on empirical grounds: the thesis, which is asserted to be necessarily true, is not so. There is, then, a methodological rationale (Smith, 1984a, b) for juxtaposing propositions which are taken to be necessary with those which are empirical, since attachment to the latter provides one way of assessing the modal properties of the former.

The rationale, briefly, is that a proposition which is necessary is defined (Hughes and Cresswell, 1972) as one whose negation is not possible. An empirical proposition is one which states that some proposition, including a negative proposition, is possible. Thus the conjunction 'Proposition *p* is both necessary (its negation is not possible) and its negation is possible' is contradictory. The obvious way in which the contradiction can be removed is by denying one of the conjuncts. In consequence, an empirical proposition which has escaped stringent falsification may be retained in preference to a philosophical proposition which is asserted to be necessary. Two examples (cf. Smith, 1987) in which this argument is actually deployed by Piaget are, firstly, the infant's 'understanding' of logic which precedes the infant's use of language, and secondly, the child's acquisition of operational knowledge prior to the use of a formal operational structure. Piaget would claim that there is good empirical evidence for his views about the abilities of the infant and child, which evidence is incompatible with germane philosophical theses.

If this argument is accepted, it may be deployed with respect to the account of equilibration. Equilibration is defined as 'the successive construction with constant elaboration of new structures' (Piaget, 1978, p. v*). One way in which this claim may be construed is as the claim that, necessarily, the use of one type of structure leads to the use of some other type of structure. For example, use of a grouping structure leads to the use of a group structure – and necessarily so. So construed, the claim is not merely that the formal features of one structure include those of the other (cf. Feldman and Toulmin, 1976, p. 409). Nor is it the claim that there is inductive evidence for claiming that there is a constant order of succession. Rather, the claim is a necessary claim about structural growth in a structure's use. With deliberate ambiguity, the necessity in question is constructive necessity, which leaves open its relation to other types of necessity (logical, empirical). Now even if the nature of constructive necessity is left unspecified, the modal argument may still be deployed. If the claim is really a necessary (in the constructive sense) claim, then empirical testing should result in propositions which are entirely compatible with that claim. Thus if there is empirical evidence which runs counter to that claim, a preferred attachment to the latter may be grounds for rejecting the former. The fact that Piaget's account of equilibration is one which includes both necessary and empirical elements is not, in principle, a reason for regarding that account as unintelligible. Such juxtaposition provides one way of establishing which actually are the necessary and empirical elements of the account.

In general, there is both psychological (Apostel et al., 1957a; McCloskey, 1983; Russell, 1982, 1983) and epistemological (Kuhn, 1977; Piaget and Garcia, 1983) evidence for the view that propositions which are taken to be necessary, possible, or impossible, by one set of individuals may be assigned respectively different modal characteristics by others. Piaget's account of equilibration is not, then unintelligible just because its elements are stated to be necessary and empirical.

Equilibration as the elimination of modal error.   The modal concepts of possibility, impossibility and necessity are utilized, in Piaget's constructivist account, in his articulation of a model which is explanatory of equilibratory change. Certainly, these concepts are explicitly used in Piaget's structuralist writings, for example in the claim that 'formal thought brings about from the outset a synthesis of what is possibly with what is necessarily the case' (Inhelder and Piaget, 1955, p. 220/158, p. 251*). Such concepts are central to the account of how children understand deductive necessity. Yet in Piaget's recent works (1981, 1983, 1986), these concepts are used to account for the process of structural change itself.

Piaget's argument has three steps. Firstly, development is defined as a process leading from initial indifferentiation to differentiation and subsequent integration (Piaget, 1983, p. 7). So construed, development is not a process leading from absence to presence (cf. Smith, 1985). Secondly, instances of modal concepts are conflated. Children conflate what is observed to be with what is necessarily the case (Piaget, 1981) just as Aristotle is taken (Piaget and Garcia, 1983, p. 73; Piaget, 1986) to have conflated the factual with the normative. Modal error (cf. Smith, 1984c) may assume two forms. A false-positive modal error occurs when an individual judges to be necessary (possible, impossible) that which is not so. A false-negative modal error occurs when an individual judges to be not necessary (possible, impossible) that which is so. Piaget (1981, 1983) provides exemplars. Thirdly, development is therefore the serial reduction and elimination of modal errors.

If this argument is accepted, there is a sense in which development has to be the process that it is. In order to define the categories of experience, reference must be made to the modal concepts whose use makes experience the experience that it is. The claim does not prejudge the issue of whether other types of concept are also required in the specification of those categories. Thus if an individual's categories of experience are partially defined through that individual's use of modal concepts; and if that use is itself a mistaken use, since modal error is one of its characteristics; and if, finally, that individual is to undergo development, then that development must assume one form and could not assume any other form. Development must be the reduction and elimination of modal error. It is not necessary that development should occur but it is necessary that development in knowledge is the process that it is, when that process does occur.

Since Piaget's account is structural, it is content free. No claim is made that any specific proposition is implicated in development. Indeed, Piaget (see, for example, Piaget, 1986) accepts that certain normative principles are regulative in their employment: the principle of contradiction proscribes contradiction but fails to describe which propositions are in fact contradictories. To accept the principle of contradiction is not to have any guidance as to what are its instances. Similarly, the modal concepts which partially define the categories of experience are regulative in that they fail to give guidance as to their instances. Thus it is always an empirical question as to which specific modal error is made by an individual on any occasion.

Taken in this way, the growth of knowledge occurs on the basis of structural change. This process is necessary (in the constructive sense) in that development must be the elimination of modal error. The process is also empirical since which specific modal errors are made is always an empirical matter.

4.2 *Equilibration: critique*

The account of equilibration is dependent upon distinctive theses, including those outlined in sections 2 and 3 above. In this final section of the discussion, three types of criticism of Piaget's account are briefly reviewed.

One criticism of Piaget's account is that it derogates the social element which is intrinsic to the formation of knowledge (Atkinson, 1983; Hamlyn, 1978, 1982). In consequence, there are doubts about the adequacy of an equilibratory model, which is focused upon the individual's cognition of objects, as a model which is explanatory of social understanding (Labouvie-Vief and Lawrence, 1985). One reply to this criticism is the reminder that Piaget's account explicitly includes a social element which is taken to be one necessary condition in the growth of knowledge, an element which is open to equilibratory analysis (Kitchener, 1981; Mays, 1979; Piaget, 1967c; Smith, 1982b). That is, if this criticism states that there is a social element in the formation of knowledge, there is no doubt that it is not a criticism of Piaget's account. By contrast, if the criticism states that the social element is both necessary and sufficient for the formation of knowledge, it is a criticism of Piaget's account. The former version is not a criticism since an account which takes equilibratory change to be one necessary condition does not exclude there being some other element which is equally necessary. The latter version is a criticism since an account which construes the social element as both necessary and sufficient is incompatible with an account which takes the same element to be merely necessary. An adequate defence of the latter version of the criticism requires the investigation not only of the presence of the social element in the acquisition of knowledge but also of the non-necessity of equilibratory factors. It is still an open question as to whether this requirement has been satisfied.

A second criticism of Piaget's account of equilibration is that it suffers by comparison with rival accounts. A notable example of this criticism arises from research in artificial intelligence in which the virtues of testability, specificity, and applicability (Boden, 1979, 1982; Johnson-Laird, 1983) are noted with some approval. In essence, the criticism states that Piaget's account of inferential understanding may be set aside in favour of a computational account of children's understanding. This criticism rests upon an assumption, namely that structuring is itself *not* open to change. Yet this assumption is not obvious; it is rejected in Piaget's account. Moreover, the argument (Fodor, 1980) that structuring could not change over time begs the question at issue. This argument requires a commitment to a conception of learning, which conception is rejected in Piaget's account (Smith, 1987). This is not to claim that Piaget's account is correct. It is to claim that it is still an open question as to whether the assumption concerned is correct. There are considerable conceptual problems here (Boden, 1982) and it would be premature to 'write off' one account in consequence of this admission.

A final criticism of the account of equilibration is that it is incomplete. It is incomplete not merely in the trivial sense that it has suffered from a relative neglect even in Genevan research but also in the fundamental sense that equilibratory factors constitute at most necessary conditions of knowledge growth. The clearest indication of this incompleteness is Piaget's frequent use of the expression *tôt ou tard* (sooner or later). This expression litters Piaget's classic works (cf. Inhelder and Piaget, 1955, p. 250/1958, p. 283; Piaget and Szeminska, 1941, p. 212/1952, p. 166). The 'definitive' account of equilibration also contains ample examples: use of a scheme *sooner or later* leads to disturbance (Piaget, 1978, p. 82) and in consequence an individual will *sooner or later* make a modal error (p. 26), leading *sooner or later* to reflective abstraction (p. 193) and culminating in upper-bound equilibration (*equilibration majorante*) – *sooner or later* (p. 40). The account of equilibration is supposed to state conditions under which knowledge is formed but these conditions are incomplete. Does knowledge grow sooner (and if so, under what conditions?) or later (and if so, under what conditions?)? In short, the exclusive use of Piaget's account makes it impossible to determine whether knowledge is formed sooner, or later, or not at all (Smith, 1981).

5 CONCLUSION

One conclusion to draw is that Piaget's account is open to differing interpretation. Indeed, this discussion will have achieved its major purpose if future evaluation of Piaget's account does take seriously the fact that this is so. The strategy used here has been to outline certain elements in one reinterpretation of Piaget's account, namely one in which the notion of necessity is used in three distinctive ways.

A second conclusion is that the preferred interpretation is given a textual support. Central to this discussion has been an attempt to show that the interpretation has a basis in Piaget's writings. Interestingly, such a stance may generate the response that the discussion is 'defensive'. It is, however, evident that no claim has been made here that the preferred interpretation is the only interpretation. Indeed, the preferred interpretation is extracted from Piaget's writings rather than being one which is elegantly formulated in one central place. Reinterpretation is one form of evaluation and a 'defensive' discussion – if such it is – has some role in the context of critical evaluation of the sort adverted to in section 1. Crucially, an argument has been presented and its grounds have been elaborated. What is clear is that the next step required of anyone who does accept this argument is an indication of how the argument may be independently supported.

A third conclusion is a reminder that one benefit in accepting the argument is the interpretive value it provides in the evaluation of philosophical and psychological critiques of Piaget's account. It is a signal virtue that one account should be capable of attracting interdisciplinary scrutiny. If 'the central core of Piagetian theory has yet to be clearly and systematically articulated' (Sigel, 1983, p. 138), there is an evident role for both philosophical and psychological contributions. In fact, the major attraction of Piaget's account may well be its capacity to allow interdisciplinary scrutiny with consequential benefit to independent disciplines.

NOTE

1 Modifications to a standard translation are indicated by the use of a French and English reference, for example (Piaget, 1947, p. 55/1950, p. 48–9). A major difference between a standard translation and my own is indicated *, for example (Piaget, 1975, p. 50/1978, p. 43*).

REFERENCES

Apostel, L., Mays, W., Morf, A. and Piaget, J. 1957a: *Les Liaisons Analytiques et Synthétiques*. Paris: Presses Universitaires de France.

Apostel, L., Mandelbrot, B. and Piaget, J. 1957b: *Logique et Equilibre*. Paris: Presses Universitaires de France.

Atkinson, C. 1983: *Making Sense of Piaget*. London: Routledge and Kegan Paul.

Boden, M. 1979: *Piaget*. Brighton, Sussex: Harvester Press.

1982: Is equilibration important? – A view from artificial intelligence. *British Journal of Psychology*, 73, 165–73.

Brainerd, C. J. 1973: Judgments and explanations as criteria for the presence of cognitive structures. *Psychological Bulletin*, 79, 172–9.

1978: The stage question in cognitive-developmental theory. *The Behavioural and Brain Sciences*, 2, 173–213.

Bransford, J. 1979: *Human Cognition*. London: Wadsworth.

Breslow, L. 1981: Re-evaluation of the literature on the development of transitive inferences. *Psychological Bulletin*, 89, 325–51.

Brown, G. and Desforges, C. 1979: *Piaget's Theory: a Psychological Critique*. London: Routledge and Kegan Paul.

Bruner, J. 1959: Inhelder and Piaget's *The Growth of Logical Thinking*. *British Journal of Psychology*, 50, 363–70.

Bryant, P. E. 1984: Piaget, teachers and psychologists. *Oxford Review of Education*, 10, 251–9.

Bryant, P. E. and Trabasso, T. 1971: Transitive inferences and memory in young children. *Nature*, 232, 456–8.

Carney, J. D. and Scheer, R. K. 1964: *Fundamentals of Logic*. New York: Macmillan.

Case, R. 1985: *Intellectual Development*. London: Academic Press.

Chalmers, M. and McGonigle, B. 1984: Are children any more logical than monkeys in the five-term series problem? *Journal of Experimental Child Psychology*, 37, 355–77.

Cherniak, C. 1981: Minimal rationality. *Mind*, 90, 161–83.

Chisholm, R. M. 1977: *Theory of Knowledge*, 2nd edn. Englewood Cliffs, NJ: Prentice-Hall.

Donaldson, M., Grieve, R. and Pratt, C. (eds) 1983: *Early Childhood Development and Education*. Oxford: Basil Blackwell.

Egan, K. 1983: *Education and Psychology: Plato, Piaget and Scientific Psychology*. New York: Teacher's College Press.

Feldman, C. F. and Toulmin, S. 1976: Logic and the theory of mind. In W. J. Arnold (ed.), *Nebraska Symposium on Motivation*, vol. 23. Lincoln, Nebr.: University of Nebraska Press.

Flavell, J. H. 1963: *The Developmental Psychology of Jean Piaget*. London: Van Nostrand.

1977: *Cognitive Development*. Englewood Cliffs, NJ: Prentice-Hall.

Flew, A. 1975: *Thinking about Thinking*. London: Fontana.

Fodor, J. A. 1980: On the impossibility of acquiring 'more powerful' structures. In M. Piattelli-Palmarini (ed.), *Language and Learning*. London: Routledge and Kegan Paul.

Furth, H. G. 1981: *Piaget and Knowledge*, 2nd edn. Chicago, Ill.: Chicago University Press.

Gallagher, J. M. and Reid, D. K. 1981: *The Learning Theory of Piaget and Inhelder*. Monterey, Calif.: Brooks/Cole.

Gelman, R. and Baillargeon, R. 1983: A review of some Piagetian concepts. J. H. Flavell and E. Markman (eds), *Cognitive Development*, vol. 3 of P. Mussen (ed.), *Carmichael's Manual of Child Psychology*. New York: Wiley.

Gettier, E. L. 1963: Is justified true belief knowledge? *Analysis*, 23, 121–3.

Goldman, A. I. 1978: Epistemics: the regulative theory of cognition. *The Journal of Philosophy*, 75, 509–22.

Halford, G. S. 1982: *The Development of Thought*. London: Erlbaum.

Hamlyn, D. W. 1971: Epistemology and conceptual development. In T. Mischel (ed.), *Cognitive Development and Epistemology*. New York: Academic Press.

1978: *Experience and the Growth of Understanding*. London: Routledge and Kegan Paul.

1982: What exactly is social about the origins of understanding? In G. E. Butterworth and P. Light (eds), *Social Cognition*. Brighton, Sussex: Harvester Press.

Hughes, G. E. and Cresswell, M. J. 1972: *An Introduction to Modal Logic*, 2nd edn. London: Methuen.

Inhelder, B. 1982: Outlook. In S. and C. Modgil (eds), *Jean Piaget: Consensus and Controversy*. London: Holt.

Inhelder, B. and Piaget, J. 1955/1958: *De la Logique de l'Enfant à la Logique de l'Adolescent*. Paris: Presses Universitaires de France/ *The Growth of Logical Thinking*. London: Routledge and Kegan Paul.

1964: *The Early Growth of Logic in the Child*. London: Routledge and Kegan Paul.

Inhelder, B., Garcia, R. and Voneche, J.-J. (eds) 1977: *Epistémologie Génétique et Equilibration*. Neuchâtel: Delachaux et Niestlé.

Johnson-Laird, P. N. 1983: *Mental Models*. Cambridge: Cambridge University Press.

Kirkham, R. L. 1984: Does the Gettier problem rest on a mistake? *Mind*, 93, 501–13.

Kitchener, R. F. 1981: Piaget's social psychology. *Journal for the Theory of Social Behaviour*, 11, 253–77.

Kuhn, T. S. 1977: *The Essential Tension*. Chicago, Ill.: University of Chicago Press.

Labouvie-Vief, G. and Lawrence, R. 1985: Object knowledge, personal knowledge and processes of equilibration in adult cognition. *Human Development*, 28, 25–39.

Leibniz, G. W. 1949: *New Essays concerning Human Understanding*. LaSalle, Ill.: Open Court.

Lunzer, E. A. 1968: Formal reasoning. In E. A. Lunzer and J. E. Morris (eds), *Development in Human Learning*. London: Staples Press.

Markman, E. M. 1979: Classes and collections. *Cognitive Psychology*, 11, 394–411.

1985: Why superordinate category terms can be mass nouns. *Cognition*, 19, 31–53.

Mays, W. 1979: Genetic epistemology and theories of adaptive behaviour. In N. Bolton (ed.), *Philosophical Problems in Psychology*. London: Methuen.

McCloskey, M. 1983: Intuitive physics. *Scientific American*, 248, 114–22.

McGarrigle, J. and Donaldson, M. 1974: Conservation accidents. *Cognition*, 3, 341–50.

218   *Issues in Stage Theory*

Miller, S. A. 1982: On the generalizability of conservation: a comparison of different kinds of transformation. *British Journal of Psychology*, 73, 221–30.

Murray, F. B. 1981: The conservation paradigm. In I. Sigel, D. Brodzinsky and R. Golinkoff (eds), *New Directions in Piagetian Theory and Research*. Hillsdale, NJ: Lawrence Erlbaum.

1984: Cognitive development. In T. Husen and T. Postlethwaite (eds), *The International Encyclopedia of Education*, vol. 2. Oxford: Pergamon Press.

Norman, D. A. 1978: Notes towards a theory of complex learning. In A. M. Lesgold, J. W. Pellegrino, S. D. Fokkema and R. Glaser (eds), *Cognitive Psychology and Instruction*. New York: Plenum Press.

Piaget, J. 1918: *Recherche*. Lausanne: Concorde.

1922: Essai sur la multiplication logique et les débuts de la pensée formelle chez l'enfant. *Journal de Psychologie Normale et Pathélogique*, 19, 222–61.

1931: Le développement intellectuel chez les enfants. *Mind*, 40, 137–60.

1947/1950a: *La Psychologie de l'Intelligence*. Paris: Colin/ *The Psychology of Intelligence*. London: Routledge and Kegan Paul.

1950b: *Introduction à l'Epistemologie Génétique*, vol. 1. Paris: Presses Universitaires de France.

1953: *The Origins of Intelligence in the Child*. London: Routledge and Kegan Paul.

1966: *Mathematical Epistemology and Psychology*. Dordrecht: Reidel.

1967a/1971: *Biologie et Connaissance*. Paris: Gallimard/ *Biology and Knowledge*. Edinburgh: Edinburgh University Press.

1967b: Logique formelle et psychologie génétique. *Les Modèles de la Formatisation du Comportement*. Paris: Centre Nationale de la Recherche Scientifique.

1967c: *Etudes Sociologiques*, 2nd edn. Genève: Droz.

1969: Quelque remarques sur les insuffisances de l'empiricisme. *Studia Philosophica*, 28, 119–27.

1970/1977a: *Psychologie et Epistémologie*. Paris: Denoel–Gonthier/ *Psychology and Epistemology*. Harmondsworth, Middx.: Penguin.

1972a: Discours de Reception. *Praemium Erasmianum MCMLXXII*. Amsterdam: Stichtung.

1972b: *Principles of Genetic Epistemology*. London: Routledge and Kegan Paul.

1975/1978: *L'Equilibration des Structures Cognitives*. Paris: Presses Universitaires de France/ *The Development of Thought*. Oxford: Basil Blackwell.

1977b: *Recherches sur l'Abstraction Réfléchissante*, vol. 2. Paris: Presses Universitaires de France.

1980: The psychogenesis of knowledge and its epistemological significance. In M. Piattelli-Palmarini (ed.), *Language and Learning*. London: Routledge and Kegan Paul.

1981: *Le Possible et le Nécessaire*, vol. 1. Paris: Presses Universitaire de France.

1983: *Le Possible et le Nécessaire*, vol. 2. Paris: Presses Universitaire de France.

1986: Essay on necessity. *Human Development*, in press.

Piaget, J. and Szeminska, A. 1941/1952: *La Genèse du Nombre*. Neuchâtel: Delachaux et Niestlé/ *The Child's Conception of Number*. London: Routledge and Kegan Paul.

Piaget, J. and Garcia, R. 1983: *Psychogenèse et l'Histoire des Sciences*. Paris: Flammarion.

Plato, 1956: *Meno*. Harmondsworth, Middx.: Penguin.

Quine, W. V. 1960: *Word and Object*. Cambridge, Mass.: MIT Press.

Russell, J. 1981: Children's memory for the premises in a transitive measurement task assessed by elicited spontaneous justification. *Journal of Experimental Child Psychology*, 31, 300–9.

1982: The child's appreciation of the necessary truth and the necessary falseness of propositions. *British Journal of Psychology*, 73, 253–66.

1983: Children's ability to discriminate between types of propositions. *British Journal of Developmental Psychology*, 1, 259–68.

Samuel, J. and Bryant, P. E. 1984: Asking only one question in the conservation experiment. *Journal of Child Psychology and Psychiatry*, 25, 315–18.

Seltman, M. and Seltman, P. 1985: *Piaget's Logic: a Critique of Genetic Epistemology*. London: Allen and Unwin.

Shultz, T. R., Dover, A. and Amsel, E. 1979: The logical and empirical bases of conservation judgments. *Cognition*, 7, 99–123.

Sigel, I. 1983: Cognitive development is structural and transformational – therefore variant. In I. S. Liben (ed.), *Piaget and the Foundations of Knowledge*. Hillsdale, NJ: Lawrence Erlbaum.

Smith, L. 1981: *Piaget's Genetic Epistemology*. Unpublished doctoral thesis, University of Leicester.

1982a: Class inclusion and conclusions about Piaget's theory. *British Journal of Psychology*, 73, 267–76.

1982b: Piaget and the solitary knower. *Philosophy of the Social Sciences*, 12, 173–82.

1984a: Genetic epistemology and the child's understanding of logic. *Philosophy of the Social Sciences*, 14, 377–83.

1984b: Philosophy, psychology and Piaget. *Philosophy of the Social Sciences*, 14, 385–91.

1984c: *Ability Learning*. London: Further Education Unit.

1985: Making educational sense of Piaget's psychology. *Oxford Review of Education*, 11, 181–91.

1986: Jean Piaget. In A. J. Chapman and N. Sheehy (eds), *Who's Who in Psychology*. Brighton, Sussex: Harvester Press, in press.

1987: Children's knowledge. *Human Development*, in press.

Stroud, B. 1979: Inference, belief and understanding. *Mind*, 88, 179–96.

Tulving, E. 1985: How many memory systems are there? *American Psychologist*, 40, 385–98.

Vuyk, R. 1981: *Piaget's Genetic Epistemology*. London: Academic Press.

Wheldall, K. and Poborca, B. 1980: Conservation without conversation? *British Journal of Psychology*, 71, 117–34.

Winer, G. A. 1980: Class-inclusion reasoning in children: a review of the empirical literature. *Child Development*, 51, 309–28.

10

Piaget on logic and number: the philosophical background

Wolfe Mays

I

INTRODUCTION

Piaget's theories of logic and number are often taken as if they had sprung from his head ready made, in the way Athena is said to have sprung from Zeus. However, they were at least partly derived from the views of his teachers Leon Brunschvicg and Arnold Reymond[1] who both took judgements rather than propositions or concepts as playing an essential role in the construction of logic and number. Piaget also took over Brunschvicg's view that number originated from the practical activities of mankind, before it became embalmed in logical definitions.

Piaget points out that few notions are as clear and distinct as those of elementary arithmetic. But, he remarks, if we consider such a simple proposition as $1 + 1 = 2$, we shall see that it has given rise to a host of difficult epistemological problems. It has been asked (Piaget, 1950, p. 57): is it a self-evident truth, a convention or a tautology? Does it arise from experience, or is it an *a priori* construction or object of an immediate intuition? And is number itself a primary notion or a synthesis of simple logical notions?

Piaget's answers to these questions are intimately connected with Brunschvicg's and Reymond's views as to the nature of number. These are closely related to the role they believe judgements play in the origin of number. Numerical reasoning is regarded as involving both analytic and synthetic judgements. They also did not believe that concepts or universals had an independent existence, but took them rather as arising through such judgements.

Brunschvicg believes that acts of judgement enter in both the construction of logic and number. In the former we deal with the assignment of a predicate to a particular individual or subject, and in the latter with the way we combine elements into a new unity. Nevertheless, he continues, logic and number are basically distinct. We may clearly see this if we compare logical and mathematical classes. A logical class unlike a mathematical one has, he says, an indeterminate character, as the precise number of elements it refers to is not explicitly stated. Thus if we say, 'the class of *Normans* is included in the class of *Frenchmen*', we mention neither the number of *Normans* nor the number of *Frenchmen* (Brunschvicg, 1922: p. 403).

But, Brunschvicg goes on, Frege and others have however tried to define number in logical terms. Thus, for example, a number such as 12 has been defined as a class of equivalent classes. On this view the class of Jesus' apostles, the class of Napoleon's marshals, the class of the signs of the zodiac, and so on, are all taken as elements of the class constituting the number 12.[2]

Brunschvicg notes that Jesus' 12 apostles form a logical class in so far as each manifests the attachment to the master which characterizes the apostle. But, as he continues, if we instead conceive Peter, John, James, and so on, as members of the class of 12 rather than the class of apostles, we no longer deal with a specific identity, which forms the basis of the logical class, but with a numerical identity – the basis of a numerical collection. We no longer deal with independent individuals falling under a specific class. We introduce a relationship between them foreign to the notion of a logical class, the element 'and' or numerical addition (Brunschvicg, 1922, p. 404).

The apostles, marshals, and so on, then form a class because there exists between the different members of a similar class the bond of addition. If we overlook the specific differences between apostles and marshals and only consider their numerical identity, we can then in each such class establish a one-to-one correspondence between an apostle numerically determined and a marshal similarly determined. It is this relationship Brunschvicg claims, which is at the root of mathematical equality and which constitutes a number such as 12 (pp. 404–5). But before we can establish such a relationship taken as defining the cardinal number 12, it is necessary, Brunschvicg argues, to presuppose an ordered series.

There is, he says, no purely ordinal or cardinal number. A collection given *en bloc* in perception is not a number, it only becomes one if we successively distinguish the different elements in it. Conversely, he goes on, a series of units of which we are conscious only becomes a number if a position (or order) is assigned to each unit in terms of its predecessors, and this succession is grasped simultaneously. We cannot, Brunschvicg concludes, separate ordination from cardination – the series of successive acts by means of which the mind runs through each of the elements of the collection, and the synthesis which brings them together into the unity of an intellectual object (that is, the specific number) (pp. 478–9).

Brunschvicg sees number as primarily in origin an operational activity arising from our practical life, as when one object is exchanged against another in barter. The whole operation of numbering by 'pairing', he tells us, is fairly primitive. For example, the inhabitants of the Marquese Islands counted fish and fruit by means of their fingers taken as standard units (p. 472). As Brunschvicg remarks, the exchange of one against one is based on an economic situation. Where material interests occur, men faced with other men not only act from their ówn point of view, but by a common rule of action which justifies them in each other's eyes. Such a rule, he goes on, is not given in things, but arises from them as a result of specifically human activities of which the loyal and equitable practice of exchange is the simplest (p. 471).

Arnold Reymond was Piaget's first teacher of logic and philosophy at Neuchâtel, and his views on logic and mathematics have much in common with Brunschvicg's.[3] Reymond (1908) too distinguishes between qualitative classes and numerical ones. Thus, he tells us, that whereas in logic we understand by a 'man' or a 'sheep' a being distinguished by its qualitative characteristics as by its unity (p. 150), in the case of arithmetical unit, the qualitative disappears almost completely. Between several arithmetical units having a cardinal number, there is only a difference of ordinal position to distinguish them (p. 167).

Reymond further tells us that from a formal point of view mathematical sets designate a collection of objects having certain definite numerical properties. Among the most important of these is what he terms the law of succession or mathematical induction.

Like Brunschvicg, Reymond is critical of the Frege–Russell attempt to reduce mathematics to logic (pp. 170–5). Russell's error, Reymond says, is to think that we can give number a purely cardinal interpretation and to construct by its means an ordinal theory. We cannot, he goes on, extract a law of succession from the class of correspondences which define cardinal number. We cannot assume that after each element of the compared sets there is always another and so on indefinitely as long as the operation is continued (p. 179). Cardinal number will, he says, need completion by ordinal theory which considers number as consecutive and as defined by this very succession. The theory of ordinals implies an indefinable alien to logic (p. 167).

Number for Reymond is then not definable in terms of a simple characteristic: it is a complex notion which has both ordinal and cardinal properties. It might seem, he says, that one can separate numerically the ordinal properties and define cardinal numbers by themselves by means of one-to-one correspondence. However, we cannot do this since such a correspondence already presupposes the activity of enumeration and that of colligation – the combining of the enumerated elements into a new unity. Number is therefore not a set of simple autonomously given elements, but results from the activities of enumeration and colligation.

On the other hand, Russell has attempted to define the succession of numerical units in purely logical terms. This he does by means of the intensional property of 'hereditary'.[4] If Russell's attempt is valid then Reymond's objection that the principle of succession is alien to logic, cannot hold.

But as against Russell, Reymond argues that the general meaning of 'hereditary', at least in its everyday and biological sense, cannot by itself form the succession of general numbers. It assumes for all the terms of a series except the first the existence of a predecessor, but it does not imply that every term will necessarily have a successor. Although every organism is derived from an earlier ancestor, there is no guarantee that a biological line may not become extinct. To fulfil the function which Russell wishes to assign to it, the property of 'hereditary' needs, Reymond argues, to have a *sui generis* numerical meaning which follows from mathematical induction, but we cannot use it without *petitio principii* to define this property (pp. 175–6).

In all this Reymond's view resembles Brunschvicg's, and they both seem to have influenced Piaget's own view of logic and number. For example, the operations of colligation, seriation, and correspondence, enter for Piaget into the construction of logical *groupements* and mathematical groups. However, since his approach is basically a genetic one he is concerned not only with number as a conceptual operation, but also with the perceptual recognition of number.

HUSSERL AND PIAGET ON 'FIGURAL NUMBER'

It is not clear whether Piaget had much first-hand acquaintance with Husserl's philosophical writings, although he sometimes shows himself critical of them. However, there is a marked resemblance between their respective views as far as the nature of number is concerned. This is especially the case in the distinction they both draw between the perception of number and our intellectual comprehension of it. It is also not clear how far Brunschvicg and Reymond were acquainted with Husserl's work, as his name rarely appears in their writings.

In his account of number Husserl (1891, chap. 4) attempts to get back to the individual's spontaneous activities of collecting and counting. He distinguishes two basic concepts: 'collective combination' indicated by the verbal expression 'and'; and the concept of 'something' (*etwas*), which he regards as the basis of the arithmetical unit. To arrive at this notion we need to abstract all the specific characteristics from the particular objects (real or conceptual). To grasp a number of things is therefore simply to grasp certain objects as mere 'somethings' and as related by the term 'and'. Piaget takes up a somewhat similar position when he attempts to base the numerical unit on the concept *quelconque* (anywhatsoever).

Despite Frege's criticism of Husserl's view that it was a form of psychologism, and his criticism of the latter's concept of 'something' as a 'bloodless ghost' (cf. Frege, 1894, pp. 313–32), Husserl would say that he was putting forward a concept of number based on the way we actually use number. He was not concerned to base number, as both Frege and Russell did, on the abstract properties of concepts.

Husserl discusses in some detail our actual perception of number, and tries to show how it differs from our categorial understanding of it. In his *Philosophie der Arithmetik* (1891), he describes the way we make estimates of plurality and number at a glance, as when in perception we recognize groups of two, three, or four objects. This he contrasts with true collecting and counting, where we apprehend each item or member of the group separately. These perceptual properties of number he described as figural or quasi-qualitative *Momente*. A figural quality is not a property of the individual elements of an aggregate, but of the aggregate as a whole. Husserl tells us that number as distinct from 'multitude', only becomes present to us when we apprehend the individual parts as standing to each other in relations of 'more', 'equal' and 'less' (cf. Husserl, 1891, chap. 11).

In *The Child's Conception of Number*, Piaget (1952, p. 199) showed an acquaintance with Husserl's discussion of number. (Although it has been suggested that he might have derived this knowledge from one of his collaborators.) Piaget follows Husserl in distinguishing figural knowledge from operational (categorial) knowledge, and he refers to a short passage in Husserl's *Logische Untersuchungen* (Husserl, 1970) where this distinction is made.

Piaget asks: can the beginnings of addition be found in Husserl's notion of colligation (that is, collective combination)? Husserl, he points out, 'makes a fundamental opposition between colligation which gives rise to sets that are categories, and global qualities that are merely perceptual, which he calls quasi qualitative Momente or figural Momente'. Piaget claims that this distinction can be observed at the different stages at which the child comes to arrive at the concept of number. Thus at the start the young child evaluates quantities in terms of figural qualities, and only later categorially (Piaget, 1952, p. 199).

Piaget refers here to his experiments on the conservation of number. He tells us that when a child at the first stage is asked to compare two rows of counters and to decide whether they are equal in number, the child uses as a criterion not the number of elements but certain figural qualities exhibiting such relationships as 'more or less long' or 'more or less wide'. For the young child there is only a figural (qualitative) correspondence. As soon as the row is altered he apparently bases his evaluations on one criterion alone, either the length of the row, the width of the figure or its density, and so on.

Thus in the case of two rows of counters which the child takes to be perceptually equal, when the counters in one of the rows are spaced out, the rows are no longer considered equal. The child, we are told, has not yet acquired the operational concept of number which would enable him to put together the various parts of the figural perception if it is broken up. But for the adult, if the row is spaced out the elements keep their ordinal number, which they also do if the row is closed up. Variations in length and density do not affect his evaluations (pp. 86–7).

That Piaget agrees with Husserl's view on the way we immediately recognize the number of groups of objects in the form of figural perceptions, is not surprising. Throughout their writings they are particularly concerned with the importance of part–whole relationships for epistemology.

It is also worth mentioning that when writing his *Philosophie der Arithmetik* Husserl was working with Stumpf at the University of Halle. At that time Stumpf was interested in the phenomenon of musical whole qualities, as, for example, when we hear a succession of separate notes as a melody. Husserl seems to have applied this kind of study to the perception of number. Von Ehrenfels, who was one of the founders of *Gestalt* psychology, was also working with Stumpf at that time, and Husserl (1970, p. 799, n. 2) compares his quasi-qualitative *Momente* with von Ehrenfels' *Gestalt* qualities.

The genetic dimension introduced by Piaget in his account of number brings out a difference between his studies and those of someone like Brunschvicg. For Piaget logical and mathematical operations have their root in the concrete ordering and classifying activities of the child.[5] Although Brunschvicg was interested in anthropological studies of the development of number among primitive peoples, when it came to the question of number as it occurs among individuals in our culture, he largely concerned himself with adult thought. He was therefore not concerned, as Piaget was, with the problems of conservation, which arise when the young child has to rely on the changing figural perceptions in his evaluations of number. At the level of adult thought the conservation of concepts during logical and mathematical operations has already been achieved.

Piaget's experiments on the development of the concept of number, are, among others, an attempt to see how far his theoretical account can obtain an empirical application. As his model of one-to-one correspondence is based on the exchange of one against one in simple practical situations, it is not surprising that there should be some fit between his theory and actual practice. To the objection that this type of experiment is highly artificial and found only in the laboratory, Piaget could reply that it mirrors in microcosm the practical activities of mankind.

PIAGET AND THE CONCEPT OF NUMBER

Piaget has been criticized for not accepting Russell's definition of number in terms of equivalent logical classes, and indeed sometimes for seeming to accept such a view. But although Piaget believes number has logical aspects, his account of it differs radically from Russell's. This is primarily because he considers logic to have an operational (that is, constructive) character and not a purely analytic one.

On the other hand, Piaget (1950) is critical of the view that number is a product of a rational intuition (pp. 92–5). Poincaré was perhaps the leading modern exponent of this view, although Brouwer's intutionism would also come under this head. For Poincaré, Piaget tells us, there exists a primitive intuition of $n + 1$ or reasoning by recurrence, which he takes to be a power of the mind to conceive an indefinite repetition of the same act. This Poincaré identifies with the principle of mathematical induction, which he states as follows. 'If a property is true of the number 1, and if it is established that it is true of $n+1$ provided it is true of n, it will be true of all whole numbers' (Poincaré, undated, p. 149). Unlike logical deduction he believes that mathematical induction can give us new knowledge.

Poincaré goes on to ask: why do we need this principle, why cannot we conceive of a mind powerful enough to see at a glance the whole body of mathematical truth? He points out that although a chess player can prepare for two or five steps ahead, however remarkable a player may be, he cannot prepare for more than a finite number of moves. Similarly, Poincaré goes on, in arithmetic we cannot conceive the general truth by direct intuition alone. The only way we can make general statements about all numbers is through mathematical induction (Poincaré, 1952, p. 11).

Piaget does not agree with Poincaré's analysis. He argues that Poincaré, by concentrating on his own adult thought, has overlooked that before reasoning by recurrence can occur, we must first have constructed invariant units and collections of such units. The faculty of conceiving that a unit can be added to a collection of units, which for Poincaré is the essence of the pure intuition, assumes the capacity of ordering the elements and of forming cardinal collections. If this is the case, Piaget (1950, pp. 93–5) concludes, the sequence of natural numbers cannot be based simply on a primitive intuition of reasoning by recurrence: as an intuition it is already complex.

Piaget claims that his own position is a viable alternative to Poincaré's intuitive account of number and to Russell's purely logical view. Piaget's main theme is that there is a reciprocal relationship between number and logic. Number has logical aspects, but logic itself contains the notion of number in an indeterminate sense, as it refers to such notions as 'none', 'some', and 'all'.

Piaget's account is rooted in Brunschvicg's and Reymond's view that in number, cardination and ordination are essential to each other, just as intension and extension are in the case of logical classes. 'L. Brunschvicg', Piaget says, 'has decisively shown that, in the finite, ordination presupposes cardination and vice versa' (1950, p. 68). In ordination, for example, if the successive units are homogeneous, this order can only be distinguished by referring to the collection formed by this very succession. On the other hand, cardinal collections can only be evaluated in terms of the ordered succession of units, if the same unit is not to be counted twice.

Piaget restricts the reciprocity of ordinality and cardinality to finite numbers, and would not extend it to Cantorian infinite ordinals and cardinals. Unlike finite numbers they are distinct from each other in much the same way as logical classes and serial relations are. And he draws our attention to certain affinities between the relations holding between Cantorian infinite sets and those between logical classes.[6]

The duality which finite number possesses can already be found, according to Piaget, in the psychological genesis of number. At first, he tells us, the young child cannot carry out enumeration and colligation as a function of each other. Thus his perception of a collection as a heap and his perception of the counters examined successively have nothing in common.[7] At a later stage, Piaget goes on, enumeration and colligation are seen to be intimately connected. Every perceived configuration of a given set can now be changed into any other of the same set, without the child saying that the number of elements in it has changed. When he counts the elements, he is able to understand that the order of each item in the series is defined in relation to the set of seriated elements, which now forms an invariant whole (Piaget, 1952, pp. 200–1).

But Piaget does not simply take over Brunschvicg's and Reymond's views relating to the formation of number, he also tries to show, more than perhaps they do, that the operations of enumeration, colligation, and correspondence have their logical counterparts. Piaget, however, sub- stitutes the notion of seriation (the operation of serially relating terms) for enumeration, as he takes it to be a more primitive notion entering into both logic and number. In logic these operations are concerned with classes, relations and the possible connections between them, which make up Piaget's theory of *groupements* (Piaget, 1942, pp. 262–6; 1966, pp. 263–6).

The following summarizes the basic features of these operations.

Colligation. In the logic of classes this refers to the combination of different individuals into a single class. For example, we put individual men under the general concept man. In relations we refer to the combination of a succession of partial relations into a more inclusive one. In number we deal with the operation 'and' or 'plus', which combines a plurality into a simple numerical whole.

Seriation. In number it refers to the different combinations in terms of which the related elements may be orderd. In the logic of classes it is to be seen in the hierarchical inclusion of one class in another, namely, $A<B<C$, whilst the enumeration of the elements in each class again involves seriation.

Correspondence. Piaget distinguishes two kinds: qualitative and mathematical. He gives as an example of qualitative correspondence, a child who puts angles in his copy irrespective of whether he knows how many there are in the original. Another example is the homologies of comparative anatomy: thus the vertebrae of an ostrich will correspond with those of a camel or a fish. Mathematical correspondence (or any whatsoever) is one where each element is understood as a unit irrespective of its qualities. Thus in two equal sets of counters, a blue counter in one set will be taken as corresponding to a red one in the other.

Piaget has been criticized for allegedly assuming that there can be an isomorphism between qualitative classes. Isomorphism, we are told, is 'a mathematical concept and does not, and cannot, refer to qualitatively different states of existence' (Seltman and Seltman, 1985, p. 194). As a counter-example we may mention D'Arcy Thompson's apparently successful attempt to set up an isomorphism between different types of organic structures in his *On Growth and Form*. In any case, Piaget distinguishes sharply between the correspondence of the D'Arcy Thompson type, and mathematical correspondence where we essentially deal with terms only distinguishable from each other by their order.

This distinction forms the basis of Piaget's criticism of Russell's attempt to define number in terms of equivalent classes. He argues that Russell's account is flawed by his failure to take this distinction into account. To illustrate this point we may refer to the example discussed early, where 12 is defined in terms of equivalent classes of apostles, Napoleon's marshals, signs of the zodiac, and so on. The equivalence established, Piaget would say, is a non-qualitative one, and this already involves an implicit numbering. Cardinal number, he therefore claims, is not reduced to a qualified logical class, but to one which is quantified from the start.

PIAGET'S FORMAL MODEL OF THE DEVELOPMENT OF NUMBER

We have seen that Piaget in his theoretical account of the development of the concept of number is not attempting to give, as Russell does, a definition of number in logical terms. He is trying to give a formalization of the sorts of activities which occur during the development of our capacity to use number. Piaget's model should not be taken as referring to what is actually going on in our conscious minds, as we also learn to number on a concrete behavioural level.

Piaget (1942) states that units seriated by means of the relation $\overset{1}{\rightarrow}$ or their sums by 'types of order'[8] form the ordinal numbers. He also brings out the reciprocity of the ordinal and cardinal aspects of number:

> ordinal number and cardinal number are both distinct and inseparable from each other.[9]
>
> They are distinct because cardinal number in common with logical classes is characterised by the act of colligation which combines the terms $(A + A = B)$ or $(1 + 1 = 2)$ by commutative addition, whilst ordinals in common with asymmetrical serial relations are seriated in a succession of linear relations . . . the cardinals and ordinals are inseparable because without the ordinal seriation of positions, the collection $(A+A+A)$ would give by tautology only A and not the number 3, and without the cardinal sum of the units already counted, the relation between one position and its successor would not be distinguished from the other relations. The 3rd therefore implies the cardinal number 3 as the latter implies the three ordinals 1st, 2nd and 3rd.
>
> This duality shows that the structures of classes and relations subsist in number, where they are fused in a truly operational whole. (Piaget, 1942, pp. 211–12)

Piaget is here largely expounding Brunschvicg's and Reymond's view that number is a complex notion resulting from acts of enumeration and colligation. There is, however, a difference between their respective positions. For example, Brunschvicg has spoken of enumeration as a series of successive acts, and colligation as the act which brings these successive acts into a unity of an intellectual object. Piaget, on the other hand, transforms Brunschvicg's mental acts into operations, and takes the further step of formalizing these in logical terms.

It is of interest that at the same time that Piaget was probably meeting with Brunschvicg during his stay in Paris, he was reading Couturat's *Algèbre de la logique* in the *Bibliothèque Nationale*. He tells us

> When I read Couturat's *Algèbre de la logique* in the *Nationale* ... I found that the elementary logical operations which I studied with difficulty in Couturat's symbolism, provided me exactly with the model I required in order to understand the difficulties my children had in solving Burt's problems. Inclusion, addition and multiplication of relations, the linking of transitive asymmetrical relations, etc, were no longer abstractions: I saw them constructed between 7 and 12 years. ... The abstract model provided by an algebra of logic became essential for me in the analysis of the genetic facts. (Piaget, 1960, p. 60)

In his early work Piaget tried to understand the difficulties children had in grasping simple logical problems by using Couturat's logic. Now in his normative model he is using the logic of classes and relations as an intellectual tool for the analysis of the genetic data relating to number. The authors of a recent book on Piaget's logic, have however transmuted his normative model into an ontology. We are told that for Piaget 'logico-mathematics is the true essence of being' (Seltman and Seltman, 1985, p. 230). Apart from Piaget clearly distinguishing between logic and mathematics, logical and mathematical operations arise in the first place for him from concrete behavioural activities, and are therefore prior to the development of the main abstract formal operations. For Piaget, concrete meaningful actions come first in the child's behaviour, and internalized mental activity arises from it at a later date.

II

BRAINERD'S CRITIQUE OF PIAGET'S ACCOUNT OF NUMBER

There has been a good deal of criticism of Piaget's account of number. One of his most trenchant critics has been Brainerd. It is worth looking at some of his criticisms as they exemplify typical misunderstandings of Piaget's position. Brainerd tells us (1979, p. 76) that Piaget's approach to the logical foundations of the number concept appears to be entirely unique to him and his collaborators in Geneva. He also states that Piaget has 'concluded that it is correct to view mathematics, generally, and number, particularly, as reducible to logical concepts. But he continued to believe that there was something logically incorrect about saying that numbers are merely classes of similar classes' (p. 83).

Piaget's views on number are certainly not unique to him and his school.

They might indeed be said to be a distillation of those of Brunschvicg and Reymond. There are frequent acknowledgements to their work in his writings. Further, Brainerd seems to be moving on a different level of abstraction from Piaget himself. He does recognize that Piaget's views on number have epistemological and psychological connections. But he fails to realize that Piaget's account of number is largely an epistemological one, and that he is not just giving, as Russell tries to give, a purely logical analysis of number.

It is in any case false to assert that Piaget believes that number is reducible to logic. This indeed is the main burden of his critique of Russell, that although number, as we generally think about it, has logical aspects it is not simply reducible to them. Piaget believes there is a radical distinction between logic and number. In the former, he would claim, the rule of tautology applies, in the latter the principle of iteration or succession. He would also assert that it is not just a question of Russell's account being logically incorrect, but that it was epistemologically false, as well as false as a matter of natural history. Russell would have responded that he was not concerned with epistemology or natural history, but with the logic of number.

Brainerd now tells us that according to Piaget, Russell is unable to set up an equivalence between unqualified classes in his account of number. He continues

Without such a 'qualitative equivalence', one-to-one correspondence is impossible. The only way that Russell was able to effect such correspondences, so the argument goes, is by assuming, without knowing it, that he knew the number of which given classes were instances. This is an exceedingly elliptical argument in which there appears to be no merit whatsoever. (pp. 83–4)

But Piaget does not say that it is impossible to establish a one-to-one correspondence between unqualified classes. This is precisely what his correspondence 'anywhatsoever' comes to. The nub of Piaget's argument is that Russell, in his attempt to derive number from a class of equivalent classes, assumed that the logical identity thus established entailed a numerical one. Piaget holds that this is not the case, as these two kinds of identity are basically different. The only identity we can establish between such varied collections as apostles, months of the year, signs of the zodiac, and so on, he would claim, is a numerical one – as pluralities they only possess the property of twelveness.

Further, Piaget would argue that we cannot derive the principle of succession (or mathematical induction) essential to the generation of number from logical concepts. For example, Reymond (1908, pp. 175–6) has tried to show that although Russell thought otherwise, in trying to define this principle in terms of the property 'hereditary', he assumed it in his definition. This does not seem to be an entirely worthless argument, and may indeed have some point to it.

Brainerd (1979) continues by trying to show that it is unnecessary to have a knowledge of the terms involved in order to establish correspondences.

> it is not true that in logic we must know that, for example, Napoleon always corresponds to Josephine as a precondition for concluding that there is a one-to-one correspondence between the class of monogamously wedded men and the class of monogamously wedded women. The relation of monogamy suffices to guarantee the correspondence independent of links between specific members of the two classes. (p. 84)

Brainerd's contention that we can establish a one-to-one correspondence between the terms of two classes without knowing their specific links is irrelevant here. Piaget's account of number does not in the first place depend on such a correspondence. Before it can be established that for him, number must already have been constructed in its dual aspect, cardinal and ordinal. Further, if we establish a relation of monogamy between a certain class of males and a certain class of females, the knowledge obtained is no help in the derivation of number. All we are told is that the elements in the two classes are equal. We are not told how many there are. For this we need numerical information.

Brainerd now puts us in the picture as to what method he thinks Piaget actually uses in his derivation of number.

> The method that Piaget ultimately decided on is that of ordering the terms of classes. If we are allowed to order the respective terms of two classes Rx and Ry, then we may say that Rx has a first term x_1, a second term x_2, and so on, and we may say that Ry has a first term y_1, a second term y_2, and so on.... Two terms are mapped together if and only if they have the same ordinal number. ... Moreover, the method can be applied to all classes, finite or infinite, without exception. (pp. 84–5)

In talking of Piaget's so-called ordering method, Brainerd identifies it with 'ordering the terms in classes', and thereby fails to grasp Piaget's point that although an ordered succession of terms is necessary for number, we also need cardinals to number them. Piaget notes that 'This is what Russell among others does when he defines ordinal number by the "class of similar serial relations"' (Piaget, 1942, p. 210, n. 1). But Piaget would say that Russell fails to take into account the reciprocity between the ordinal and cardinal aspects of number. Hence, number for Piaget is not simply derived from establishing a correspondence between the class of elements x_1, x_2, and so on and that of y_1, y_2, and so on. Before such an equivalence can be set up for him, number in its dual aspect has first to be constructed. He also makes it clear that his claim that number has such a duality is only applicable to finite inductive ones and not to Cantorian infinite sets.

Early on in his critique Brainerd tells us that on Piaget's view it is incorrect 'to base the natural number system exclusively on either ordinal numbers or cardinal numbers. Instead natural numbers should be identified with both the ordinals and the cardinals (1979, p. 76). However, some pages later he informs us, 'Piaget obviously assumes that Russell was correct when he maintained that the natural numbers should be identified with cardinal numbers' (p.85). It is difficult to reconcile these statements. If the former is correct the latter must be false. There seems two possible explanations of this apparent inconsistency. Either Brainerd has forgotten his earlier statement, or he believes that Piaget's *malgré lui* was putting forward a cardinal view of number. If it is the latter it has, to quote his own words, 'no merit whatsoever'.

Brainerd produces another objection to what he takes to be Piaget's view that we need to use the 'ordering method', to establish a correspondence between classes containing equally many elements. Brainerd tells us that it is unnecessary to do this.

> Suppose we have the class of all natural numbers and the class of all even natural numbers, but neither is arranged in any particular order.... Given any natural number x, we do not need to know its position (ordinal number) in the series to find its even correspondent. We simply multiply by 2.... Given any term from either class, therefore, we can map it with a unique term in the other class without knowing the ordinal number of either term.... The terms in any infinite class can be placed in one-to-one correspondence with the terms of subsets of the class. (pp. 86–7)

Interestingly enough Piaget has used a similar example to make the point that Cantorian infinite numbers are of a radically different kind from finite inductive numbers. Piaget tells us that Cantorian infinite cardinals and ordinals like logical classes and relations, are independent of each other and can therefore be specified separately. That only finite numbers have for Piaget a dual character is made clear in the quotation from Piaget which Brainerd puts at the head of his critique. 'Finite numbers are therefore necessarily at the same time cardinal and ordinal' (p. 76). Brainerd seems unaware that a limitation is being introduced here.

Piaget notes that Cantorian infinite numbers have the property of being reflective, namely, we can establish a one-to-one correspondence between an infinite class and its subsets. Brainerd's counter-example is therefore beside the point, as Piaget is only concerned here with finite inductive numbers in which the reflective type of correspondence does not apply. Because of this Piaget does not regard Cantorian infinite sets as true numbers, but as being more akin to logical classes and relations (see note 6).

Brainerd now tries to show that Piaget misconceives the very nature of the correspondence relationship.

> In logic, correspondence is not a mapping 'operation' which mechanically links one element with another, as Piaget seems to think it is. . . . Correspondence depends on the relations which obtain between classes. Correspondence is . . . a 'property' of certain kinds of relations. Some relations are invariably one-to-one . . . there are some relations which are invariably one-to-many or many-to-one or many-to-many. (p. 87)

Piaget's whole conception of logic is radically different from Brainerd's. He would reject the view that correspondence is a mechanical linking between two sets of terms. He considers it to be an operational (synthetic) activity combining them. Earlier on Brainerd had stated, 'Piaget seems to confuse the everyday "concrete operation" of correspondence with the formal relational concept' (p. 84). But Piaget would argue that all forms of correspondence – concrete or conceptual – involve an active bringing together of sets of elements. He would also claim that formal relations, when considered apart from the terms they relate, are really abstractions. He would not deny that there are various ways of relating elements in classes. But he would say that Russell in his logical account of number, is primarily concerned with the one-to-one relation of equivalence.

As another objection to Piaget's so-called 'ordering method', Brainerd refers to Russell's remark that order is not the essence of number, and he quotes Russell's cardinal definition of ordinals. 'We may therefore define the ordinal number *n* as the class of serial relations whose domains have *n* terms, where *n* is a finite cardinal number.' Brainerd goes on, 'The crucial point is that it is completely superfluous to "add" ordinal number to Russell's definition of cardinal number as Piaget does.' He concludes, 'In all of Piaget's extensive writings on the number concept, there seems to be no evidence that he is aware of either of these facts' (p. 89).

Not only was Piaget aware of these facts, he also refers to Russell's definition. But he would say that it only gives one side of the story, that unless we had an ordered succession of terms we could not set up such a class of similar serial relations. In other words, cardinals and ordinals imply each other. Piaget does not, therefore, have to accept Brainerd's directive that whether we choose an ordinal or cardinal approach, we must in any case choose between them. Piaget need do neither, as he is involved in a different sort of enquiry. He is not, as Brainerd assumes, giving a logical analysis of number, trying to base it on the smallest number of axioms; but a formal model of what he terms a 'natural' arithmetic.

CONCLUSION

As we have suggested, Piaget is giving in his account of the origin of number, not only a description of the operations entering into the development of a 'natural' arithmetic, but also a formal model of them. This seems to be the point of his comments on Frege's criticism of Husserl's philosophy of arithmetic, which Frege took to be a form of psychologism, namely that it proceeded from empirical observations to normative statements about the formal properties of number.

Piaget (1952) tells us,

> Husserl would have been able to continue doing good psychology without falling into 'psychologism'. All he needed to know was that he studied a 'natural' arithmetic without claiming to legislate for the logic of number. He could then construct limited logical models corresponding to what he found, and compare them with the completely abstract models constructed by Frege, Schröder, etc. There would not then have been any psychologism in the sense of an inference from fact to norm. (p. 143)

Piaget, then, believes that an account of the origin of number ought not to proceed from abstract concepts relating to the properties of classes as the Frege–Russell account does, but from the way we actually use number in our daily lives. However, together with Brunschvicg and Reymond he also holds the stronger thesis, and here they have something in common with Poincaré, that a purely logical account of number is inadequate. They argue that attempts to define the principle of succession in intentional terms fail. And here they seem to be legislating for the logic of number despite Piaget's assertion that they need not.

English-speaking readers of Piaget's *The Child's Conception of Number* may overlook that in his experiments described there, Piaget is giving among other things an empirical application of Brunschvicg's and Reymond's views on number as developed by him. Consequently, it is often assumed, as Brainerd does, that the inspiration for Piaget's views came from Russell's logical account, and that one might regard it as a 'freak' variety of the latter. But this can only lead to a misunderstanding of Piaget's position. In his account of the dual aspect of number, in his emphasis on iteration as a basic feature of numerical formulae, as well as in his critique of Russell's attempt to define number in logical terms – in all these respects his account closely follows Brunschvicg's and Reymond's.

A standard objection by philosophers to Piaget's views on logic and mathematics is that they commit the fallacy of psychologism. To this Piaget would reply that his enquiry is primarily an epistemological one. The operations he describes exhibit implicatory or meaningful relations and not causal ones. In his early work, for example, he tried to explain the conditioned reflex in terms of implication rather than habit, conceiving it as a relation of meaning between sign and thing signified (Piaget, 1953, pp. 399–407). He would also distinguish between the operations of classifying and seriating and the product of these operations – the more formal systems constructed from them. These have a normative character and are only dependent for their truth on formal tests of validity.

On the empirical side the results of Piaget's experiments on, for example, the conservation of number, and also his manner of their interpretation have been questioned. But even if his experimental results were to be shown false or incorrectly interpreted, his experiments would nonetheless remain of interest. He has shown in them, among other things, how theoretical models of number can be given an empirical application. It ought not to be forgotten that the relation of one-to-one correspondence used by Frege and Russell in their logical definition of number, has its roots in the pairing operations which primitive peoples use in their counting, and which is closely related to the act of exchange.

APPENDIX: PIAGET ON MATHEMATICAL REASONING AND POSSIBILITY

Piaget (1942) contends that mathematical reasoning engenders new conclusions. Thus in the equation $1 + 1 = 2$, the operation of addition gives rise to a new element 2. On the other hand, he tells us, if we believe that mathematical reasoning concerns itself with tautologies, then 2 becomes by definition equal to $1 + 1$. The operation of addition is no longer a conceptual one, but a sign, and on this interpretation, logic and the whole of mathematics becomes a simple language.

Mathematical reasoning for Piaget, as it does for Poincaré, goes beyond the syllogism to arrive at conclusions not contained in the original premises. As he sees it, the feature of mathematical construction is that it can be continued indefinitely, so that, for example, ∞ is to be taken as expressing the operation $n + 1$ indefinitely repeated. He argues that if we reject a constructionist approach in terms of operations, it becomes necessary to situate ∞ somewhere in a physical, logico-linguistic or logico-ideal reality. Some such assumptions seems to have been implicitly made by Cantor when he constructed his infinite sets. Piaget seems to overlook that there could be a *tertium quid*, Popper's 'third world'. But although Piaget believes that the propositions of logic and mathematics have a normative character, he would not wish to give them the status of eternal Platonic truths.

Piaget argues that although logical classes and relations result through constructive thought, mathematics alone exhibits the property of generating new knowledge. Such knowledge, he claims, results from the unlimited ways in which mathematical entities can be combined. Logical classes and relations, on the other hand, do not possess for him this property, as they only engender tautological truths.

In a more recent publication Piaget (1976) has discussed the nature of possibility, which he takes to be the central problem of a constructivist epistemology like his own. He first looks at the view held by some biologists of a preformist tendency. On this view a sufficiently powerful mind would be able to deduce every possibility from the start by means of combinatory procedures. For example, the DNA molecule which is the origin of hereditary properties is said to be made up of elements combined in innumerable ways. The evolution of human beings could therefore be conceived as the simple product of these combinations, so that its creativ : character becomes illusory.

Against this approach Piaget argues that possibilities especially as they occur in mathematical reasoning, are not static and are continually developing. A possibility, he tells us becomes possible in the degree where we become able to conceive it as such. Each possibility is therefore the result of an event which has, as it were, produced an 'opening up' on a new possibility. From this it follows that the notion of 'the set of all possibles' is an illusory whole, since its boundaries are not sharply drawn and are continually changing. If this is so, he concludes, the capacity to conceive of an ever wider range of possibilities cannot be simply due to a recombination of existing elements, as is the case in a combinatory system.

Although Piaget's account of possibility has something of the 'Sorcerer's Apprentice' about it, it is clear that his view is radically opposed to the current conception of 'possible worlds', where all possibilities are already present if we have the wit to make them out. Invention and novelty are then eliminated from mathematical reasoning, which then becomes more like a voyage of discovery, where we discover truths which up to then had been hidden from us. On the other hand, for Piaget human reasoning, whether it be in mathematics, science or literature involves the capacity to create new ideas, which are more than a recombination of old elements.

HISTORICAL NOTE

Piaget arrived in Paris in 1919 and left in 1921. During this period apart from attending a course on psychological pathology, he studied logic and philosophy of science with Lalande and Brunschvicg. The latter, he says, influenced him considerably because of his historico-critical method and his appeal to psychology. Piaget then had the opportunity to work in Binet's old laboratory in a Paris school, so as to standardize Burt's reasoning tests on Paris children. It was during this time that he read Couturat's *Algèbre de la logique*.

NOTES

1   Leon Brunschvicg (1869–1944) was Professor of Philosophy at the Sorbonne, and Arnold Reymond (1874–1958) was Professor of Philosophy at the Universities of Neuchâtel and Lausanne.

2   Bertrand Russell (1948, p. 18) defines number as '*The number of a class is the class of all those classes that are similar to it.*'

3   Brunschvicg brings out the origin of number in our practical activities by introducing an intellectual experiment which might be a precursor of Piaget's own experiments on children.

   Suppose, he says, we give a young child who cannot count, four sous and ask him to exchange a sous for an apple at the greengrocer. He will give a sous and be given an apple in return, and he will continue until he has run out of sous. Brunschvicg tells us that the repetition of this action highlights a constant factor – a certain rule manifesting itself in the act of exchange. Whilst the exchange of a sous for an apple is not a mathematical operation, the exchange of four sous for four apples is already one. Arising from these exchanges the boy has added to his perceptions the conception that the two groups, sous and apples are related – that they are equivalent (Brunschvicg, 1922, pp. 465–6).

   Brunschvicg states that he accepts Kant's view of number that it is not a concept or judgement but a law of reasoning.

4   According to Russell (1948, p. 21) 'A property is said to be "hereditary" in the natural-number series if, whenever it belongs to a number n, it also belongs to $n + 1$, the successor of n.'

5   Piaget considers conceptual operations to be actions which are internalized, reversible in the sense of being carried out in both directions and co-ordinated into structured wholes. By concrete operations he means those accompanying language, but not conceived solely in terms of propositions or verbal statements, as they are carried out on concrete objects.

6   Piaget (1942, pp. 218–31; 1950, pp. 126–31; 1972, pp. 197–8) discusses the difference between finite and infinite numbers.

7   Piaget does not think enumeration by itself implies addition without colligation entering in. It has sometimes been said, he tells us, that because the child can carry out a primitive form of enumeration, he also has the concept of number. Piaget quotes Preyer who 'regards as a beginning of addition the behaviour of a child who picked up all the ninepins of a set one after the other, each time saying "one, one, one", then "one, another, another" '. 'To this', Piaget (1952, p. 198) says 'K. Buhler rightly objected that true addition cannot occur without a clear awareness of the sum.'

   The above might be compared with the example given by Brunschvicg to show what it would be like to have enumeration without cardination. He quotes the curious fact noted by P. Bourdin in his *Objections* to Descartes's *Meditations*.

   A man was woken by a clock striking four, which he counted as one, one, one, one. This seemed to him absured and he cried out: 'The clock has gone crazy: it has struck one four times.' As he was half asleep his habitual reaction did not occur – he was unable to form the numerical notion four as exhibited in the basic equation: four times one equals one times four. In other words, he was unable to combine the enumerated units into the cardinal number four (Brunschvicg, 1922, p. 475).

8 Piaget (1942, p. 211) tells us 'And if we define the ordinals by "types of order", we have the numbers $1 = 0 \xrightarrow{+} 1_1; 2 = (O \xrightarrow{+} 1_1 \xrightarrow{+} 1_2); 3 = (O \xrightarrow{+} 1_1 \xrightarrow{+} 1_2 \xrightarrow{+} 1_3)\ldots$ etc., which results from the same seriation.'

9 As Piaget (1942, p. 212, n. 1) puts it 'M. Brunschvicg has shown in an enlightening fashion in *Étapes de la philosophie mathematique* (478) the inseparable nature of ordination and cardination.'

REFERENCES

Brainerd, C. J. 1979: *The Origins of the Number Concept*. Berlin: Praeger.

Brunschvicg, L. 1922: *Les Étapes de la Philosophie Mathematique*, 2nd edn. Paris: Félix Alcan.

Frege, G. 1894: Review of *Philosophie der Arithmetik* by Husserl. *Zeitschrift fur Philosophie un Philosophische Kritik*, CIII, 313–32.

Husserl, E. 1891: *Philosophie der Arithmatik: Psychologische und Logische Untersuchungen*, vol. 1. Berlin: Pfeffer.

1970: *Logical Investigations*, vol. II, trans. J. N. Findley. London: Routledge and Kegan Paul.

Piaget, J. 1942: *Classes, Relations et Nombres*. Paris: Librarie Philosophique J. Vrin.

1950: *Introduction a l'épistémologie génétique.*. Tome 1. *La pensée Mathématique*. Paris: Presses Universitaires de France.

1952: *The Child's Concept of Number*, trans. G. Cattegno and F. M. Hodgson. London: Routledge and Kegan Paul.

1953: *The Origin of Intelligence in the Child*, trans. M. Cook. London: Routledge and Kegan Paul.

1960: Les modèles abstraits sont-ils opposés aux interprétations psychophysiologiques dans l'explication en psychologie? *Revue Suisse de Psychologie Pure et Appliquée*, 29, 67–96.

1965: *Sagesse et Illusions de la Philosophie*, trans. M. Cook. London: Routledge and Kegan Paul.

1966: *Mathematical Epistemology and Psychology*, trans. W. Mays. Berlin: Reidel.

1972: *Essai de Logique Opératoire*. Paris: Dunod.

1976: Le possible, l'impossible et le necessaire. *Archives de Psychologie*, 44, 271–83.

Poincaré, H. undated: *Science and Method*, trans. F. Maitland. London: Dover.

1952: *Science and Hypothesis*. London: Dover.

Reymond, A. 1908: *Logique et Mathématiques: Essai historique et critique sur le nombre infini*. Neuchâtel: St. Blaise.

Russell, B. 1948: *Introduction to Mathematical Philosophy*. London: Allen and Unwin.

Seltman, M. and Seltman, P. 1985: *Piaget's Logic: A Critique of Genetic Epistemology*. London: Allen and Unwin.

PART V

An Overview

11

Varieties of perspective: an overview

Carol Feldman and Jerome Bruner

For the last 20 years or so, in some measure because of the influence of Jean Piaget on Anglophone psychology, problems in the psychology of mental development have tended to be formulated as questions about how the child comes to know the world. They were epistemological questions, with epistemological answers given in terms of mechanisms, procedures, operations that were the proposed means by which knowledge might be constructed. The operations were described by means of a model drawn from symbolic logic. Meanwhile, students of adult cognition were building a new field called 'cognitive science' with a very different model of mental processes. Here the mechanisms, procedures and processes were drawn from computer theory. It was at first urged that the mysterious, in-accessible procedures of mind could be approached by adopting the digital computer, whose procedures were transparent, as a model. In the early stages, model and data were kept distinct. For many purposes, and especially for modelling human computational activity, the digital computer was a powerful model, but it failed to give a satisfactory account of that great variety of species-specific states that had formerly seemed to both psychological and philosophical students of mind to be essential to mind itself – beliefs, doubts, wonder, expectation and so on, what are now called intentional states, not to say disbelief, disappointment, amazement and satisfaction.

Cognitive science hoped to replace cognitive psychology more broadly defined. It hoped that the computer model would give the full and complete account of mind. When it seemed that in principle the machine model would never be adequate to account for certain aspects of mind, some cognitive scientists said it was a limited model. But others, unable to live with that conclusion, began to deny that there were any real mental events that lay outside the boundaries of the model. A new philosophy of mind developed to explain the status of their claims to these cognitive scientists. The new philosophy of mind insists that as the computer is the best possible (the complete, the only intelligible, the only scientific, the most basic, and so on) model of mind, any aspects of mind, such as intentionality, that it cannot model are not *real* and that (therefore) explanations of intentional states that lie outside the computer (or scientific) model will always be non-scientific. (see especially, Stich, 1983)

This view, a kind of 'computational realism', looks for the mechanisms of the computer – switching mechanisms, end-gates, addresses in memory, random access, and the like, or its nearest possible homologues – in nature. It condemns psychology to a theory of mind that looks just like a description of a machine, a theory that is not even expanded to include the less compelling 'real', and more mind-like, programs that can be run by the machine.

With the emergence of this new philosophy of mind, the ground has shifted. No longer are the philosophical questions raised by psychological research in cognition epistemological. Now they are metaphysical. What is brought into question is the very reality of mind itself, and the arguments are arguments about whether mind as we know it, the everyday and literary mind of intentional states, is real. Underlying these arguments is a strong metaphysical stand in favour of physical monism. If there are mental events that have no physical representation they cannot be real. Acceptable physical representations may be machine states, or they may be neurological, or they may be both.

We find the philosophers of mind arrayed in metaphysical ranks, monists (physical rather than mental) arrayed against the dualists with their, from the monist's point of view, impossible task of getting an abstract mind connected to a physical body, and even such complex and creative proposals as Searle's (1984) dual-aspect monism – a mind 'expressed by and realized in' the physical matter of the brain. The disputes are about what is real, what really exists. Eventually, they are proposals about substance. Is all substance physical as the physical monists would have it, or are there two kinds of substance – mental and physical – each irreducible to the other, as the dualists would have it, or one (physical/neurological) substance with two aspects as Searle would have it?

What makes these disputes sound strange to modern ears is that we have no accepted procedures – no philosophical procedures, no empirical procedures – for answering questions like these. In modern procedures, we begin with premises, with a universe, with some stipulation. For the new metaphysicians, the kinds of issues that have been handled by stipulation in modern science are now being treated as matters of discovery themselves. These are matters so basic that one approaches them without premises, without a beginning. And beginning at this inchoate beginning all directions seem equally well justified, for there is nothing to constrain the argument. Nor does anyone have any idea what a well-formed, knockdown argument for the existence of one kind of substance rather than another would look like.

The nature of reality, the ultimate nature of reality, is not a matter then that can be resolved by modern forms of argument, whether empirical or theoretical. Far better to say, as one generally does in science, that we prefer to make different stipulations – for that is all it is, a preference of taste, of intuition, perhaps of interssts. Or to put it in Goodman's (1984) terms, better to say that we begin with different world versions, none of them ultimately real, and many of them right. If the current metaphysical arguments were framed as differing stipulations, they would be benign. Everyone's stipulation would be a beginning for some sort of further discovery. We would make choices finally by seeing where they led. And all we would give up would be the possibility of claiming that some stipulations are real and others not.

Whether or not we should go on with the enterprise of modern cognitive psychology is thought to hinge on the resolution of this seemingly scholastic argument. The implication is that if we cannot make an intelligible metaphysical case for the existence of mind, then it is a fiction, and we who study it are counting the angels who dance on the head of a pin.

The last time metaphysical issues dominated philosophy was a time before there was a philosophy of mind proper, and they were concerned with the reality of theological abstraction within the often encumbering constraints of church dogma (see Carre, 1946). And certainly it was also a time before the discovery of the powerful notion of observation as the standard against which theories should be tested. The pattern of theory-testing empirical research framed the enormous growth of scientific knowledge since the Renaissance, and, in consequence, empowered the procedures of theory testing through observation in everyone's mind. So the return now to metaphysics seems oddly anachronistic and strangely unfamiliar. One hardly knows where to begin. And the transformation of philosophical issues in modern cognitive psychology into questions about existence is a juxtaposition that boggles the mind.

Nevertheless, that is the state of the philosophy of mind today, and this collection captures it as a well-wrought prism. Conveniently for the reader, the central metaphysical issue recurs in most of the chapters, and is easily recognized by the common use of the phrase 'folk psychology', after Stich (1983). For those who think intentional states are not real, they cannot be studied scientifically, and are a *mere* matter of folk psychology.

This volume is concerned not just with mind but with the development of mind. The emphasis on development raises another difficult issue that has also taken a new form in recent years. To be specific, there are now doubts as to whether anything mental could or does develop. To gloss the argument crudely, if the mental is real (as the dualists would have it), then it exists as a substance, and knowledge and concepts are made of mental stuff. If we have this substance in adulthood, we must have had it in childhood, for (to put the problem in its essential and most medieval form) how could we make substance out of no substance? Therefore if knowledge is real, then all knowledge must be innate. Fodor (1981) has been the leading exponent of this view, and several chapters in this volume try to make the notion of mental development intelligible again.

The current metaphysics thus challenges the legitimacy of studies of intentional aspects of mind and of mental development, by challenging their reality. But these stipulated realities have led to some of the richest empirical work so far done in psychology. Within the context of the current metaphysics, cognitive psychology is at a very important crossroads from which it has only two possible futures, both of them unpalatable: it can either proceed in a manner that increasingly loses touch with the very mysteries we created the field to explain, or carries on studying them but tarred as unscientific and with the burden of having to justify that its phenomena are real.

This book presents these important new debates from a variety of points of view but with a common set of issues addressed. It thus makes as clear as possible the nature of the crossroads that students of mind have reached in its most intractable form. Many of the authors in this volume are prepared to give up claiming that the psychology of intentional states is scientific, but none of them is willing to give up altogether the possibility of having some (say, a non-scientific) psychology of intentional states. In several cases, this takes the form of trying to create an intelligible model of folk psychology.

One hopes that there are a variety of ways out of this muddle and that the two unpalatable alternatives above are not the only possibilities, for if they are, we have ourselves programmed a field of scientific research for extinction. But then there are the phenomena of mind and of development, and they, of course, will not go away.

For the most part, the authors of these chapters share the view that in a scientific psychology, any terms in statements about mind must refer to physically real entities. Nevertheless, there is a good deal of discomfort with this conclusion among them. But, we disagree. All that is required of a scientific psychology is that it give a model or theory that accounts for our observations about people.

Indeed, the best way to escape the present dilemma is to avoid metaphysics; that is, to refuse to accept the metaphysical framing of the questions. One important approach is metaphysical atheism (Goodman, 1984, for example) that denies that there is any underlying, ultimate reality awaiting discovery. Another less radical proposal is a metaphysical agnosticism that leads us to frame our efforts within the patterns of modern science. In the modern scientific pattern, the two categories of theory and data need not be different natural kinds, need not be essentially different. Rather, they are distinguished functionally, by playing different roles in the process of discovery – theory being a hypothetical account, a stipulation, and data being observations suggested by the theory that serve to confirm or infirm the theory as a lens through which to view the world. We can carry on working within this richly productive pattern without ever raising metaphysical questions, provided that we can keep its functional constituents distinct and the pattern clear. Indeed, it could be argued that this functional frame is precisely what has made the rich productivity of modern science in the last 400 years possible.

The impulse to reify models, to project theories into the phenomena they were meant to describe, in short to collapse the theory into the data, continues to haunt and needlessly to confuse discussions of models and mental events. This error seemed some years ago (Feldman and Toulmin, 1976) to be especially relevant to the Piagetian case, where it created mayhem. Once Piagetian theory was understood, psychologists went about looking for evidence for it not as they should have, by looking for data that the theory could explain, but too often, by looking for expression of the statements of the theory as part of the baggage of their subjects' mental lives. Not finding the theory (for example, the INRC group, a mathematical four-group that was, at first, used to describe abstract reasoning) among their subjects beliefs, they inferred that the theory was defective. The theory may have been defective, but if so, it was for other reasons – for example, because the kind of holistic, saltatory change that was embodied by Piaget's notion of stage was not confirmed by observation. The inferred defect was actually due to the scientists' failure to keep distinct the phenomena to be explained and the manner (model, theory, story) of explaining them. Evidently, this confusion and the impulse to 'entify' theory cannot be attributed specifically to the characteristics of Piagetian theory or its exemplification, for as we shall see, it is a central muddle in cognitive science as well. Perhaps it is a general problem in cognitive psychology.

Or worse, in psychology generally. For in psychology, mind, however unwelcome, tends to intrude on the tidy, reductive schemes that we keep inventing to manage or to avoid it. In the period of Watsonian behaviourism in America, thought was handled by psychologists who denied that it was real, as 'nothing but subvocal speech'. The worst offender of that era was, perhaps, not Pavlov (for he was rather relaxed on this issue, thinking of himself only as a physiologist) but his contemporary Bekhterev (1932) who, by reducing all mental phenomena to their putatively causal reflex origin, could dismiss them as without significance, as ways of talking in common sense (folk psychology) about scientific matters. During this period of puritan zeal even 'sensations' and their absolute and differential thresholds had to be laundered into respectability by being reduced methodologically to 'button pushings' and 'vocal responses'.[1]

In the case of cognitive science, we would argue, the computer is first, foremost, and most intelligibly a *model* of thinking – that is, a picture, story, maybe an emergent theory. And, then, at some moment in the development of the field of cognitive science (for example, see Harnad, 1982), the mind is said to *be* a computer and the computer *is* the mind. Thus the theory becomes, by fiat, the data it was meant to account for, and everything that is not the model, it is said, cannot be in the world. In the neuroscience version of this argument, everything truly in the mind must have a representation in the brain. Absent a real representation in the brain, and putative mental events are not real and talk about them cannot be scientific. As Wilkes argues (this volume), first, a scientific theory must aim at empirical adequacy; but 'postulated psychological functions must not merely be competent to account for cognitive development; they must be functions which are really there – which the brain can and does perform', a requirement that Wilkes calls 'realism'. Among Piagetians it was said that if a procedure was in the model it must *actually* be in the world; among the neuroscience advocates, everything in the model must actually be in the brain; among the computer scientists it is said that if it is not in the model, it cannot *actually* be in the mind. It is puzzling that in cognitive psychology we should keep making this mistake. No physicist would expect to find the law of displaced bodies in the bathwater or to find $E = mc^2$ in the fissioning metal.

Why do we tend to conflate theory and data in this way when we try to do the science of cognitive psychology? In cognitive psychology, the data we want to explain are not physical events but mental events. This leads to four related issues that derive from the seemingly excessive subjectivity of the data. First, the data may seem to be too dependent on theory – what we see seems to be unduly dependent on the theoretical stand with which we observe. But now it turns out that this is true too of the data of modern physics. Second, mental states may seem to be insufficiently foundational to have undergone too much prior construction by other mental processes that moreover depend on the constructs of the culture. But if Goodman (1984) is right, all of the furniture of our worlds, 'black holes' no less than beliefs, share this characteristic. Third, the findings in the data do not exhaust the meanings (neither intensional nor extensional) in the theory. But of course no theory has ever been fully unpacked by its data. Quine says of modern physics that it is '99% theory and 1% data'.

Or, fourth, do we conflate theory and data in psychology because we are simply misled by their being entities of much the same natural kind? In cognitive psychology, the data we want to explain are, like the theory, mental events. But mental events, however much they may seem to be like the theories that explain them (of course, theory construction *is* itself a mental event), are still the *data* in this case – that is, their functional role is as the thing to be explained.

We believe that, as in science generally, the psychology of intentional states can, in principle, be scientifically described by any model provided that the model is a stipulation distinct from the data – that is, is *anything but* the intentional states to be explained themselves. How good the science is depends on how much of what goes on gets accounted for, now parsimoniously, how perspicuously, and all the rest of it. But, equally, a mind seen as nothing but a computing machine described by a model that is a computing machine is *not* scientifically described in that the most basic pattern of science is violated – there is no theory distinct from the data.

There is, however, in cognitive theory a special and serious difficulty in making sense of how a theory 'accounts for' the data. The law of displaced bodies accounts for the behaviour of the bathwater by predicting how high it will rise. $E = mc^2$ may be used to predict the amount of energy that will be released by fissionable material. No cognitive theory has every predicted what people will think or do. And neither of course will cognitive science. Is this then a bona fide reason for agreeing that theories of intentional mind must be unscientific?

With people we cannot control all the conditions as we can in the bath, but even if we could, people are not inert bodies. They think, and they are free to think in a variety of ways; they act, and they are free to act in a variety of ways. People make choices and defy prediction. On the other hand, to permit into cognitive theories only statements that do predict behaviour, would be to restrict them to a very specialized and uninteresting component of human activity – say, the behaviour of people trapped on all fronts, deprived of freedom, without resources, forced to act. This is not being scientific, this is failing to do the science of the great bulk of human behaviour, perhaps of any human behaviour. For, even prisoners do many surprising and unpredictable things.

It seems, then, that cognitive theories cannot account for the data by predicting them. Rather, cognitive theories should be expected mainly to interpret and construe (and, perhaps, occasionally, to predict), as Morton (1980) suggests. This seems to be the most intelligible goal of explanation of human intentionality, as it is of explanation of intentional systems generally (Dworkin, 1985, chap. 6). For some, this limitation in the nature of our accounts will make them seem to be essentially unscientific, and a science of human action essentially impossible. But, if interpretation is the only kind of account appropriate to intentionality, we would argue that that is the form that genuinely scientific accounts of human behaviour must take.

This volume begins with three extremely thoughtful chapters that all come to grips with the difficulties of defending the reality of mental events in a manner consistent with the possibility of scientific explanation of mental development.

Wilkes poses the doubly vexed question of what we can mean when we ascribe belief states to the infant. Wilkes notes that we do not think that the concepts of infants, that is, the contents of their beliefs, are much like our own, and indeed there is a good deal of empirical work to suggest that the concepts of infants are very different from those of adults, and that they undergo systematic reorganization in development. She then says, 'If we are unable to say what is the content of any belief [the infant] has . . . then we cannot say whether it is true or false; and once we lose *that* hook we are at sea when discussing much more.' She finds the conclusion that we cannot therefore talk about the beliefs of infants 'disastrous', and looks for a solution. She argues that *every* attempt to identify the content of beliefs, including those of adults, runs into similar difficulties, and concludes 'Thus we should start from the beginning – *dismissing* the arguments . . . that impose unrealistically high conditions on content identification, but searching for conditions that *in fact* govern our ascriptions of . . . mental states.' Wilkes's solution is to distinguish science from common sense. For Wilkes, scientific explanation requires empirical adequacy (what Wilkes calls 'instrumentalism') and 'realism', while common-sense explanations require only empirical adequacy and the possibility of identifying beliefs without 'entifying' them. Wilkes solves the problem of explaining belief states by eliminating the requirement of realism, but concedes at the same time the possibility of scientific explanation.

Woodfield begins by observing that the notion of 'concept' is itself unclear and that there are no satisfactory psychological accounts of concept formation. He asks whether the notion itself, a term drawn from folk psychology, may be an unsuitable candidate for scientific study. 'Folk psychology models inner states on sentences; but the inner states of the pre-verbal child are not sentence-like.' Moreover, 'concepts are individuated by their contents' but 'content is not an objective property'. Woodfield then poses the dilemma at the crossroads this way: 'It is an open question whether content-based developmental psychology will gradually give way to a content-free computational approach. At the present state of play, I think we ought to try to give concepts a good run for their money. This means making a serious effort to solve the problems I am now about to state.' Woodfield then reviews Fodor's arguments for the innateness of concepts and rejects Fodor's conclusion as counter-intuitive.

Woodfield's solution begins with a careful discussion of the nature of concepts that leads to a more exact framing of the puzzles posed by concept acquisition. He then says,

> concepts come in bundles by their very nature. This fact imposes a tough constraint on any theory of concept acquisition. Given the graduated holism, it makes no sense to suppose that there was ever a time when subject S possessed just *one* concept, and no sense to suppose that constitutively linked concepts

were acquired *one by one*. . . . It appears that the acquisition of a minimal system of concepts is *not* a gradual process in which parts of the system are acquired at different times, precisely *because* the system is holistic. Yet, any observer of children will say that light does dawn gradually. How is this possible? (p. 23)

Woodfield then poses two objections that others have raised against the possibility of concept acquisition. First, concepts are identified by their contents. If the contents of concepts change in development, then the earlier and later concept are, strictly speaking, different concepts. Second, we can only know the concepts of others who are essentially similar to ourselves, 'but infants evidently do not think like adults'. Woodfield's solution is to concede the technical points – that concepts cannot, by definition, change their contents, and that we can only specify subjective contents of people who are conceptually similar to ourselves, but to insist nevertheless that something concept-like does develop.

His solution is a proposal for a developmental pattern that begins early with representations he calls 'recognition-schemas' that are not yet concepts because they do not yet form an inferentially integrated network like our own, 'but which are, so to speak, destined to attain that status later. Let us call these precursors "protoconcepts".' The programme he outlines is this: First, 'describe how schemas do actually get formed in the human infant's mind/brain'. Second, devise a theory of protoconcept formation. Third, give an account of the 'various ways in which protoconcepts turn into concepts'.

The last chapter in this section addresses the problem of introspection, a topic that, as Lyons says, is rarely thought worthy of investigation in its own right, yet our views about it are central to our notions of the mental. 'One way or another it is still believed or assumed that we have a second-order sense . . . for gaining immediate direct information about our first-level perceptual and cognitive appetitive life', by perceiving or monitoring or registering first-level events. 'This core model . . . is, it will be argued, fundamentally mistaken.' What follows is an interesting historical review of the notion of introspection leading to Lyons's central objection: 'The more we learn about the brain, the less it seems that there is any correlation of an informative kind between the output of our introspective reports – in terms of beliefs, intentions, desires, and so on – and the cognitive operation of the mind as revealed by neuroscience.' Intro-spective data, then, cannot be a literal report produced by scanning dis-crete brain states or processes. Difficulties like these were partly responsible for functionalist accounts of mind, accounts in terms of inward operations performed between environmental output and be-havioural output. This description might avoid having to say anything about the composition or nature of inner processes, or not, but it leaves 'the basic story – that in introspection we have direct, immediate, and reportable knowledge of inner states and processes' – intact.

Lyons sets out to give a new account of introspection. He begins by observing that introspection has no phenomenology of its own, and that our descriptions of it are not of '*what it is like*' to introspect, but rather of its contents – of '*what*' we introspect. Lyons rejects the claim that the ability to introspect is acquired in development as learning to analyse one's own overt actions and to reconstruct them on the plane of thought. He objects that any such reconstruction is 'on the plane of memory and imagination, and in "folk psychological" terms'. Moreover the claim is based on our particular cultural conventions: 'we claim the very ability to introspect occurrent mental or brain events because it is embedded in our culture that we have the ability to do this'.

There is experimental evidence that ought to unsettle those who hold that introspection is private access with unique reliability. The evidence that Lyons finds unsettling is the wealth of information that we have but fail to attend to, and the result that many times our reports are unreliable. Equally, our reports about how we remember something may be un-reliable. Rather than reporting on our actual deliberations in these cases, we seem to be 'adopting a likely rationale for *a* person exercising a choice in such a situation'. Though these are not knock-down arguments, they should be taken as 'hints that introspection when explained as any form of monitoring ... of data in respect of cognitive–appetitive processes is a myth of our culture, an invention of our "folk psychology" '.

Lyons offers an alternative proposal. When we introspect, 'we engage in a process of perceptual replay ... "with edited highlights" or "in dramat-ized form" '. 'Introspection is not a special and privileged executive monitoring process over and above the more plebeian processes of per-ception, memory and imagination: it is those processes put to a certain use.' In introspection we imaginatively construct a version of overt behaviour 'which we describe in our "folk psychology" as thinking, hoping', and so on, 'a highly interpreted and abstracted level of talk about behaviour'. These may be wrong or fanciful, and someone else's account may be better than mine. The only corner of incorrigibility I retain is privileged access to *my* version or *my* replay, however, mistaken.

With this gloomy conclusion about self-knowledge, Lyons turns to his surprising and interesting conclusion: introspection is crucial for under-standing and predicting the behaviour of others. Through its use, we form a general model of another person's mind from observation of his behaviour, by imagining 'what it is like' (to borrow a phrase from Nagel, via Morton, 1980) to be the other person. Via similar processes of inference from behaviour, introspection helps us to build up something we do need – a 'holistic' concept of ourselves, a 'macro model of the cognitive activities of the brain ...' 'in terms of such concepts as deliberating, deciding, wanting, and so on'. These non-scientific models may influence psychologist's models and vice versa so that in the end 'the gap between ordinary amateur "folk" psychologizing and proven psychological explanations may be reduced to a sliver'. Finally, mental development, including the development of 'introspection' is a matter of developing sufficient maturity to understand and take part in our 'folk psychology'.

The next chapter is by Adam Morton. It raises the folk psychology versus cognitive science argument head on, and offers an exemplary and lucid discussion that frames the issues, with illustrations of the model he recommends taken from Marr's work on perception. Russell's chapter offers a rich and detailed discussion of theory and data in perceptual development. He rejects the claim that nothing perceptual develops in cognitive development and moreover denies that in thinking this he is adopting a folk psychological 'illusion': his central claim is that cognitive development can *only* be understood as increasing ability to locate perceptions in the web of intention.

Robinson's chapter is a defence of dualism and, specifically, of that sort of dualism in which it is claimed that mind is a mental substance. His central interest is to 'investigate what psychological development might consist of for someone who thinks the mind is an immaterial substance'. In the course of his discussion, he makes a case against physical monism and for the existence of systems of belief. And then he tries to rescue substance dualism from the charge that it cannot account for development. His proposed solution is this: 'If we accept that the immaterial self is a simple substance with a capacity for (at least) consciousness and thought, then the framework for development is established, for none of these capacities are realized except through the body and learning how to realize these capacities is [done] from scratch.'

In one way or another all of the chapters up to this point attempt to defend a psychology of intentionality against attack by the cognitive scientists. The chapters from 7 on take a different tack. All of them assume the reality of intentional systems and defending such systems against charges or irrealism is not part of their work. The last four chapters – Hopkins, Matthews, Smith, and Mays – are on aspects of Piagetian psychology and are written within the Piagetian theoretical framework. They thus do not take on the host of issues around the folk psychology versus cognitive science debate that frame the concerns of the earlier chapters. Conversely, they raise a number of interesting issues in interpreting Piagetian theory in the various areas that they discuss: self-concept, moral development, necessity and number. The importance of these discussions in the context of the other chapters of this book is that Piaget's theory is the only well-known, fully developed theory of cognitive development that assumes that mind is real and that it does develop. For Piaget, the intellectual enterprise was to discover how. His effort was a substantial contribution but it was flawed in various ways as these chapters point out. But if we are going to be able to save the idea of a psychology of mental development from the assaults of cognitive science, eventually we will have to get on with the business of theory building again. The last four chapters warn us of some rocks in the water.

'Folk psychology' cannot be simply jettisoned. Too much of the behaviour that we would like a scientific psychology to explain (or predict) is transactional, involving people's conceptions of each other's intentional states: what they think, feel, intend, and so on. Worse, these conceptions are organized in holistic patterns that go by such names as the 'self', which are in turn shaped by such still larger patterns of shared convention as culture.

In a word, the cycle of action and interaction becomes so 'thick', so linked to the *content* of intentional states, that it is not possible to describe what is going on without reference to those intentional states and their content. If one seeks to do so in terms of 'cognitive science' and omits the role of such states, the result is a description so *thin* that it must fail to capture the events that others think they are involved in but that, as it were, do not exist for the cognitive scientist. In the end, then, the cognitive scientist might as well run computer simulations for their own sake – for their own sake in the sense that they are models that only other people who share his explanatory intentions will find interesting. As for the rest of human intentions, we will have to invent other and more complete ways of explaining them, new explanations with a more hospitable attitude toward the folk psychology that guides our ordinary ways of looking at the world.

NOTE

1   A second approach to the problem of mind in that era, as today, was to introduce two 'substances'. The first was basic sensation to be described by mechanical models. The second was higher intentional processes that acted on sensation once they had been formed. But intentional set was found to affect such basic matters as sensory threshold, muddying the distinction between them. Interestingly, the fall of classical psychophysics can be dated from the encounter with set. Postman and Bruner (1946) argued that *all* sensory activity was governed by a system of intentional states. Brunswick (1934) rejected the dualist solution and proposed instead a thoroughgoing functionalism in which he denied that there was a single correct version of mind. His world of objects and events (the *Gegenstandswelt*) was a set of constructs created by the requirements of living. That was why *A Study of Thinking* by Bruner et al. was dedicated to him.

REFERENCES

Bekhterev, V. 1932: *General Principles of Human Reflexology: An Introduction to the Objective Study of Personality* (Russian edn, 1923). For a version of this same defence, see also two early papers of K. Lashley (1923): The behavioristic interpretation of consciousness. *Psychological Review*, 30, 237–72; 329–53.

Bruner, J., Goodnow, J. and Austin, G. 1986: *A Study of Thinking*. New Brunswick, NJ: Transaction Books.

Brunswik, E. 1934: *Warnehmung und Gegenstandswelt: Grundlegung einer Psychologie vom Gegenstand her*. Vienna: Deuticke.

Carre, M. 1946: *Realists and Nominalists*. London: Oxford University Press.

Dworkin, R. 1985: *A Matter of Principle*. Cambridge, Mass.: Harvard University Press.

Feldman, C. and Toulmin, S. 1976: Logic and the theory of mind. *Nebraska Symposium on Motivation, 1975*. Lincoln, Nebr.: University of Nebraska Press.

Fodor, J. 1981: *Representations*. Cambridge, Mass.: MIT Press.

Goodman, N. 1984: *Of Mind and Other Matters*. Cambridge, Mass.: Harvard University Press.

Harnad, S. 1982: Neoconstructivism: a unifying theme for the cognitive sciences. In T. Simon and R. Scholes (eds), *Language, Mind and Brain*. Hillsdale, NJ: Lawrence Erlbaum.

Morton, A. 1980: *Frames of Mind*. Oxford: Oxford University Press.

Postman, L. and Bruner, J. 1946: The reliability of constancy errors in psychophysical measurement. *Journal of Psychology*, 21, 293–9.

Searle, J. 1984: *Minds, Brains and Science*. Cambridge, Mass.: Harvard University Press.

Stich, S. 1983: *From Folk Psychology to Cognitive Science*. Cambridge, Mass.: MIT Press.

Notes on contributors

JEROME BRUNER is George Herbert Mead University Professor at the New School for Social Research and Fellow of the New York Institute for the Humanities at New York University. Over a long period at Harvard and Oxford he has made contributions to the fields of perception, education, social psychology and cognition – an area that he helped to launch as a legitimate area of psychological study in the 1950s. He has since been working on language and is currently doing research on narrative thinking.

CAROL FELDMAN is Adjunct Associate Professor of Psychology and Fellow of the New York Institute for the Humanities at New York University. After a graduate career in both fields, she has for many years been interested in problems in the philosophy of psychology. Her empirical research, she writes, 'is a sort of empirical philosophy on a variety of problems in language and thought'.

JAMES HOPKINS is currently a member of the Philosophy Department at King's College, London, having previously held posts at Oxford and Cambridge. His research interests include the philosophy of Wittgenstein and the philosophical foundations of psychoanalysis. He is the co-editor, with Richard Wollheim, of *Philosophical Essays on Freud* (Cambridge University Press, 1982).

WILLIAM LYONS is Professor of Philosophy at Trinity College, Dublin. He has studied or taught at universities in Australia, New Zealand, Canada, Italy and Scotland. His main interests are in the philosophy of mind and philosophical psychology. As well as numerous articles in journals, he has published *Gilbert Ryle: An Introduction to his Philosophy* (Harvester and Humanities Presses, 1980), *Emotion* (Cambridge University Press, 1980) and *The Disappearance of Introspection* (Bradford Books/The MIT Press, 1986).

GARETH B. MATTHEWS is Professor of Philosophy at the University of Massachusetts. He has also taught at the Universities of Virginia and Minnesota. Although much of his work is in the history of philosophy, an important recent focus of attention is 'the philosophy of childhood' – conceptions of childhood, theories of cognitive and moral development, children's rights and the place of children in society. As well as numerous articles, he is the author of *Philosophy and the Young Child* (Harvard, 1980) and *Dialogues with Children* (Harvard, 1984).

WOLFE MAYS is currently a Fellow of the Institute of Advanced Studies at Manchester Polytechnic, having previously been Reader in Philosophy at Manchester University for a number of years. He was personal assistant to Jean Piaget in Geneva and was a founder member of the *Centre International d'Epistémologie Génétique* there. He has translated four books by Piaget and co-authored two books with him and others. He is also the author of *The Philosophy of Whitehead*, *Arthur Koestler* and *Introduction to Whitehead's Philosophy of Science and Education*.

ADAM MORTON is Professor of Philosophy at the University of Bristol, having previously taught at Princeton, Ottawa and elsewhere. He has, he writes, 'two academic personalities: one does rather loose philosophy of mind, sometimes bordering on ethics, and the other does rather tight philosophy of language, bordering on logic. I am trying to marry the two personalities by working on decision theory, but the marriage is not yet consummated.' His books include *A Guide through the Theory of Knowledge* (Dickenson, 1977) and *Frames of Mind* (Oxford University Press, 1980). He is currently working on a book called *Disaster and Dilemmas*.

HOWARD ROBINSON is currently a Senior Lecturer in Philosophy at Liverpool University, having previously researched and taught at Nottingham and Oxford. He has written a book, *Matter and Sense* (Cambridge University Press, 1982), criticizing materialism, and co-edited, with John Foster, *Essays on Berkeley* (Oxford University Press, 1985). He has also written articles on ethics and ancient philosophy. At present he is working on books on the philosophy of perception and in defence of an immaterialist account of self.

JAMES RUSSELL is currently a Reader in Psychology at Liverpool University, having previously taught at Glasgow University and been educated at the Universities of Oxford and London. His empirical research concerns children's understanding of the way language creates different logical contexts, and his theoretical work is on the nature of explanation in developmental and cognitive psychology. He is the author of *The Acquisition of Knowledge* (Macmillan, 1978) and *Explaining Mental Life* (Macmillan, 1984).

LESLIE SMITH is currently a member of the Department of Educational Research at the University of Lancaster. He was previously a school teacher for a number of years as well as a student in philosophy and a graduate researcher in psychology. His main interests lie in the educational, psychological and philosophical issues which arise in Piaget's constructivism. He has published papers in such journals as *Human Development*, *British Journal of Developmental Psychology* and *Philosophy of the Social Sciences*.

KATHLEEN WILKES is Lecturer in Philosophy at Oxford University and Fellow and Tutor in Philosophy at St Hilda's College. Her publications include *Physicalism* (Routledge, 1978), *Real People* (Oxford University Press, forthcoming) and articles on several aspects of philosophy – especially the philosophy of science and of psychology as a science. A book on psychology-as-a-science is in preparation, entitled *The Autonomy of Psychology*, and another on Aristotle's ethics and the philosophy of mind, entitled *Aristotle's Absences*.

ANDREW WOODFIELD is currently a member of the Philosophy Department at Bristol University, having previously held posts at the Universities of Sheffield, Oxford and California. He is the author of *Teleology* (Cambridge University Press, 1976) and editor of *Thought and Object* (Oxford University Press, 1982). He has published a number of articles on the philosophy of mind and is currently interested in philosophical problems concerning cognitive and biological development.

Index

Abraham, K., 146
adualism 153–7, 169
Aquinas, St Thomas, 18
animism
  in children, 134–5, 177–8, 185
  in infants, 157–8
Anscombe, G. E. M., 86–7
anthropology, 40–2
appearance–reality distinctions
  in childhood, 105–6, 107, 111–2
  in infancy, 160–2, 163
archetypal symbols, 133–7
Aristotle, 23, 60, 120, 129, 130, 184, 212
Armstrong, D. M., 5, 25, 28, 35
Augustine, St, 19, 33, 40, 60

Baldwin, J. M., 95
Bartlett, F. C., 28
behaviourism, 34–5, 37, 56, 122, 247
Bekhterev, V., 247
belief ascription, 3–9, 12–14, 18, 24–5, 69–79 *passim*, 108, 124–5, 244, 248, 254
'blindsight', 83, 95
Boden, M., 18, 214
Bower, T. G. R., 27, 82, 96, 99, 102, 155, 159, 161, 163
Bradley, F. H., 109
Braine, M. D. S., 106
Brainerd, C. J., 196, 200, 230–4
Bruner, J. S., 106, 208, 254

Brunschvicg, L., 220, 221–2, 224, 225, 227, 229, 230, 231, 235, 238
Bryant, P. E., 84, 196, 203, 204
Butterworth, G. E., 32, 82, 111

Campion, J., 83, 110–11
Campos, J. J., 154, 158, 159–60, 165, 167
Carpenter, G., 166, 167
Churchland, P. M., 18, 60, 67, 68, 69, 72, 73, 74, 75, 124
Churchland, P. S., 20, 60, 67
class inclusion, 201, 202, 203–4, 208, 221, 228, 230
Cohn, J. F., 166
computational psychology (or cognitive science), 35, 36–7, 71–8, 85, 97, 107–8, 120, 121–4, 127, 243–5, 247–8, 253, 254
concept acquisition, 17–30
  by displacement, 23–5, 176–8
  and natural kinds, 179–83
conservation, 194, 196, 203–8, 225, 236
Cromer, R., 84

Davidson, D., 6, 24, 124
Dennett, D. C., 37, 60, 79, 98, 125–6
'depressive position', the, 150–1, 164, 165
Descartes, R., 120, 129, 130, 131, 195
direct perception (theory of), 82, 97